A HISTORY OF
EUROPEAN LITERATURE

A HISTORY
OF
EUROPEAN LITERATURE

BY

LAURIE MAGNUS

KENNIKAT PRESS
Port Washington, N. Y./London

A HISTORY OF EUROPEAN LITERATURE

First published in 1934
Reissued in 1970 by Kennikat Press
Library of Congress Catalog Card No: 75-103233
SBN 8046-0870-9

Manufactured by Taylor Publishing Company   Dallas, Texas

CONTENTS

BOOK III
THE AGE OF SHAKESPEARE

· BOOK IV
THE FRENCH RULE AND ITS SEQUEL

BOOK V

NOTE

WHEN Laurie Magnus died suddenly at the end of April, 1933, he had completed and corrected in typescript with some manuscript additions, the " copy " for this volume. He did not, however, live to see any of the printed proofs. At the request of Mrs. Magnus I have read these for press. Misprints have been corrected and some pure verbal emendations have been made. But it should be noted that Magnus did not have the opportunity of making any of the final emendations which often occur to a writer when he sees his work in proof.

This volume closes with a quotation from George Saintsbury. It is a significant coincidence that Laurie Magnus's last public utterance, following a paper read by me before the Royal Society of Literature, was a tribute to Saintsbury's work in the field of the comparative study of literature. In that field Magnus had won for himself a widely recognised position, especially by his *Dictionary of European Literature*. The present volume will, I believe, be welcomed both by the student and the general reader as summing up and interpreting the most mature results of his labours in his chosen field.

F. S. BOAS.

September, 1933.

PREFACE

THIS book has been written to supply the need expressed many years ago by the late Professor Edward Dowden for a one-volume history of European literature. In an essay on ' The Teaching of English Literature,' Dowden declared that he

' would have the student start with a *General Sketch of European Literature*, somewhat resembling Mr. Freeman's *General Sketch of European History* in its aim and scope and manner of treatment. . . . When Boccaccio,' he went on, ' is spoken of in connection with Chaucer, when Tasso or Ariosto is spoken of in connection with Spenser, or Boileau in connection with Dryden or Pope, or Carlyle in connection with Goethe, he ought at least to be able to place Boccaccio and Tasso and Ariosto and Boileau and Goethe aright in the general movement of European literature, and in some measure to conceive aright the relation of each to the literary movement in our own country.'

Since Dowden's day many excellent books on the comparative study of literature have been published, including the twelve-volume *Periods of European Literature*, under the editorship and part authorship of the late George Saintsbury, and special works by the late Sir Sidney Lee, W. P. Ker, C. H. Herford and others. To all these, students are indebted. But the " General Sketch " has not yet been written ; and, after one or two attempts and one or two interruptions, and after collecting my material in a *Dictionary of European Literature*, first published in 1926, I have now completed this volume to the scale of the original design.

I was in correspondence with Dowden about it shortly before his death in 1913, but whether it would satisfy him, I cannot say. Perhaps he did not visualise all the difference between a history of Europe and a history of European literature. The part is fuller than the whole, in the sense that there have been more writers than rulers and, happily, more songs than wars. Still, I am aware of shortcomings. I should like to review my own book, but, failing that unlikely commission, may I beg my critics to take more account of what is in than of what is out? Omission and compression have both been used, but the former more than the latter, since I have always tried to avoid a tail of names. At the same time, the book is a history, not an essay in criticism or taste, and such moral as it may display, in the sense of Seeley's dictum, ' The history of England ought to end with something that might be called a moral,' arises out of construction and is not dragged in by a partisan.

The general reader, if he survives in a world of specialization and broadcasting, may share the student's need for this book. The interests of both have been consulted by dividing it into five ' Books,' by providing a ' Foreword ' to each, by dividing each into ' Sections,' with two extra ' Intersections,' and by giving titles to the paragraphs. Thus the Contents-table, into which some dates have been introduced, and the Index, wil facilitate reference.

L. M.

The Athenæum, S.W.1.
1933.

BOOK I
THE BACKGROUND

FOREWORD TO BOOK I

THE period covered by this Book is shorter than it looks. Nominally, it includes (1) the Old (Hebrew) and the New (Greek) Testaments, and (2) the Greek and Latin writers of Hellas and Rome, from the 9th century B.C. to the 5th century A.D.; or from Homer to Boethius (Boece), described by Gibbon as 'the last of the Romans whom Cato or Tully (Cicero) would have acknowledged as their countryman'. Actually, it includes those books and writers only in the forms in which they were known at the dawn of modern literature, say, from the epoch of Dante who was born in 1265 A.D. For the Hebrew and Greek languages, through many centuries after the capture of Rome by Alaric the Visigoth in 410 A.D., had been unfamiliar in the West. The Bible was current in a Latin version, commonly called the Vulgate, of which St. Jerome in the 4th century A.D. was the chief author; and the Greek classics, so far as they were known at all, were likewise current in Latin versions, often very much changed from the original texts. In the following pages Homer and Aristotle will be selected as typical examples of a loss or corruption of Greek texts (an 'occultation' of literature, to borrow an astronomical term) which was almost universal. Many Latin classics, too, went unread, despite the general use of the Latin language, owing to the disappearance of numerous manuscripts and the paucity of copies of others. '

Accordingly, the first task of men of letters in the 13th and succeeding centuries, when the literature of the modern nations took its start, was to lift the veil from the background and to recover the hidden works of Antiquity in their Hebrew, Greek, and Roman forms. It is as the objects of this research that writers before the Christian era are essential to the study of European literature. The early makers of that literature recognized this essentiality, and devoted immense efforts to the then extremely difficult tasks not only of learning the old

3

languages but also of finding the old books. Out of their strenuous endeavours came the Renaissance and its sequel, the Reformation, which added up to a new civilization. The founders of the literary Renaissance are usually called Humanists because they turned back to human (or lay) from divine (or sacred) preoccupations, and their early home was in Italy, where Cicero was still honoured as philosopher and statesman and Virgil as prophet and poet.

THE BACKGROUND

AN attentive reader of early English books is struck by a curious phenomenon. Recurring among their writers is a note of self-insufficiency and experimentation. The writer confesses, sometimes with surprise, that the instruments at his disposal are inadequate. His language is inexpressive, his metres are inharmonious, his style is not worthy of his material, and he tries experiments with new words and measures. Or else—and it is the same thing reversed—a writer in an older tradition rebukes the innovators and experimenters, and says in effect that what was good enough for their fathers should be good enough for them. The evidence for the experimentation, in other words, is found in the reaction from it.

An Example from Chaucer. One or two examples may be given. Even if they are not at once fully understood, their intention will be clear. Chaucer, for instance, declares in the prologue to one of his *Canterbury Tales* :

> ' I am a Southren man,
> I cannot gestë *rum, ram, ruf* by lettre.'

What did he mean by it ? Plainly that the non-Southern men, the English writers from the North or North-West, were still employing a style which he had given up and would not use. These old alliterative versifiers were writing their tales of gestë (Latin, *gesta*＝heroic deeds), in a *rum, ram, ruf* kind of ding-dong, which impressed the ear 'by letter' not by rhythm. Chaucer had abandoned this style for that of the Kentishmen in the South, and he would not go back to it. North and South were foreign to each other in the England of the 14th century, and Chaucer explains his difficulty at the opening of another book. Because, he writes,

5

B

> ' there is so greet diversitee
> In English, and in wryting of our tonge,
> So preye I God that none miswrytë thee (his poem)
> Ne thee mismetre.'

It was a necessary prayer, though we need not now explore the details. The point is that there was this ' great diversity ' between the old and the new, and that Chaucer chose the new Southern road. As a fact, too, he was miswritten and mis-metred for several centuries. Indeed, his text was not properly written till 1775, when Thomas Tyrwhitt, his first complete critic, edited the *Canterbury Tales*.

An Example from Caxton. Take another example, this time from the 15th century. William Caxton, a Kentishman by birth, went further South than his own county in his search for new things in English literature. At his printing-press in Westminster, the first which was set up in England, he published Malory's *Morte d'Arthur*, and observed in the preface that—

' There was a king of this land named Arthur . . . And he is more spoken of beyond the sea, more books made of his noble acts, than there be in England, as well in Dutch, Italian, Spanish, and Greekish, as in French.'

He adds that the copy delivered to him by Malory had been taken ' out of certain books of French', and Malory himself refers some fifty times to his obligation to those books. Thus the English version of a native epic material had foreign affiliations and debts.

An Example from Marlowe. Take an example from the 16th century. Christopher Marlowe, the Elizabethan dramatist, declared in the prologue to one of his plays—

> ' Albeit the world thinks Machiavel is dead,
> Yet has his soul but flown across the Alps.'

In other words, he claimed inspiration from Machiavelli, the Florentine political philosopher who trained kings in the doctrine of absolutism ; and Roger Ascham, Queen Elizabeth's tutor, was moved accordingly to protest that English

6

Italianizers at that date were importing from abroad ' plenty of new mischiefs never known in England before ', thus supplying evidence to the innovators by his reaction from them.

The Light from the South. We need not multiply examples. Whether for mischief or benefit to English literature—and, generally, it was for good—we see that, century after century, its chief makers went abroad for light. Chaucer went as far south as Italy, and discovered there Francis Petrarch, poet, scholar and antiquary. His ' rethoryke sweete ', by Chaucer's own testimony, ' enlumined al Itaille of poetrye ', and Walter Savage Landor, in the 19th century, was moved by the record of that encounter to write an ' imaginary conversation ' between Chaucer and Petrarch in which the English poet says to the Italian :

' I will attempt to show Englishmen what Italians are : how much deeper in thought, intenser in feeling, and richer in imagination, than ever formerly ; and I will try whether we cannot raise poetry under our fogs, and merriment among our marshes.'

Leaving till Book II the light which Petrarch spread in Italy, here we would compare its reflection on Chaucer in England with what Schiller wrote to Goethe in Germany at the end of the 18th century :

' Had you been born a Greek or only an Italian, your way would have been infinitely shortened. But as you have been born a German, as your Greek spirit has been set in the Northern world, you have no other choice than either yourself to become a Northern artist, or with the aid of your intellect to supplement your imagination, thus . . . bringing to birth a new Greece.'

It was the same thing in Germany in the 18th century as in England in the 14th. Northern writers were conscious of insufficiency. They sought to supplement their resources out of the South. They sought to bring to birth a new Greece ; in one word, to effect a Renaissance.

Why Italy ? Why Greece, we ask ? Why, in fine, this self-insufficiency of English writers, this history of English literature incomplete without rays from the distant and the past ? Why Chaucer, confessing himself a Southernizer and seeking sunshine from Petrarch; why Malory, importing French books, and Marlowe inspired by Machiavelli ? We have touched but the fringe of our subject and have selected our examples almost at random, but already it is plain, from the direct evidence of the writers themselves, which is so much more impressive than what is written about them, that Greece and Italy had gifts in their keeping which, though dimly and through a fog, those writers sought for their own enlightenment.

§ 2. THE PAGAN VIEW.

The Heritage from Greece and Rome. And now for one sentence written about them. Sir Richard Jebb, an indisputable authority, writing in the *Cambridge Modern History*, says of this age of Petrarch and Chaucer :

' The pagan view was now once more proclaimed that man was made, not only to toil and suffer, but to enjoy.'

It is essential to our purpose thoroughly to understand Jebb's meaning. If we can get that clear it will help considerably to simplify and to co-ordinate the history of European literature.

The pagans, of course, were the Greeks and Romans. The pagan view was to be recovered from the literature and art —the cultural way of life—of the dead civilizations of Greece and Rome. When Schiller regretted that Goethe had not short-circuited his task by being born an Italian or a Greek, he was wishing him a native claim to this ' pagan view'. When Chaucer sought the light poured on Italy by the sweet rhetoric of Petrarch, he was reaching out after the same pagan writers. For, since these were the objects of Petrarch's constant worship, Chaucer's recourse to Petrarch was at the same time an attraction to the ancient lights behind him—to the light in which Petrarch longed to shine. Indeed, Chaucer's visit to Italy in 1372 and Goethe's visit to Italy in 1787 were alike journeys of revival and exploration. With four centuries between them, both poets had to seek on its own soil the storied past of ancient Roman culture. They visited the back of beyond, the pagan background reflected in modern Italy, in order to bring home the pagan view to Northern climes.

The Summons to Enjoyment. So much at the moment for the view, the way of life which was sought from Greece and Rome, and the Re-birth, or Renaissance, to be derived from it. But what about the summons to enjoyment, the proclamation, under the sign of the pagan classics, ' that man was made to enjoy ' ? This is a little more difficult to explain because it involves some knowledge of society and Church in the early Middle Ages and of the way of life of peoples in Europe when Chaucer was following Petrarch into the light of ' the pagan view'. Yet it belongs to the origins of European literature, and it is essential to consider it, if the sequel is to be understood. We would associate it first with Landor's imagining of what Chaucer may have said to Petrarch when they met in Florence in 1372 : by that contact he would try to ' raise merriment among our marshes'. Associate this again with the motto which Rabelais, the great French satirist, about a hundred and fifty years after Chaucer, say, about 1530, wrote on the fly-leaf of his romance : ' Le rire est le propre de l'homme'. For this claim to merriment and laughter, to free expatiation under the sun with less fear of the frown of authority, whether without or within, this open eye to the humour of the human spectacle, unaffrighted by divine inhibitions, this re-adjustment of the territories of the sacred and profane, in favour, however timidly, of the latter, all this was a part of the 'pagan view', and lay in the keeping of the pagan classics. Greeks and Romans in the dead and buried past had laughed and loved and followed beauty. They had thought and built and reasoned and fought and conquered and died, not *ad majorem Dei gloriam*, for the greater glory of an unseen God, but for the greater glory of Athens or Rome, for the advancement of the glory of mankind. There is a verse in the Psalter which says : ' The heavens are the heavens of the Lord, but the earth has He given to the children of men'. But for men and women in the dawn of modern Europe, for whom obedience to the Church in their lifetime was the first condition of Paradise after death, this demarcation was less exact. Earth itself was but an ante-chamber to heaven, and there were dire penalties for enjoying it as a room apart, perils of persecution and even death. Dante's *Divine Comedy* of the 13th century is crowded with witnesses to the belief that the joys of Paradise would be withheld from those who had played too freely in the human comedy and had claimed too large a share of the fruits of earth.

The Liberty of Knowledge. Not even the liberty of knowledge was to be enjoyed without restraint. Least of all, perhaps, particularly that liberty since it might open forbidden doors, guarded by the authority of the Church. Thus, Aristotle himself, the ancient fount of modern knowledge, was treated by Dante as an infidel. He was a pagan unreconciled with the Church, and he had to be subdued to the 'divine' rule. The great benefits which he had conferred on mankind could not exalt him to the Paradise of saints, and Dante placed him firmly, if reluctantly, in the first circle of his divinely-appointed Hell. This treatment was congruous with the thought and almost bold for the speculation of the 13th century, when reason was awaiting its Renaissance and religion its Reformation. While those human processes were still incomplete (and, indeed, they are not complete to-day), men were weaned from mortal joy by a discipline of toil and suffering, and too eager pathfinders were limited and even persecuted. Meanwhile, those processes went on. The boundaries of the knowable were pushed back by pioneers too curious to yield to fear. By their efforts, the provinces of earth and heaven, of profane and sacred, were progressively re-adjusted. Brave men—Discoverers and Humanists—fingered lay[1] things careless of defilement, secure in the pagan-human creed that 'le rire est le propre de l'homme'. It was for the recovery of earth and its restoration to the children of men that Greek learning was sought in the 14th century. The way of literature was followed as a way of life. That way was sought physically

---

[1] 'Lay' and 'lewd' used to have the same meaning.

by the Discoverers, hardy voyagers to new lands across strange seas, and it was sought intellectually by the scholars or Humanists, re-opening with no less pains the sealed resources of the pagan classics. A sailing-ship and a Greek grammar, and, a little later, the open Bible, three commonest possessions in their modern forms, were the symbols of men's transportation into the freedom of the layman's view.

§ 3. THE LOST CLASSICS.

Loss of the Pagan View. But the visibility was bad. The pagan classics to-day are a neat row of books on a shelf, printed either in their original Greek or Latin, as restored by critics and commentators, or in the elegant translation of the Loeb or another library. They were not available in either form in the 14th century. It was not only that there were no printed books, for what had not been invented would not be missed. What was missed was what had been lost, and the authentic texts of the pagan classics were known to have vanished in the ruin of the Roman Empire in the West. Somewhere, of course, they were, preserved, the precious manuscripts of the Greek and Roman writers, the ' dead authors ' to whom Petrarch wrote letters, and out of whose guessed-at legacy eager Humanists discerned the ample power to satisfy their longing for light and liberty. Reaching out through the murk to the past, through the darkness to the dead, these scholars, conscious of their loss, felt their way through a screen of perversion to the simple forms of un-corrupted truth. There was no secure future for life in Europe unless it were built upon that past, and there was no way back to that past except by improving its visibility.

Somehow, the prospect was realizable ; somewhere, the forms, or many of them, were preserved. But the task of reaching them was as arduous as the enterprise of the Discoverers themselves. The Reformers who made the new religion, the Discoverers who opened the new continent, and the Humanists who sowed the new learning by reviving the old, were all pioneers in the same field. The Bible, the sailing-ship, the Greek grammar : of these three the last was not the least either in the labour of its acquisition or in the dangers that attended its use. All that is worth having in our civilization is due to the spirit of those times.

Three Legacies. Thus, in the background of European literature are the legacies of Israel, Greece and Rome. These legacies had to be exhumed by the diligence and even the daring of the pathfinders. A thick belt of darkness and smoke hid them from common use and wont. To the recovery of the Old and New Testaments in their Hebrew and Greek originals we shall come back in a later Section. Like them, the texts of the Greek and Roman writers were exiled and forgotten, laid away in mouldered or over-written manuscripts which were physically far to find, and, when found, difficult to decipher. These, briefly, were the problems which confronted the Humanists and Reformers, the men of the Renaissance and Reformation who built bridges from antiquity to modern life. This was the work which they were to achieve from the 14th century onwards, always at infinite pains, often in personal peril, and even with the ordeal of war. *Tantæ molis erat Romanam condere gentem* ; so heavy was the task of founding the culture of modern Europe.

Roger Bacon's Sense of the Loss in Science. The illiteracy—the self-insufficiency—of scholars in the 14th century (only six hundred years ago) may be illustrated from contemporary witnesses, who bear frequent evidence to the lack of light. Roger Bacon, for instance, on the century's edge (he died in 1294), a man of such immense learning that he was accounted a magician in the Middle Ages, declared :

'Ignorance of the truths set forth by the ancients is due to the little care that is spent on the study of the ancient languages . . . It is impossible to obtain a perfect knowledge of the Scriptures without knowing Hebrew and Greek, and of philosophy, without knowing Arabic as well.'

(Jews and Arabs had treasured the writings of Greek philosophers during their sojourn in the East, and translated them and commented on them.)

'There are not five men in Latin Christendom,' he continued, ' who are acquainted with the Hebrew, Greek and Arabic Grammar. . . . So it is now with nearly all the Jews, and even with the native Greeks. . . . Even when they *do* understand the languages, they know nothing of the separate parts of philosophy, that the falsities and defects in the Latin copies may be discovered.'

(The same was true of the Hebrew and Greek Testaments, familiar only in the Latin ' vulgate ' version.)

'The scientific works of Aristotle, Avicenna[1], Seneca, Cicero, and other ancients cannot be had except at a great cost; their principal works have not been translated into Latin. . . . Thus far there have only been three persons who could form a true judgment of the small portion of the whole of Aristotle that has been translated.'

Petrarch's Sense of the Loss in Poetry. So much for the disappearance of Aristotle, or, more exactly, the loss of some and the corruption of others of his writings. We select him as the father of Western science, ' the Master of all who know', as Dante called him with conscious discipleship, when he committed him authoritatively to Hell.

And next, what of poetry? What of Homer, for example, the eldest son of the Western muse, who ' enlumined ' all Hellas of poetry, as Aristotle ' enlumined ' it of philosophy? His *Iliad* was as familiar to the Greeks as the Bible is to modern Europeans. His influence was poured on Virgil and through Virgil on Dante, and spread beyond the Middle Ages to the epic verse of Ariosto and Tasso, of Spenser, Milton and Tennyson. Yet the authentic text of Homer came late into the possession of Western Europe. In 1280, on the edge of the 14th century, a certain Hugo of Trimberg bore witness that Homer, ' sticking among his Greeks, has not yet been rendered '[2] into Latin, then the only language familiar to Western readers; and, again, in the middle of that century, Petrarch declared in 1353 that

[1] An Arabic Aristotelian; died A.D. 1037. Observe how Roger Bacon includes the Eastern commentator with the Greek and Roman writers.
[2] *Apud Græcos remanens nondum est translatus.*

there were not ten men in Italy who 'knew and loved' Homer—four or five in Florence, two in Verona, one in Bologna, the seat of a university, one in Mantua, Virgil's birthplace, one in Sulmona, and none at all in Rome, the former centre of the Empire in the West. The irony of the situation was that a Greek from Constantinople, visiting Petrarch at Avignon, had brought with him a manuscript of the *Iliad*. This most precious and unique possession was a dead letter in Petrarch's hands. Homer was 'Greek' to him literally and colloquially. He exerted himself almost in vain to unseal its hidden delights. No dictionary or grammar was available. He went to his wealthier friend, Boccaccio, to whom, too, we shall come in the next Book, to supplicate his aid, and Boccaccio, yielding to this urgency, took a boorish Greek into his household at Florence and employed him for two or three years to translate the manuscript into Latin.

Foreground and Background. These two conspicuous examples of the leading philosopher and poet illustrate the difficulties which obstructed the pursuit of Greek studies in the West. Still keeping to the same examples, we observe that the immense significance of Homer in modern literature is as recent as that of Chaucer, and that scholars did not enjoy the freedom of Aristotle uncorrupted till a date later than Dante, whose Hellenism was subject to inhibitions. The pace quickened from the Renaissance onwards, but the darkness was prolonged to a late dawn. Truly does a modern witness say :

' It would not be easy to exaggerate the impression produced on thirteenth-century Oxford by the discovery that Aristotle's logic was only part of a larger philosophy, hitherto unknown, and by the translations which made his writings on natural philosophy, metaphysics and ethics for the first time familiar to the Western World. It meant a new birth of science. It was the greatest event in the intellectual history of the age.'[1]

Note the phrases used by the historian : 'discovery', 'unknown', 'for the first time', and 'new birth' which is a synonym of renaissance. Remember that this 'greatest

[1] Sir Charles Mallet, *History of the University of Oxford*, Vol. I, p. 76.

event in the intellectual history of the age ' occurred sixteen centuries after Aristotle's birth in 384 B.C., and more than two thousand years after the birth of Homer, the recovery of whose works was just as recent. We may then ask with lively curiosity, Why did their works disappear ? How and why did it occur, that long period of the occultation of the pagan view and the exile of Hellenism in the East ? And how were the Greek and Roman legacies preserved for transmission to modern life and letters ?

§ 4. HIDDEN TREASURES.

A vast history of the dead, of the dead who were brought to life again, lies behind the literature of modern Europe. Without them, that literature is very imperfectly intelligible, like a flat landscape without perspective. A full answer to these questions, accordingly, must be sought in such books as the Oxford *Legacy* volumes of Greece and Rome and the *History of Classical Scholarship* by Sir John Sandys, with historical sidelights from Bryce's *Holy Roman Empire*, and Gibbon's *Decline and Fall*. Not everyone can read them all. But everyone can seize the salient fact that modern history, including modern literature, has its roots in antiquity and that the ancients in a real sense are the moderns. Aristotle, Homer and the rest, reborn in the 14th century for their new life, passed into the stream of modern letters. The background and foreground are one picture.

History of the Loss. As to the cause of the occultation, the bare facts are probably familiar. Constantine the Great, the first Christian Emperor, transferred under duress the seat of Empire from Rome to Byzantium, which he re-named Constantinople. He died A.D. 337. Prior to that date the invasions of the Barbarians from the North-East of Europe had threatened the majesty of Rome, and after that date the menace increased. In 376 the Goths crossed the Danube. In 410 Alaric captured Rome. Attila and his Huns came in the middle of the 5th century, and the end of the Roman Empire in the West is dated at 476. The ebb and flow continued through several centuries, and Charlemagne in 800 was the first Emperor to be crowned again in Rome.

Illustrated by Homer. So much for the outline of the story. There went east with Constantine and his builders a civilization as well as a city, and, roughly, for a thousand years, from the 4th to the 14th century A.D., the legacies of Greece and Rome, the pagan classics and the ' pagan view', were in exile from the Western world. Great Homer, the glory of Hellas, persisted as a poor, shrunken fellow, the mere shadow of a name. The Trojan war, the topic of his *Iliad* (Ilion is Troy), was degraded from poetry to a kind of history, which no one was scientific enough to recognize as legendary. Some time between the 4th and 6th centuries, two of these unscientific historians re-wrote the tale of Ilion in a prose-narrative, from the Trojan and the Greek sides, respectively, and that dull epitome of the Homeric poems, ascribed to Dictys and Dares, a Phrygian and a Cretan, became the synonym of ' Homer ' in later centuries. Even so, they could not quite conceal the poet. The indestructible romance of Homer still appealed to the imagination of poets, and a Norman, Benoît de Sainte-Maure, and a Sicilian, Guido delle Colonne, working up all the available material, both written and oral, produced Troy-books in verse before 1300, which began to show the way back to the splendid original. When Petrarch, in 1353, first handled a manuscript of the *Iliad*, he and Boccaccio and a few others were aware of its value for learning and life—for the new life under the sign of ancient Hellas—and their hired translator was the forerunner of a long line of wandering scholars from the East who found a way to and a welcome in Italian cities, even before the Turkish capture of Constantinople released its treasures and their keepers in 1453.

Illustrated by Aristotle. The story of Aristotle in occultation is much the same as that of Homer. In his lifetime in the golden age of Greece he was a member of Plato's Academy at Athens, and became tutor to Alexander of Macedon, the Napoleon of the ancient world. With the fall of Rome his works passed into outer darkness. His physics and natural history were decocted in the East into 'bestiaries', or beast-tales, half-fabulous and wholly popular. The science was boiled out of them and only their story-value remained. His logic and metaphysics (a word which Aristotle did not use) were diluted by Arab and Jewish scholars into a *materia philosophica*, which, in Latin renderings from the Oriental text-books[1], passed at last into the curriculum of the Schoolmen at their seats of learning in Paris and elsewhere. This Scholastic philosophy maintained itself, somewhat precariously at times, as a discipline of the Church, and Dante, a contemporary of Roger Bacon, was as keen a Schoolman as he. The Schoolmen studied the Arabic doctors. Avicenna, mentioned by Bacon above, and a greater Aristotelian, Averroes (1126-98), were recommended to modern readers by Dante; and another carrier of Hellenism from East to West was Avicebron (Solomon ibn Gabirol), a Spanish Jew of the 11th century, who frankly regarded Aristotle as ' the only man whom God had permitted to attain the highest summit of perfection.' The full story of Aristotelian studies in those centuries without Aristotle is a romance of the East, and well does a modern scholar say : ' Arab and Moor and Syrian and Jew treasured his books while the Western world sat in darkness.'[2]

The Recovery of Homer. The darkness was dissipated in the 14th–15th century. Thus, the restoration of Homer, to keep to that typical example, may be traced almost year by year after Boccaccio came to the aid of Petrarch's Greek studies. A brilliant group of eager Hellenists gathered in Florence, Boccaccio's city, at the Platonic Academy, under the patronage of Lorenzo de' Medici. We shall come back to this circle : here we are specially concerned with the name of Politian, a member of the Academy, who died in 1494 at the early age of forty, and who was known in his lifetime as ' Homericus juvenis' in recognition of his primacy as a Homerist. He was not alone in his labours. In 1488, the first authentic Greek text of the *Iliad* and the *Odyssey* was printed at the new press in Florence, and commentary, criticism and

---

[1] They were sometimes translated and retranslated in and out of foreign languages, which took them further and further away from the original Greek.
[2] Professor D'Arcy Thompson, *The Legacy of Greece*, p. 160.

translation, with a 'Homeric question' invented by modern scholars, were multiplied rapidly in every land. Antiquity was unsealed for its new sovereignty over the hearts and the minds of living men. 'I go to awaken the dead,' cried Ciriaco, an antiquary of Ancona, who has been called the Schliemann of the 15th century, and pen and spade alike were employed in bringing the dead back to life and rebuilding the past for present use. This revival was greeted by contemporaries with almost lyrical fervour. Politian's Latin verse-declamations which accompanied his lectures on the Classics have been described by Symonds as 'leaping' and by Saintsbury as 'exultant', and the instant sense of exhilaration at the restoration of 'the pagan view' is a measure of the loss to the intellectual outlook which had been caused by the long night of its obscurity.

§ 5. THE LATIN BIBLE.

We have been discussing the legacies of Greece and Rome in two signal instances of Greek writers who disappeared and were found. They are to be taken as types of a story which is repeated in the rest. Even greater is the 'legacy of Israel', as it is called in the Oxford book of that name. For what would be the present state of European literature without the vernacular Bibles ? A famous passage in Green's *History of the English People* helps us to reply for our own literature :

'The disclosure of the stories of Greek literature had wrought the revolution of the Renaissance. The disclosure of the older mass of Hebrew literature wrought the revolution of the Reformation. . . . As a mere literary monument the English version of the Bible remains the noblest example of the English tongue, while its perpetual use made it, from the instant of its appearance, the standard of our language.'

Difficulties of Approach. Looked at dispassionately (without the passion of religion), it is an unexpected tribute to a foreign book, translated from Hebrew and Greek, and the tribute reflects immense credit on the English translators of 1611. But, surely, it is even more significant in relation to the centuries when Englishmen did *not* possess that 'noblest example of the English tongue'. For the Bible, too, was in the background of modern literature. Like Homer, Aristotle and the rest, it had its period of occultation, its dead age of a shadow-life in a Latin version. The darkness did not lie on it as heavily as on the pagan Classics. The Latin Bible was read familiarly and in full. But the darkness was heavier in the sense that the real light was more jealously shut out. All textual criticism was difficult in the absence of dictionaries and grammars and in many instances of the texts themselves. But Biblical criticism particularly was difficult because it was specially selected for discouragement by the Church. If, as we are told,

'Christian writers up to the first half of the 5th century regarded the old literature, especially poetry, with grave mistrust';

if 'its very charm seemed carnal and made them afraid'; if

'at the back of their minds was the feeling that the pagan view of life was not wholly destroyed, and that to give undue encouragement to the older culture was like playing with the embers of a fire that was not yet wholly extinguished,'[1]

how much more powerful would be the ecclesiastical opposition to a lay study of Holy Writ. A new reading derived from the original text might do worse than let in a 'pagan view': it might let in an heretical opinion; and in order to protect the Church from sacrilege of that kind, an obscurantism, or a manufactured darkness, was added in Biblical studies to the obscurity common to all scholarship. It was not only the absence of grammars, to which Roger Bacon bore witness ('it is impossible to obtain a perfect knowledge of the Scriptures without knowing Hebrew or Greek'): that was common to all students of dead languages; there was further the active prohibition of lay criticism of Holy Writ

[1] F. W. Hall, *A Comparison of Classical Texts*, Oxford, 1913; p. 64.

just because it was holy. It was this chief and extra barrier to Biblical studies which had to be broken down at the end of the 15th century, when the Renaissance was passing into the Reformation; and, when we fit our language to the standard of the English Bible, and spend its legacy in our literature, we cannot forget the saints and martyrs, the critics, scholars and translators, who brought it out of darkness into light and changed a stagnant pool in a dead tongue into a fountain of living waters.

Restorers of Biblical Study. In the background of European literature we have found the Bible and the pagan Classics. But we have not found them at large or in full. We may consult contemporary evidence once more. Erasmus, the schoolmaster of Europe, wrote in 1516:

' The mysteries of kings it may be safer to conceal, but Christ wished His mysteries to be published as openly as possible.'

He expressed his longing for the books of the Bible—

' That the husbandman should sing portions of them to himself as he follows the plough, that the weaver should hum them to the tune of his shuttle, that the traveller should beguile with their stories the tedium of his journey.'

And in both these passages he was plainly anticipating a liberty which men and women did not then possess. Luther, the liberator, was preparing it, but long years of opposition lay in front, and it was not till 1611 that ' the revolution of the Reformation' brought the Authorised Version to our own shores. There had, of course, been earlier bids for freedom. St. Jerome, in the Syrian desert, had translated the Bible into Latin in the 4th century A.D., and his version, the famous Latin Vulgate, became the sacred Book of the Church of Rome. John Wiclif, a thousand years afterwards, translated the Latin Vulgate into English (1389), and up and down that busy millennium there had been workers in every country at like tasks. But the full liberty of Holy Writ was not enjoyed without let or hindrance until the vernacular Bibles were established in the foreground of modern literature.

Pushing Back the Mysterious. We pause at this point to say one word in passing about the phrase used by Erasmus : ' the mysteries of kings . . . the mysteries of Christ.' His foresight, in 1516, was remarkable. For a time was to come, though Erasmus did not know it, when it would no longer be safe to conceal the mysteries of kings. The work of the revolutionaries in France was added to that of the reformers in Germany, and the last shred of mystery was stripped from the last human ruler by divine right when Louis XVI perished by the guillotine. The Revolution of the 18th century was the sequel to the Reformation of the 16th, and the two mysteries noted by Erasmus were both published openly at last.

Thus pausing, we may go a step further and ask if all the mystery that hampers the progress of mankind was removed in 1793. When the light of the French Revolution was added to the twin lights of the German Reformation and of the Italian Renaissance, did all Western life become a sunshine ? The story of Europe in the 19th century and the experience of Europe in the 20th must answer these questions, and students are likely to reply that, though the centre of curiosity has been shifted, still mystery remains. Roger Bacon wanted Greek and Hebrew grammars in order to open the sealed books of philosophy. Petrarch wanted a Greek-Italian dictionary in order to read ' dead authors ' and to unlock the ' pagan view'. Erasmus in Luther's generation wanted to open the Bible to popular knowledge. The Discoverers opened the New World, and the fall of the Holy Roman Empire in 1806 made a pathway for national consciousness. But still the curiosity of man, his eager, unsatiable humanism, finds mysteries to explore. He still wants tools of investigation and new grammars to further knowledge unrevealed. For in this ' mysterious universe', wrote Sir James Jeans as recently as 1930—

' Every conclusion that has been tentatively put forward is quite frankly speculative and uncertain. We cannot claim to have discerned more than a very faint glimmer of light at the best '.

Courage of the Pioneers. We return from this brief

digression, the object of which has been to show that modern life, illumined with so much pains, has not yet reached its height of achievement, to the light of the early Humanists. Their first and most urgent business was to explore the background of literature. They asserted the right and found the means to bring back classical studies out of the night, for they partly knew and partly conjectured the uplift, in an expressive American phrase, which these would impart to their own life. ' The idea that the Classical writers were of real practical use, and that a transformation of contemporary life was to be accomplished by means of them, pervades the whole period of the Renaissance.'[1] To this end, not easily attained, men sought not only the mechanical aid of dictionaries, grammars and the like, with the collaboration of scribes and translators and searchers for manuscripts and other treasures : a whole society and apparatus, though unorganised and mostly unskilled ; they sought, too, and even less easily, the moral atmosphere in which to pursue their fearful joys. They sought release from the inhibitions on lay learning and freedom for the physical energies of man. They claimed the right, as science dictated, to call the earth flat or round, to tend the body independently of the soul, to love a woman without merging flesh in spirit, to follow fortune without surrendering the fruits. Their claim was disputed by the authorities and resisted by dark counsellors all the time, but still, bit by bit, they made way. They were moved by the common human instinct of a man conscious of his powers and not to be constrained by a higher power to use them for ends not his own.

§ 6. DANTE ALIGHIERI (1265–1321).

Dante's Double Loyalty. Recall Dante's way with Homer and Aristotle, whom we have selected as typical pagan writers. His guide to the Inferno made him enter

[1] F. W. Hall, *op. cit.*, p. 99.

' The foremost circle that surrounds the abyss.
There, in so far as I had power to hear,
Were lamentations none, but only sighs,
That tremulous made the everlasting air.
And this arose from sorrow without torment,
Which the crowds had, that many were and great,
Of infants and of women and of men.'

It was hell, but not the worst hell: just ' sorrow without
torment ' in the first circle of the Inferno, and Dante's guide,
who was Virgil himself, explained their situation to his
disciple :

" Now will I have thee know, ere thou go farther,
That they sinned not ; and if they merit had,
'Tis not enough, because they had not baptism,
Which is the portal of the faith thou holdest ;
And if they were before Christianity,
In the right manner they adored not God ;
And among such as these am I myself [*i.e.* Virgil].
For such defects, and not for other guilt,
Lost are we, and are only so far punished
That without hope we live on in desire.'

Dante was sorry for them, but he acquiesced. It was inevitable
in his creed, which represented the sublimest creed of the
13th century (Dante was born in 1265), that these unbaptised
men, women and children, whose fate it had been to live
before Christianity, should be ' lost ' through all eternity
' for such defects', and should live on ' without torment '
but ' without hope', bearing the punishment of insufficient
merit. It was inevitable and it was just.

In this company, then, were Homer, Horace, Ovid, Lucan,
and Virgil himself, and these Big Five, Dante tells us a little
naïvely, turned to him

' with signs of salutation,
And more of honour still, much more, they did me,
In that they made me one of their own band ;
So that the sixth was I 'mid so much wit.'

As a poet, he was proud to be of their company ; as a baptised
Christian, he was prouder still to leave them in hell.

With the pagan poets were congregated the philosophers.
In the same circle of the Inferno, Dante tells us,

> ' The Master I beheld of those who know [Aristotle]
> Sit with his philosophic family.
> All gaze upon him and all do him honour.
> There I beheld both Socrates and Plato,
> Who nearer him before the others stand,'

and numberless great thinkers of antiquity, including

> ' Tully [Cicero], Livy, and moral Seneca,
> Euclid, geometrician, and Ptolemy,
> Galen, Hippocrates, and Avicenna,
> Averroes who the great Comment made.'

' I cannot all of them portray in full,' protested Dante, the
disciple of the Schoolmen who taught Aristotle obediently
to the Church, as he quitted them in order to visit yet lower
circles.

An Escape from Dante. The revelation sought by the
Humanists so very shortly after Dante's lifetime was of
an antiquity not subject to inhibitions. They wanted Aristotle
outside the Church, and his ' philosophic family ' out of the
Inferno. Petrarch was living when Dante died ; he was born
in 1304 and Dante died in 1321. Boccaccio, who was born
in 1313, occupied the first Dante Chair founded in their
common city of Florence. But between the antiquity which
satisfied Dante's sense of seemliness and the antiquity explored
by Petrarch and Boccaccio there was a difference which
cannot be measured by the few years dividing the elder from
the younger writers. For the Humanists of the 14th century,
however timidly and tentatively, sought a moral permit for
the pagan view. If we were to say that they fetched out of
hell Homer, Aristotle, Cicero and the rest, we might be using
too graphic a locution. But we may borrow from a trustworthy
modern writer a phrase which expresses our meaning, and
call Boccaccio—

'The escape from Dante. The dreamer awakes,' we are told, ' and tastes the air, and sees the colours of life and feels the delight of moving his limbs. He is among men and women. He has touched ground after his dizzy flight of the spirit; he has come out of the prison-house of theological system, nobly and grimly architected, and is abroad again in the homely disorder of our familiar world. Small blame to him,' adds the critic,[1] ' if he laughs,'

and we remember the forecast of Rabelais: ' le rire est le propre de l'homme'.

Claims of the Humanists. So, the new researchers of antiquity, Classical and even Biblical, sought it at large and in full. They claimed a right to the pagan view and possession in the joys of earth, estopped through so many pious centuries by the subordination of human action to divine ends. Complete victory was not theirs : perhaps it is a constant endeavour from which victory ever recedes. But the challenge was made. The pioneers of Renaissance, Reformation and Revolution had entered the lists. They did not know all that lay before them. The gentle scholar in his study, poring over the manuscript which he had recovered from the back of beyond, did not know that the genie of antiquity which he was seeking to release would shake the bases of his world and transform its traditional beliefs. But he may have partly conjectured it, for Petrarch (we are thinking particularly of him) associated the revival of Latin studies with a renewal of the Roman rule in modern life ; so that, even if he had known it, he might not have been overmuch afraid. His joy was to feel certain that he was doing right, and this new self-confidence distinguishes him from scholars before the dawn and links him with the discoverers to be. He had shifted the boundaries of *fas* and *nefas*. Curiosity, the beginning of philosophy, was no longer in his view a secret vice to be cultivated with a consciousness of guilt. He might still be persecuted for indulging it. ' The prison-house of theological system ' still reared its grim and noble lines. The Bastille stood till 1789, and the origin of species was disguised till 1859. But the old

[1] Walter Raleigh, *Some Authors*, Oxford, 1923 ; pp. 3, 4.

system was inevitably to fall. The contribution of the early Humanists to the cause of intellectual and moral liberty would prove greater than they knew, and yet they were aware that it was great. For they were vindicating a principle at the same time as they were changing a practice. They were asserting for modern men and women, subject to the domination of authority, the right to think, act, live for themselves in unrestricted freedom of venture and of knowledge. The increase of light is to be measured by the courage of the enquirers rather than by the patches of ground on which they threw their little beams.

Dante's Message to His Times. So Dante stands in this background of European literature, sublime, solitary and supreme as the representative of a passing age. The hills of antiquity are not yet stormed. The Hebrew and Greek Testaments are untranslated into any language except the Latin of the Roman Church. Aristotle is in the keeping of the Christian Schoolmen, Homer is the shadow of a name, and these two are typical of the occultation of the Classics of Greece and Rome. The pagan view is not yet proclaimed for the free acceptance of humankind. Though the love of woman cannot be resisted, since men have always been men, yet it is refined for poetic use by a kind of mystical sublimation, in which common carnal desire, rarified to a yearning of the soul and, therefore, remote from experience, turns in subdual to—

'The Love which moves the sun and the other stars.'[1]

This, very briefly, is Dante's message, in his *Vita Nuova* ('New Life') and *Commedia*, known later as the 'Divine Comedy.' This was his way of a man with a maid, the human way transmuted to the divine way, the fleshly to the spiritual. This was the Beatrice of Dante, of whom he sang:

'Beatricë is gone up into high Heaven,
The Kingdom where the angels are at peace,
And lives with them, and to her friends is dead.
Not by the frost of winter was she driven

[1] The last verse of the *Divine Comedy.*

Away, like others, nor by summer heats,
But through a perfect gentleness instead.
For from the lamp of her meek lowlihead
Such an exceeding glory went up hence
That it woke wonder in the Eternal Sire,
Until a sweet desire
Entered Him for that lovely excellence,
So that He bade her to Himself aspire,
Counting this weary and most evil place
Unworthy of a thing so full of grace.'

But it was a harsh condition for common human lovers, who
counted love worthy and earth fair. These fastened their hopes
on the world's rewards and pains and turned eagerly to new
counsellors. They sought the sanction of happiness not in
heaven but on earth. In the full noon of the Renaissance we
shall hear, like a peal of bells, the opening verses of Shakespeare's *Sonnets*, which reaffirmed the dignity of man from
this sublime ascription of unworth and repaired the standard
of moral values :

'From fairest creatures we desire increase,
That thereby beauty's rose might never die.'

The romance of the rose that never dies is a theme at the
front of modern literature, and it is of the essence of the
theme that immortality comes by enjoyment, not renouncement.

His Learning. Dante is at once very simple and very
difficult, very learned and very ignorant, according as we look
at him against his background or try to read him as a poet
among modern poets. He wrote Italian, though he lived in
a Latin age : his defence of the ' illustrious ' vernacular tongue,
in a Latin treatise *De Vulgari Eloquentia*, is a critical document
of prime importance, and philology is grateful to him for
the terms *d'Oïl*, *d'Oc* and *de Si*, chosen from the respective
particles of affirmation (' yes ') to describe the three current
dialects of Northern France, Southern France, and Tuscany.
He believed in kingship, though in the kingdom of God on
earth, and another of his Latin treatises, *De Monarchia*, ex-

pounded in a riven State the highest ideal of a united Italy, where Cæsar should be just and Peter should be wise. He wrote love-verse, but as a theologian, and his early songs transferred to the mainland of Italy the love-lyric and dance-music of Sicilian Troubadours. The sonnet, the elegy, the ballad, the pastoral, the serenade, the virelay, the madrigal, the rondeau and other verse-forms, including rhyme-royal and its variants, are derived from those schools of song, in which Guido Gunicelli of Bologna, who died in 1276, was acknowledged by Dante himself as the chief inventor of a *dolce stil nuovo*, a sweet new style in Italian poesy. But such love-verse had an unearthly ending. Dante was always a son of his own century, with its superstitions, its inhibitions and its exclusions, and with the unconquered hills behind. He raised to its very highest power—so high that its white candour almost blinds us—the poetry of a Christian thinker without the pagan view, or with the pagan writers conforming to the Church. Leaving all the unbaptised far below him in circle after circle of Hell and Purgatory, ' I ', says Dante,

> ' who to the divine had from the human,
> From time unto eternity had come,'

found the ardour of desire stilled in Paradise. Finite ends were consumed in the Infinite, a little longing in a great light, the candle in its flame.

His Limitations. It is a strange, grand and awful world, very distant from common understanding, that of Dante and his Beatrice. Part of the *Commedia*, like the whole of the *Vita Nuova*, is the biography of the poet; part of it is the history of his country (' a ship without a pilot in great tempest '), tossed between rival factions, known after the names of royal families as Guelfs and Ghibellines, and struggling for predominance in the State; and all of it is immense and vast, something bigger than common kinds of poetry, and more comprehensible by what went before than by what will come after. Yet it is not wholly comprehensible in any century except his own, which lay in a brief and almost breathless pause, so far as literature is concerned, between the Schoolmen and the Humanists, between the other-worldly

and the this-worldly points of view, between the followers
of learning under the sign of theology and the unbound
pursuers of experience, of whom Christopher Marlowe was
to write in 1587 :

> ' Our souls, whose faculties can comprehend
> The wondrous architecture of the world,
> And measure every wandering planet's course,
> Still climbing after knowledge infinite,
> And always moving as the restless spheres,
> Will us to wear ourselves and never rest.'

We 'escape from Dante' on this perception. We quit the
background of European literature in his company. It is
pertinent to his biography to remark that Beatrice, mystically
transformed and raised to a throne of pity, is represented by
the poet as a real person, Bice Portinari, whom he first met
when he was nine years old and who died in 1290. It is
pertinent, too, to remark that his guide through Purgatory
and Hell to the portals of Paradise was Virgil, the epic poet
of Rome, who came very near to Christian hearts and prophecy,
and from whom Dante took his ' beautiful style,' for the
special significance of Virgil to Dante belongs to the magic
of that suspended age.[1] Biographers, too, would have us
recall that Dante was exiled from Florence in 1302, and knew

> ' how savoureth of salt
> The bread of others, and how hard the road
> The going up and down another's stair'.

The Pope who drove him out was Boniface VIII, whom he
committed to the third trench of the eighth circle in Hell
(*Inferno*, XIX).

Temporary Expedients. More literary interest attaches to
that numeral nine mentioned just now. In an age which

---

[1] 'Dante is the culminating figure of the Middle Ages ; he is also the creator
of modern literature ; and Virgil was Dante's acknowledged and adored
master. From him Dante took, as one torch kindling from another, not only
the vision of the ordained divine government of the world, and the prophetic
and operative faith in the unity and supremacy of Roman Italy, but also the
long-lost *bello stile*, the beauty of language which he regained for European
poetry.'

J. W. Mackail, The Æneid, Oxford, 1930 ; pp. lxxiii–iv.

ignored the frontiers between science and magic, a mystical value was attached to certain 'perfect' indivisible numbers. Thus, King Alfonso the Wise of Spain (d. 1284), an older contemporary of Dante, had seven letters in his name and compiled the *Siete Partidas* or 'seven parts' of the Castilian code of laws. The number three and its multiples fascinated Dante. His *Commedia* was divided into three books, each with thirty-three cantos, in a metre of linked threes (*terza rima*), with 3 × 3 circles in Hell. To the same province of literature belongs the use of the devices of personification, allegory and dream. Each had a long descent in Oriental extensions from Latin beginnings, and each served a practical purpose in the Middle Ages. It supplied a cloak in which to wrap up a meaning which it might be imprudent to state literally. We remember what Erasmus said about the mysteries of Christ and of kings. Both alike had been concealed. Popes and princes were quick to resent an affront to their authority and to see one even in unlikely places. So these useful rhetorical devices were cultivated for expediency and became a part of the art of the men of letters. The criticism which the Church prohibited and which was discouraged by the State found an outlet in the freer realm, where, as Chaucer wrote in the *House of Fame*, the most Dantesque of his poems,

> ' spirits have the might
> To makë folk to dreme a-night '.

Even the opening verses of the *Commedia*,

> ' Midway upon the journey of our life
> I found myself within a forest dark,
> For the straightforward pathway had been lost ',

concealed Florence in the forest.

§ 7. The Rose of Beauty.

The quotations from Marlowe on page 29, and from Shakespeare on page 27, which were cited to illustrate the contrast of the Elizabethan age with the age of Dante, help to show us in detail how the revolution of ideas in the 14th century was quickened in the 16th. The courage, the liberty, the independence, worldly values and the dignity of life on earth, sought in dreams and through a fog by the early Humanists, were realized by the sons of the Renaissance :

> ' That thereby beauty's rose might never die ' . . .
> ' Still climbing after knowledge infinite.' . . .

Love and learning pursued their own infinite without clutching at the robe of theology, and a compromise of human aims became as unnecessary as a disguise of their expression.

' *Roman de la Rose*'. If this difficult perception be understood—and it points the way out of the Middle Ages—we may follow backwards for a moment the romance of Shakespeare's ' rose'. Still keeping in the background of European literature, we come to a poem of that name, the famous and inescapable *Roman de la Rose*, which was written by two Frenchmen in the 13th century, Guillaume of Lorris (*c.* 1237) and Jean of Méun (*c.* 1277). The elder writer probably died young, for he left his *Rose* unfinished at verse 4,070, and Jean, who took it over when it was growing in popularity, found it a convenient model on which to drape another 18,004 verses of adventurous tales and moral reflection. It was the first omnibus-book in European literature. Part of it, about 1,700 verses, was translated by Chaucer, whose English version was completed by two other writers, and it enjoyed in several centuries and many countries a fame not at all in excess of its mingled sweetness and strength and of its value as a source-book of European poesy.

It contained all the elements that have been mentioned : the dream-convention

> (' That it was May, thus dreaméd me
> In time of Love and Jollity ') ;

the love-lore

> (' Hard is his heart that loveth not
> In May when all this mirth is wrought ') ;

the personification (Sir Mirth, Lady Gladness, Fair Welcome,

Sweet-Seeming, False-Seeming, and many another who helped or hindered Amant, the lover, in his quest of the Lady of the Rose), the allegory, and so on.

The Contribution of Ovid. Particular notice is due to the share contributed by Ovid to Guillaume's portion of the *Roman.* Publius Ovidius Naso, 43 B.C.–A.D. 17, was one of the Classical Latin writers whose works, or versions of whose works, were most assiduously read in the era before the Renaissance. He was traditionally the love-poet of the ancients, and in medieval Courts of Love his authority was sought for the rules of the game and his repertory for stories of how to play it. His *Ars Amatoria* ('Art of Love') inspired several Western redactors, and helped to codify the laws of the service and psychology of love, as practised by aspirants to chivalry and as exemplified in the manners of the Table Round. His *Metamorphoses* and *Heroides* provided the examples of the theory, and separate tales, such as those of Pyramus and Thisbe, Dido, Medea, Orpheus, Ariadne, Narcissus and many others, became part of the common stock of romantic story-tellers. Chaucer was an eager Ovidian; Marot[1] in France and Arthur Golding in England were among his translators in the 16th century; Francis Meres wrote in 1598 that 'the sweet, witty soul of Ovid lives in mellifluous and honey-tongued Shakespeare', and Dryden, Swinburne, and William Morris continued the Ovid-cult to yesterday. Truly he wrote of himself:

'Trans ego tellurem, trans altas audiar undas.'

§ 8. COMMON THEMES OF LITERATURE.

The Courts of Love and the Table Round in the last paragraph bring us back, still behind Dante, to another feature in the background of European literature. A French writer in the 13th century—his name, Jehan Bodel, has been preserved—meditating the themes which were available for

[1] See page 84 below.

chansons de geste, or narrative poems of heroic deeds, remarked in a jingling couplet :

> ' Ne sont que trois matières à nul homme entendant—
> De France, et de Bretagne, et de Rome la grant '.

The literal meaning is, of course, that there were three ' matters ' out of copyright, as we might say : the French matter, the Breton matter, and the matter of great Rome. But the ultimate meaning requires a little more explication.

The Big Three. Consider, first, the kind of audience which Bodel had in mind. It was the age of chivalry and the Crusades. The knights in their camps had to be entertained during months of inactivity, and the dames at home had to be amused in the absence of their lords. Moreover, just as to-day by broadcasting and other means we try to foster a sense of peace and a League of Nations mentality, so then a Crusader's mind and a sense of martial glory were aimed at in order to gild the edges and disguise the roughnesses of the social complex. The institutions of chivalry, with its ladies' favours, its knight-errantry and so forth, made a powerful contribution to this object ; and when there were no printed books and but the barest rudiments of a stage the ingenuity of story-tellers was drawn upon to the utmost. To tell a new tale of love and glory, or to re-tell an old tale more effectively, with a finer edge to its point of honour, or a bolder flight of adventure or with more wonderful magic for the credulous, was not only to win the rewards of authorship but to increase *morale*. So the chansonists ransacked the source-books and trimmed and adorned the tales they found. Hence the double vogue of Ovid, alike for his *ars* and for his heroes and heroines, and hence the common recourse to the stockpots enumerated by Bodel. ' France ', briefly, meant the ' matter ' of Charlemagne, the Carlovingian heroic cycle, as it is called, which expanded the life and work of that great Emperor, who died in 814, into an epopee, or collection of epical tales, and created a Charlemagne-legend based less and less exactly on the genuine exploits of the leader and his paladins, the chief of whom was Count Roland, the hero of Roncesvalles. ' Bretagne ', as briefly, meant the ' matter ' of King Arthur, leader of the

Britons in the 5th century, whose life was similarly expanded into the exploits of the Arthuriad—Tristan, Lancelot, and the other Knights—and absorbed the legend of the Holy Grail. And ' Rome ' meant all the ' matter ' of antiquity : the stories of Thebes and Troy, and the glamorous fables of the Orient, particularly of Alexander, the magic of whose conquering might was spread to fairyland and paradise.

Lesser ' Matters '. These matters belonged to every man and were the monopoly of none. They were treated by song-smith and ballad-writer, by epicist and prose-narrator, and more was added to them on the way. Other countries, too, brought their heroes. Thus, Prince Roderick in Spain, who captured Valencia in 1092 and ruled it for seven years till he died, passed at once out of history into legend as ' the conquering lord ' (el Cid Campeador), and his *Poema del Cid*, composed in the course of the 12th century, was adorned with marvellous accretions. The historical *sagas* of Scandinavia, the *lied*, or lay, of the mist-dwellers (*Nibelungen*) in Germany, and heroic tales (*byliny*) from Kiev in Russia reinforced the more commonly accessible *matières* and the delectable name of Walter of the Birds'-mead (Walther von der Vogelweide, *c.* 1170–1228), a German master of medieval love-song in the class famous as *Minnesinger*, is particularly to be mentioned.

More Familiar Treatment. With all this wealth of material for song and story there were naturally variations in the treatment. The fun of the thing began to be seen, particularly when middle-class audiences, composed of merchants, traders and travellers at the busy fairs and markets of the day, or gathered at an inn under the temporary rule of its stout, jolly host, developed a consciousness of their own and a social sense of what was due to them as a class. Out of these new conditions a new turn was given to the old themes. The worshipful ladies of the courts of love, set apart by the conventions of chivalry, gave place to women of the people whose lively tongues and easy manners opened the gates of literature to the gay, human, motley company of Boccaccio and Chaucer in the 14th, of Lesage, Fielding and Dickens in the 18th and 19th, centuries. This human comedy, as distinct from the divine, which Dante was depicting so magnificently, found its first chief outlet in French *fabliaux*. It was the characteristic of the fable to disguise the point of its wit. *Mutato nomine de te fabula*,[1] ' change the name and you are my victim,' the fabulist said, but the victim himself might miss the allusion, and anyhow it was safer in disguise. A short natty tale in verse, with a sharp edge falling on some human foible—a smug virtue or a snug vice—was the commonest form of this craft. The safest of all disguises was an animal's skin thrown over a human being, and the ' bestiary ' or beast-tale, with its obvious debt to Æsop, became universal in its vogue. The biggest and most popular of all beast-tales was that of Reynard the Fox, famous throughout Western Europe in the 12th and 13th centuries as the *Roman de Renart*. It was the grand clearing-house for fun and satire, reversing the morals of the heroic tales, and featuring, in modern film-parlance, the old Emperor Charlemagne as Noble the Lion, with his fangs worn and his authority set at nought by the nimble wit of Reynard the ready. On this basis, so simple in its appeal, was reared an immense structure of Reynard-literature, down to Goethe's *Reinecke Fuchs* of 1794 ; and it is obvious that a social satirist, using the medium of the verse-fable, just as Mr. David Low uses the graphic cartoon, would find in the animal world types of greed, vanity, stupidity, deceit, sloth and other qualities by which to rebuke offences, whether conventional or moral, in the microcosm of a local *bourgeoisie*.

§ 9.   SUMMARY.

Such then was the background of literature, when Chaucer would not ' gestë *rum, ram, ruf* by lettre ', and Petrarch was trying to read Homer, and Boccaccio was seeking an ' escape from Dante', and when ' the pagan view was now once more proclaimed that man was made not only to toil and suffer, but to enjoy.' Much, of course, has necessarily been omitted. It is a bird's-eye view, not an ordnance-survey, which has been attempted in these few, imperfect pages. But they should prove

[1] Horace, *Satires*, I, i, 69.

full and true enough to supply a guide to the country, and we rehearse them even more briefly.

First of all and far away, behind the screen of perversion, are the shining Classics of Greece and Rome. Their radiance comes dim and broken, and in place of the actual authors of antiquity—the veritable Homer, Plato, Aristotle, Cicero, Virgil, Ovid, Horace and the rest—there are Latin renderings of Oriental versions of their works, or bits and scraps preserved for special causes. Thus, all that was left of Cicero's *De Republica*, a learned volume for which Roger Bacon searched in vain, was a fragment from its sixth book, known as *Somnium Scipionis* ('The Dream of Scipio') preserved by Macrobius in the commentary which he wrote at the end of the 4th century A.D. The dream-motive referred to above, which meant so much in medieval poesy, is traced directly by Guillaume of Lorris in his *Roman de la Rose* to—

An authour that hight Macrobes [was named Macrobius],
That halt [held] not dremës false ne lees [nor untrue],
But undoth us the avisioun [reveals the vision]
That whylom mette King Cipioun ' [Scipio],

and this sanction for a poets' convention was all that medieval scientists valued in Cicero's political treatise. When later science sought the treatise itself, all the rest of it had vanished. Not dissimilarly, Cicero's philosophic *Hortensius* is known to us to-day only because St Augustine read it in A.D. 373 and relates in his ' Confessions ' how it helped to convert him to Christianity. The curiosities of literature include many records of this kind which the present is not the place or time to tell. But these two examples may suffice to illustrate the haps and chances by which some treasures of antiquity came home from the East to the West through the darkness in which so much was lost.

There were gains[1] as well as losses in that darkness. Among the gains were many new Latin books, our possession of which affords some compensation for the older books that disappeared. Thus, Augustine himself (A.D. 354–410) lends

[1] For the gains see summarily *A History of Later Latin Literature* (331–1674), by F. A. Wright and T. A. Sinclair, London, 1931.

his name to an age in which the work of Christian Latinists added immensely to the resources alike of the new religion and of the old language which were now to be so intimately bound together. His 'Confessions' and his 'City of God' (*De Civitate Dei*) would rank as great books in any epoch, and the latter particularly was important for its influence in reconstructing the moral foundations of society after the sack of Rome by Alaric in 410. Without Augustine the history of thought in Europe cannot fully be studied. Still less could it be studied, however, without the old Roman and Greek books which had passed out of common use and knowledge. Night covered them, and it was from beyond that darkness that the Humanists of the 14th century summoned the 'Renaissance' of the 'dead authors' to whom Petrarch had written letters.

Their summons of the 'Reformation' was not less hazardous. The Bible is written in Hebrew and Greek, and we quoted Roger Bacon's evidence to prove that there were no facilities in the Dark Ages for the study of those languages. We may quote modern scholars to like effect :

'While the Hebrew and Greek Scriptures, and even languages, were lost to the West for over a thousand years, the Latin Scriptures and the literature based on them remained all through that time the common possession of every scholar in Europe.'[1]

So the Vulgate Bible of Jerome (A.D. 377–420) was a great and necessary achievement, which put the Church in succeeding centuries under a deep debt of 'remembrance and thankfulness' to him. But it was not only the grammars that were lacking for the study of Hebrew and Greek. So far as the Bible was concerned, those studies were directly discouraged. The defenders of the faith were jealous of any breach in their defences : a new rendering or even an amended text might shake the seat of authority, which accordingly guarded its prerogative : and while native Bibles here and

---

[1] *A Grammar of the Vulgate*, by W. E. Plater and H. J. White, Dean of Christ Church, Oxford, 1926 ; p. 5. The Hebrew language, now revived in Palestine, was always kept alive by the Jews, to whom, as we shall see, pioneers of the Reformation took recourse.

D

there were translated out of the Latin version, it was a perilous undertaking to attempt translation from the original. The 'pagan view' in worldly affairs ran contrary to the rule of conduct perfected by Dante in the *Divine Comedy*, and the layman's view in theological affairs might involve prosecution for heresy.

Hardly less dangerous in practice was the pursuit of 'Discovery'. The Navigators extending the physical frontiers, like the Humanists extending the intellectual, were in equal risk of offence against accepted tenets of belief. They might find that the earth was round whereas authority stated that it was flat; they might make similar infringements of the set code of astronomy or of another science, as it was formulated at that date, and the penalty was severe. Not only did the individual pay it, but the advancement of knowledge was retarded by the forces of occultation and obscurantism in the background of European literature.

Sundry stylistic devices were used to circumvent the screen. As animals take the colour of their surroundings in order to avoid observation, so medieval writers learned to hide their meaning from unfriendly eyes. They employed fable and allegory instead of direct names and objects, and these disguises, which, in part at least, were at first employed for purposes of precaution, became in themselves a secondary art of literature, and supplied John Bunyan, for example, with his style in the immortal *Pilgrim's Progress*. Akin to this method was that of the love-poets who sublimated their theme, and made love an unsubstantial, objectless ideal. Once more, we may rely on modern authority :

'The poetry of the Troubadours', we read, 'shows an increasing refinement and delicacy of sentiment. Especially noteworthy is the stress laid upon the fact that without love there can be no song, an idea which led to the personification of love, and also upon the fact that by love man is ennobled, is spurred to greater effort, is superior to all other men. The earlier Troubadours strove to be their best in the hope of obtaining their heart's desire; but there came a gradual change, and, seeing that love was the inspiring force to good deeds, the later Troubadours gradually dissociated their love from the object which had aroused it : among them, love is no longer sexual passion ; it is rather the motive to great works, to self-surrender, to the winning an honourable name as courtier and poet'.[1]

Finally, in this summary, the background of European literature, explored so eagerly by writers in the 14th century, contained the great, heroic story-matters of Welsh Arthur, Frankish Charlemagne and Spanish Cid, in their local and universal variants, extended, expanded and embellished through romance, ballad and satire, during times when history and legend were inextricably confused. To these were added the hero-matters of antiquity : Ovid's tales of love and adventure, the marvellous conquests of Alexander, Helen's beauty and Ilion's towers ; and, for ' sacred representation ' in the open-air barns of strolling players, the unsurpassable repertory of the Bible : Milton's *Paradise Lost* is a direct descendant in that line.

The recovery of the past for the building of the future of European literature was the task to which, with growing self-consciousness, men now began to apply themselves, after Dante, ' the culminating figure of the Middle Ages,' had died with them in 1321.

[1] *The Troubadours of Dante : Being Selections from the Works of the Provençal Poets quoted by Dante*, by H. J. Chaytor, Oxford, 1902 ; pp. xxi–ii.

BOOK II
RENAISSANCE AND REFORMATION

FOREWORD TO BOOK II

THE period covered by this Book is the two centuries from the death of Dante to the Diet of Worms, 1321 to 1521. It is no mere figure of speech to say that Dante was all that time a-dying. For the literature of which the *Divine Comedy* was the supreme expression was then most completely replaced (or was at any rate not till then completely replaceable) by an expression of the modern mind when the liberty of religious creed was added to the liberty of lay learning. These liberties and the instruments which implemented them were two hundred years in the making, and during the next four hundred years, from the 16th to the 20th century, there were religious and dynastic wars, and wars for territorial aggrandisement, which obstructed the free enjoyment of the restored legacies of Israel, Greece and Rome. Direct links of historical causation join the Diet of Worms to the Great War of 1914–19. It may even be said, a little more fancifully, perhaps, but yet not without substance, that the Hebrew grammar compiled by Reuchlin in 1506 in order to open the treasures of the Old Testament for the leaders of the Reformation was a first step in the process which destroyed the Holy Roman Empire in 1806. Certainly, the two centuries of active preparation under review in this Book led to issues, social and political, which could not have been foreseen when the methods of Italian Renaissance students were adapted in Germany to the purposes of Biblical study.

The invention of Printing during our period rendered immense service to the advancement of knowledge. The books recovered from Antiquity and edited for current use were reproduced by mechanical means, thus becoming the common property of ever wider classes of the population. The appetite for the liberty of learning grew rapidly with its satisfaction. and the public demand for such supplies increased the confidence of the providers.

43

Some big books were written in these two centuries, but for the most part it was the schoolmaster who was abroad : antiquaries, grammarians and translators were more active than new men of letters. There was no Dante because there was no assured authority : the Renaissance was not full-grown. But trails were blazed and paths were found along which thinkers moved to new conclusions, and these proved the splendour of the vision of the early pioneer-Humanists who had penetrated the background of Antiquity.

I. FIRST PHASE

§ 1. POSITIVE VALUES.

WE take up our narrative again a few years after Dante's death. In Florence, and throughout Italy and beyond, opinion moved away from his assumptions. Men of letters discovered in his style many valuable models for imitation, but neither men of action nor men of thought were helped by what he wrote to fit their conduct or philosophy to the needs and habits of their own time. When it is said that Dante founded no school and that his genius is unique, the meaning is that from various causes the world left him behind. In a sense, he was too good to be true : the type of goodness which he represented did not correspond to reality in human affairs.

Impact of Reality. Then, as now, reality was hard to get at. Probably there was not much more pretence, not much more humbug and sham in the 14th century than in the 20th. But there was quite enough to confuse judgment. *Faux Semblant*, or False-Seeming, was a very early personification of a trait of character inevitably developed by the departure of experience from convention. In public as in private life men were not always frank about their motives.

Real and Seeming Issues in the Hundred Years' War. Take the Hundred Years' War, for example, between England and France. Nominally a royal dispute, in reality it was a commercial war. King Philip VI of France was the feudal suzerain of Count Lewis of West Flanders, and the vassal had appealed to his suzerain for support in a revolt of his own subjects. Philip came to Lewis' help, and there, from the feudal point of view, the trouble should have ended. But in West Flanders were situated the rising cities of Ghent, Bruges and Ypres. Famous in warfare in the present century, they caused a war six hundred years ago. For the wool imported from English looms was manufactured into cloth in those cities, and traders in both countries were anxious to save their mutual commercial interests from the feudal quarrel which threatened them. When Philip in 1336 required Lewis to imprison all Englishmen settled in Flanders, and when King Edward III, retaliating, stopped exports and imports and encouraged some Flemings to set up cloth-factories in Norfolk, Jakob van Artevelde, a Ghent citizen of forward vision, devised a means of suiting feudal custom to the cause of free trade. His object was to make the false motive seem the real, and, in order to satisfy that condition, he had somehow to contrive that the King of England should *seem* to be King of France. For loyal Flemings could support him as King of France against the then usurping King Philip, and as supporters of King Edward they could keep their factories in their own country. The false king had to seem the true for the sake of a real commercial policy. The Emperor proved compliant, and at a Diet of the Empire held at Coblentz in September, 1338, he solemnly invested King Edward, in virtue of his French descent on his mother's side, with the office of Imperial Vicar of King Philip's provinces on the left bank of the Rhine. Therefore, the King of England was King of France, and Flemings fighting for England were following their feudal suzerain into battle against a usurper. But what was the cause of the Hundred Years' War? Edward's right to the *fleur-de-lys* through his French mother, Isabella, or the commercial interests of England and Flanders? Napoleon called us a nation of shopkeepers, but would not a touch of the shop have kept King Philip VI of France out of a long and wasteful war?

Trade and Letters. We are nearer than might appear to literature. Geoffrey Chaucer, who was born about 1340, was employed by this very King Edward on trade missions abroad concerning wool; on one of these in 1372 he met Petrarch or Boccaccio or both, and a couple of years later he was appointed comptroller of wool-customs at the Port of London. But we need not rely on accidental contacts between foreign literature and English wool in order to establish the connection between the rise of a self-conscious middle-class and the increase of literary productivity in Western Europe. In the republic of letters, as in the feudal State, the real conditions

.had to be taken into account. Thus, the growth of fable, as we have seen, with its recourse to figurative language, enabled observant writers to attack the conventions of the dominant Church-State, and long-sighted students of antiquity sought the lights of the ' pagan view,' not only for a ' beautiful style,' but also for a conduct of life. There were standards of taste and thought which urgently craved expression, more particularly in urban society, with its active coming and going between men in the front line in various countries. King Edward III was borrowing money from Italian bankers ; the first inns were being opened for politico-commercial travellers ; scholars were exchanging manuscripts and commentaries, and middle-class men like Artevelde were sensible of motives for action not less worthy than those of lords and knights, or even of prelates and princes. So, the new men of the middle-classes began to think for themselves. They established a rule of conduct derived from self-esteem, not authority. They built upon reality, not convention, and dared to *be* instead of to *seem*. It is obvious that this changing mind would find its literary refraction.

§ 2. SOCIAL AND MORAL CHANGES.

Literature and the Black Death.   Now, turn back to Dante's Florence about twenty years after his death. 1348–49 were the years of the Plague of Europe, and the ' Black Death', which it brought in its train, and which made superstition more morbid, visited Florence among other cities. How was it likely to affect the Florentines ? Contemporary evidence is available as to the physical havoc which it wrought. But we are thinking now of the moral reaction to it. We have observed how the pagan view that men on earth are entitled to human joy had been lost with the pagan writings. The saints had substituted another joy. Constantine had converted the Empire to Christianity ; St. Jerome had given it its Latin Bible, and St. Augustine early in the 5th century had furnished it with a philosophy of conduct in his Latin treatise on ' The

47

City of God' (*De Civitate Dei*).[1] Thus provided, led and inspired, the monasteries and cathedrals of Western Europe formed centres of educational activity, and Church and Schoolmen worked in close association. From Alcuin (735–804) in the epoch of Charlemagne down to Dante five hundred years afterwards lay learning conformed or was subordinated to that tradition.

Then came the Black Death. So common and uniform a mode of dying could not seem otherwise than divinely appointed, and the normal diagnosis of the disease was an act of God in requital for sin. The supernatural became the natural. Pietists preached resignation and practised it in such retreats as that of the Brethren of the Common Lot, first founded by Dutchmen at Deventer; and an abiding fruit of their tranquil meditation, in line with ' The City of God ' and other writings of the early saints, was the 'Imitation of Christ' (*De Imitatione Christi*) of Thomas à Kempis. In the century of the *Commedia* and the *Imitatio*, between the death of Dante (1321) and the birth of à Kempis (1380), and in the very epoch of the Black Death, we hardly look for a mood less positive or devout. An assertion of living above dying, an intellectual questioning of God's will, and a free use of human reason are hypothetically improbable in the Dante– à Kempis–Black-Death epoch. But there was revolt in the air. We have marked some of its signs. Even in Dante's Florence, just dowered with his epic masterpiece, we have noted a political ferment, in which Dante himself took part. We have seen the rise of lay learning in the Florentine Academy and the new approach to pagan books. We have marked the efforts of Petrarch (1304–74), whose active lifetime fell in the Plague period, to recover the books and the view, and to restore to Florentine society, seared by that horrible ordeal, a perception later to be formulated as ' le rire est le propre de l'homme'.

Boccaccio's Reaction to Experience. And now for the evidence of Boccaccio (1313–75). We will not say that in him

---

[1] ' One of the strongest bulwarks of faith all through medieval times and one of the chief sources from which the temporal organisation of the Catholic Church drew its inspiration.' Wright and Sinclair, *op. cit.*, page 60.

It was computed that

'between March and the ensuing July (1348) upwards of a hundred thousand human beings lost their lives within the walls of the city of Florence, which before the deadly visitation would not have been supposed to contain so many people'.

Yet despite this accumulation of horror and its urgent call to surrender to the will of God, Pampinea took counsel with her friends how to save the dignity of humankind and to assert their self-esteem even in a dead city.

' I should deem it most wise in us', she said, ' our case being what it is, if we were to quit this place and betake ourselves to the country, and there live as honourable women on one of the estates, of which none of us has any lack, with all cheer of festal gathering and other delights, so long as in no particular we overstep the bounds of reason. There we shall hear the chant of birds, have sight of verdant hills and plains, of cornfields undulating like the sea, of trees of a thousand sorts : there also we shall have a larger view of the heavens, which, however harsh to usward, yet deny not their eternal beauty.'

Surely, it was a new point of view, nearer to that of Artevelde and Rienzi than to that of Dante and à Kempis, which Pampinea was moved to express by the violent stimulus of the Plague. The new conduct and philosophy of life created a new utterance of the lips—the new note sought with so much pains by the pioneers of intellectual liberty.

§ 3. GIOVANNI BOCCACCIO (1313–75).

GIOVANNI BOCCACCIO was a love-child born in Paris, but brought up in Florence by his banker-father without further sight of his unknown mother. It would be as fanciful as it is unnecessary at this date to infer any consequences from that experience, but we hear of him as a bit of a wildling, serving law and lighter lieges at Naples and spending an articulate devotion on the Countess Maria d'Aquino, who figures in his writings as Fiammetta, and who in real life was the natural daughter of King Robert of Naples and the wife of a nobleman at his court. Boccaccio returned to Florence after his donna's death and made a name as scholar and man of letters, forwarding Petrarch's Homeric studies, filling the first chair in Dante studies, and composing works which have been described on good authority as 'the first novel of psychology ever written in Europe' (*Fiammetta*) and 'the first critical treatise of the Renaissance' (*De Genealogia Deorum*, Books XIII–XIV): a pioneer, then, in various fields of learning, as well as a practical Florentine with a French mother and a taste for forbidden fruit.

Scheme of The 'Decameron'. Another epithet has been attached to him. Addington Symonds writes of his 'undesigned revolt against the sum of medieval doctrine', and these words so helpful in our present context, refer expressly to his most famous book, *Il Decamerone*, the *Decameron*, or the 'Ten Days'. There were ten days, a company of ten, and ten stories told on each day : a hundred stories in all, linked by the audience and the setting, like the *Canterbury Tales* or the tales recounted of Sherlock Holmes by Dr. Watson in Baker Street. Pampinea brings the company together. She and six other young ladies of Florence,

' connected either by blood or at least as friends or neighbours ; and fair and of good understanding were they all, as also of noble birth, gentle manners, and a modest sprightliness,'

and three young men, ' very debonair and chivalrous ',

' in whom neither the sinister course of events nor the loss of friends or kinsfolk, nor fear for their own safety, had availed to quench, or even temper, the ardour of their love',

resolve not to die in Florence but to live, if they may, outside its walls. The eternal beauty of the heavens was not changed by the Black Death on earth, and it were wisdom to seek the larger view. The medieval doctrine was subjective : the heavens were ' harsh to usward ' ; but the modern doctrine was objective—to see and hear the common sights and sounds, and to live by the senses according to the rule of reason.

The New Literary Public. Thus, in a deeper sense, Boccaccio, inventing the novel, invented its audience as well. ' Gaily we mean to live ', announced Pampinea, when the ten had reached the estate, identified with the Villa Crawford, or Palmieri, on the Fiesole slope, which should be their ' refuge from sorrow.' Man, we see, was meant to enjoy. Gaily would they live, she announced, but their liberty should not be licentious. Grief had brought anarchy to Florence and joy should bring order back to it ; for

' I,' said Pampinea, ' who initiated the deliberations of which this fair company is the fruit, do now, to the end that our joy may be lasting, deem it expedient that there be one among us in chief authority, honoured and obeyed by us as our superior, whose exclusive care it shall be to devise how we may pass our time blithely.'

They appointed each of the Ten successively as mistress or master of the revels, so that the audience should be fit for the recital and to that extent expert in the appreciation of the ten tales told each day.

Influence of Boccaccio. Where Boccaccio found his tales does not much matter. There was ample stock in folklore and legend, in fable and romance, and he ransacked all the available sources, both in the West and the East. How he left them is more significant, and how Chaucer, his younger contemporary, and all subsequent story-writers followed the founder's lead. William Painter, in his *Palace of Pleasure*, 1566, translated some of the tales in good time for Shakespeare's stage and the standard English translation appeared in 1620. France, Germany, Spain and other countries made similar use of the *Decameron*, and its influence on the novel in Europe is a commonplace of literary history. In that influence it is timely to let go the moral aspect on which we have insisted. It is possible to make too much of the analogy between the flight of the Ten from Florence and the emancipation of thought from medievalism. The story is the thing, here as in Hamlet's play, and the example of the stories is more important than the conduct of the tellers. Still, there is that change and development in the years that followed Dante's death. A truer sense of reality introduced new values into literature. Historians write of the difference in various ways. One says that ' poetry was removed from the region of metaphysics, allegory and theology, and began to be re-animated by the old classical principle of the direct imitation of nature '[1] ; another speaks, as we have seen, of the new poet who ' has come out of the prison-house of theological system nobly and grimly architected, and is abroad again in the homely disorder of our familiar world '[2] ; a third writes that ' the talent of Boccaccio for finding out new kinds of literature, and making the most of them, is like the instinct of a man of business for profitable openings '—Jakob van Artevelde's talent, as observed above—and adds that ' there is nothing more exhilarating in literary history than the way in which Chaucer caught the secret of Boccaccio's work, and used it for his own purposes '.[3] However worded, the meaning is plain. About the middle of the 14th century, and not in Italy only, though most conspicuously in Italy, which was the native soil of the Latin Classics, a road was built out of the Middle Ages. It was a narrow road and in places a rough road. Narrow, because a pioneer must concentrate on the patch before him and looks forward more reverently than he can look back ; and rough, because stone-breaking must always be a rough affair, with much to pull down of old obstructions and many common things to call by rude names. But the road led across the Alps, and spread into wide and smooth prospects, which are now the pleasaunces of European literature.

§ 4   The New Note in Petrarch (1304–74)

First, then, in his due place, Petrarch. FRANCESCO DI PETRACCA, commonly known as Petrarca or Petrarch, was nine years older than Boccaccio, and nine years nearer accordingly to the background in which Dante's

---

[1] W. J. Courthope, *History of English Poetry*, i, 300.
[2] W. Raleigh, page 25 above.
[3] W. P. Ker, *Essays on Medieval Literature*, pp. 68–9.

Divine Comedy was the culminating feature. He was more hidden a student than Boccaccio and more of an idealist than he. Much of his life was spent at Vaucluse, near Avignon, and he rarely quitted his library except in the hope of adding to it by journeys in search of new manuscripts. The journeys were arduous, the *caches* remote, and the rewards were few and exacting. His chief treasures were Cicero's *Pro Archia* and some of his letters to Atticus.[1] Cicero, indeed, his main quarry, was also his chief delight ; all literary history contains nothing quite so virginal as Petrarch's rejoicing over Cicero. It was a part of his revival of the new Italy at the founts of old which inflamed his brief zeal for Rienzi, the mock tribune, and which on another occasion caused him to visit Rome in order to be crowned as poet-laureate on the Capitol. Another vent for his constant Latinity was an epic poem, *Africa*, in which he mused and meditated on the theme of Scipio and Hannibal, and which, exotic in its own day and unreadable in ours, he preferred to his Italian lyric poems, though these made the Petrarchan measures a model for poets to be. He wrote Latin letters with prolific ease and fluency, and he preached, as we have seen, that classical culture is Greek in its origin. He was the first Hellenist in modern Europe, though he could not read Greek, and he was writing notes on the translation of the *Odyssey* when he died in his library at Arqua in the Euganean hills. His love of that hill-side scenery was a further link with the new naturalism, or return to Nature, which expressed itself in voyages of discovery, whether to the past in time or to the distant in space : free outlets for the energies of man.

§ 5. AND IN CHAUCER (*c.* 1340–1400).

Chaucer's ' Griselda '. Readers of Chaucer are instantly aware of this new note in European literature. Consider, first, the story of Griselda, which is related by the ' Clerk of

---

[1] In 1345. ' This discovery was a decisive moment in the history of the Renaissance, and from it all modern study of Cicero dates '. And again : ' We may say that the Renaissance itself was the work of Cicero's spirit '. A. C. Clark, *English Literature and the Classics*, pp. 130, 131.

Oxenford ' as his contribution to the *Canterbury Tales*. Chaucer makes it abundantly clear that the learned clerk is permitted to tell the tale as a curiosity of literature and not for its pragmatic value. He is the kind of man, we are told, in the Prologue to the *Tales*, who would rather keep twenty books of Aristotle by his bedside than rich robes and decorated psalters, and, though he has borrowed this story from Italian books, yet his audience is to remember :

> ' Grisilde is deed and eke her pacience,
> And bothe atones buried in Itaille ;
> For which I crye in open audience,
> No wedded man so hardy be t' assaille
> His wyves pacience, in hope to finde
> Grisildes, for in certein he shall faille ! '

Chaucer's counsel to wives was in another and a livelier vein. There should be no more patient Griseldas. ' Let no clerk have cause or diligence ', he enjoined the women of his own day, ' to write of you so marvellous a story. Though your husbands be armed in mail the shafts of your eloquence shall pierce it. Be cheerful and light, as a leaf on a linden-tree, and if there is weeping to be done let him have his share in it.' The new school of wives should not be founded on a medieval tradition. The tale of Griselda was now a work of art : the human comedy was composed of other motives.

Chaucer's ' Troilus '. Next, associate this departure from the moral standard taught by Griselda with the new approach made by Chaucer to the tale of *Troilus and Criseyde*. The plot of this story was derived from the old ' màtiere de Rome la grant ' (the common stockpot of Antiquity), and would be found, as Chaucer wrote,

> ' In Omer, or in Dares, or in Dyte '.[1]

There, and in the later versions by medieval romancers, Boccaccio duly had found it. In his *Filostrato*, which means literally Prostrate-in-love, he had rendered it excellently into Italian verse, and, except for its verse-form and its length,

---

[1] *Troilus and Criseyde*, Book I, verse 146, in Skeat's edition. See page 16 above for this reference to the equal authority of Homer, Dares and Dictys.

this ' Troilus ' of Boccaccio might well have made another tale for the *Decameron*. It displayed the same skill in construction, the same hard brilliance of plot, and the same conventional conduct-standards. But 'Dares, Dyte' and the other Homers at secondhand were not meat for true lovers to train on. Boccaccio had added to their lore his personal pangs for Fiammetta, but he had not universalized his experience. Chaucer, by the virtue that was in him, by his sense of real values and practical interests, and by virtue, it is not fanciful to add, of a nip in the English air which drives lovers home betimes, made a drama out of the epic. His characters speak what they act, and feel what they speak, instead of saying set pieces of repetition. The old yarn, the old framework, and, since Chaucer was always a gorgeous translator, a good deal of the old stuff is there, but Troilus and Cressida are no longer Boccaccio and Fiammetta. Her love beats in every woman's heart, and Pandarus, the future ' pander ' of all comedy, is a person and not a shadow of a quality.

His ' Canterbury Tales '. These gifts, not distantly connected, as we have tried to indicate, with the social consciousness of growing classes of the population in the market-towns and even on the countryside, were yet more lavishly displayed in Chaucer's *Canterbury Tales*. April 16th, 1387, was the day of the start of the Pilgrimage from Southwark at the Tabard Inn to the shrine of the Blessed Martyr at Canterbury, and truly we have travelled a long way since that May day in 1274 when Dante first met Beatrice and his *vita nuova* began. We have travelled out of the Middle Ages, bounded by a Church-made hell and heaven, into the world of modern men and women, whose sky is boundless and their earth is free. We cannot pause to analyse the tales. Interesting as they are both historically and dramatically, they are less important than the tellers, whose varied origin, displayed in the Prologue, struck so fresh a note in European literature. The ' verray parfit gentil Knight ' belongs to the community of chivalry, together with his son, the young squire, ' a lovyere and a lusty bacheler,' who had fought in Flanders, Artois and Picardy, as has many a young squire since. But the cook, the haberdasher and the carpenter, the dyer, the

57

miller and the shipman, and a dozen more of particular callings remind us of Dickens rather than of the Troubadours, and blow a wind through the cobwebs on old tapestries. Under the rule of the jolly host of the Tabard—and an inn was itself a new setting for the poet's art—the Canterbury pilgrims tell their tales; not, indeed, as many as were promised, (Chaucer left several works incomplete) but enough to furnish over seventeen thousand verses with additionally two tales in prose : ' God's plenty ', as Dryden said of them.

We might dwell on Chaucer's metrical innovations, illustrating here what was mentioned on page 5, his departure from the old alliterative verse-making and his adaptation of the measures which Petrarch had perfected in the modes of Tuscan invention. The rhyme-royal[1] of his *Troilus and Criseyde* and of parts of the *Canterbury Tales* is a stanza of seven decasyllabic verses, rhyming *ababbcc*, a variant of Boccaccio's *ottava rima*. Even more English by adoption is his rhymed couplet of five-foot lines, first employed in the *Canterbury Tales* and known throughout all English literature as heroic verse. It became the national measure, second only in splendour to blank verse.

§ 6. LANGLAND AND FROISSART.

Two Minds in the 14th Century. But more to the purpose than the contents of the *Canterbury Tales* or the technique of the poet is the fascination of the dual mind in Western literature, which made the 14th century so decisive as a watershed in the history of civilization. Feudal law and the wool-trade, Dante and the escape from Dante, ' *rum, ram,*

---

[1] An excellent example of rhyme-royal, more interesting because Chaucer translated it direct from a sonnet by Petrarch, is the song of Troilus (I, 400–20) :

> ' If no love is, O God, what file I so ?
> And if love is, what thing and whiche is he ?
> If love be good, from whennes comth my wo ?
> If it be wikke, a wonder thinketh me,
> When every torment and adversitee
> That cometh of him may to me savory thinke ;
> For ay thirst I, the more that I it drinke.'

And so on.

ruf by lettre ' and the Italian measures, the *Decameron* and the
Imitation of Christ, *fas* and *nefas*, curiosity and mystery—this
contrast is constantly occurring and points the way to wider
differences yet to be. The gulf revealed at the Diet of Worms
between Luther and the Emperor Charles V was but a widening
of the rift which divided those who read Cicero for his style
from those who studied him for his thought.[1]

The contrast is seen very clearly in two contemporary
authors with whose names we shall conclude this first phase.
One is known, probably wrongly, as William Langland and
lived from about 1330 to about 1400; the other was Jean
Froissart, who was born in 1337 and died about 1410.

Illustrated by (1) *Langland*.   Langland, if that was his name,
and, after all it does not much matter,[2] was born and bred,
or at least was most at home, in the swelling bosom of the
Midlands, so dear to a recent Prime Minister. Indeed, so close
is the sympathy between these statesmen (for Langland was
no less) of the thirteen-thirties and the nineteen-thirties, that
a quotation may be permitted, limited though our space is,
from Mr. Stanley Baldwin's Introduction to Messrs. Long-
man's ' English Heritage ' series. He writes :

' I could show you many a ten or twenty miles of road in
England where every turn opens out a fresh picture to make
you draw in your breath with sheer delight, where the roadside
timber is yet undisturbed, and where the black-and-white
cottage at the bend, with its garden scented with gillyflowers,
makes such an awkward corner for the motorist ; and here
and there a little inn, even as it was when Glutton met Peronel
of Flanders in the day when Langland lay on the slopes of
Malvern Hill.'

---

[1] See page 55, Note [1].

[2] ' I do not think it desirable to introduce even the appearance of scientific
reasoning into what must necessarily always remain a region of nebular hypothesis.' W. J. Courthope, *History of English Poetry*, Vol. I, p. 208, n. 2. Prof.
J. M. Manly, of Chicago, in *The Cambridge History of English Literature*, Vol. II,
Ch. i, states the case for five authors of the *Piers Plowman* poems. Skeat,
Jusserand, and Prof. F. J. Snell (*Periods European Literature*, Vol. III) assume
their single authorship. The two last-named critics rely partly on what they
regard as the ' anagrammatical clue to his own identity ', which he left in the
verse—'I have lived in londe, quod I, my name is longe Wille.' *Will Longe
Londe*. It is at any rate simpler than some alleged Shakespeare anagrams.

Well, that, except for the motorist, is the England of *The Vision of William concerning Piers the Plowman*, written in the third quarter of the 14th century by a religious reformer before the Reformation, who, as lawful Englishmen will, brought his trouble to the notice of the King in London. Four times in twenty-five years—1349, 1361, 1369, 1375—the Plague had levied its toll of English life, destroying half the population. A great tempest on January 15th, 1362, had wrought new devastation. The soldiers home from the French War after the Peace of Bretigny in May, 1360, had brought to their twice-ravaged countryside urgent problems of demobilization and unemployment. There was trouble enough, it will be seen, to rouse the dreamer on the hillside to pity and indignation and to cause him to bring the plea of Peace before Parliament. It is a real world to which Langland introduces us, for all his old-fashioned preference for the dream-motive of Macrobius and the *Roman de la Rose*, for the devices of allegory and personification, and for the alliterative verse which Chaucer was abandoning. The dream slides into further dreams : Piers the Plowman is Peter the Church, and becomes the figure of its Head ; Dowel, Dobet(ter) and Dobest expound the being of virtue ; Meed, who is the maiden of justice, is prevented by Theology from celebrating her marriage with Fals(ehood), promoted by Favel (Fable, duplicity), and, when the King would marry her to Conscience, Reason forbids the banns till priests practise what they preach. This is Langland's way of telling his story ; it was not Chaucer's way, but it was very much like Bunyan's way after him, and it was like the allegorists' way before him, with Dante as their culminating practitioner. And at the top of the way was the goal of a better England, a happier and a freer people, clear-eyed in the correction of wrong and fearless in the pursuit of right.

(2) *Froissart*. Froissart, the Frenchman, to turn at once to him, lived through the same experiences as Langland. The Peace of Bretigny brought him to England, which he visited as the guest of Queen Philippa, his countrywoman, at Edward III's busy court. Most of his full and active life was spent at the courts of princes. He had seen the French fleet destroyed

at Sluys, the French army defeated at Crecy, the surrender of Calais, and the peasants' revolt in *la Jacquerie*. The same problems as Langland's, the same social ordeals, the same Black Death, but how contrary his reaction! ' Je suis un historien', he justly claimed, and his place is secure among the chroniclers of chivalry, in the lap of which he was born and nurtured. Villehardouin (1157–1213), the French crusader who wrote the prose *Conquête de Constantinople*, the Sire de Joinville (1224–1319), saintly historiographer to a saintly king, Louis IX, and Jean Le Bel, canon of Liège, whose *Chronique* of 1326–61 immediately preceded Froissart's, are the links in the chain of his descent from the French writers of the *chansons de geste*, which made a legendary splendour of the exploits of Arthur and Charlemagne. These were the sources of Froissart's art, and their difference from Langland's is obvious—as different as is his decorative prose, with its sense of paragraph and pause, and its skill, reminiscent of Herodotus, in narrative by conversation, from the monotonous reaches of the verse of *Piers the Plowman*. We may rely on Sir Walter Scott for a criticism of Froissart which leaves no doubt as to these differences :

' With that true chivalrous feeling,' says Claverhouse ironically in *Old Mortality*, ' he confines his beautiful expressions of sorrow to the death of the gallant and high-bred Knight. . . . How he will moan over the fall of such a pearl of knighthood. . . . But, truly, for sweeping from the face of the earth some few hundreds of villain churls, who are born but to plough it, the high-born and inquisitive historian has marvellous little sympathy.'

Time has been on the side of the churls. The plowman's vision corrected the historian's. The real cause of the Hundred Years' War was better known to the merchants than to the knights ; the price was paid by the peasants, not the princes. Froissart, elegant, delightful, chivalric, heroic, patrician, is in the line of the court-chroniclers of glittering warfare ; Langland, the nameless dreamer among the hills, is a creative factor of the Reformation.

Two words more, to complete this section. Dr. E. Dale,

tracing 'national life and character in the mirror of early English literature ',[1] draws a contrast between Chaucer and Langland :

' As in Chaucer's pages,' he writes, ' we have the life of the people portrayed, so in Langland's we have the ripening conscience. . . . Here we have the two great divisions of men and character ; the one active, practical, worldly, the other contemplative, introspective, deeply religious. In Chaucer we see the world as a man of the world actually saw it. . . . In Langland we see it as it appeared to the earnest reformer. . . . The scales are falling from the Englishman's eyes, and the things he sees sit heavily on his soul. . . . We see him in the tall, gaunt figure of Langland, passing through the jostling crowds of London streets. . . . The Englishman has never been so completely idealistic as to stay long in the midst of dreams.'

All this is true and worth observing. But the bigger dualism in the 14th century, which forced the Renaissance out of the womb of medievalism, is that which is illustrated most pointedly by contrasting Froissart's *Chronicle* of war with Langland's *Vision* of peace.

§ 7. THE SPANISH RESPONSE.

Lastly and very briefly, France and England were not alone in their response to the new note. Far away in the West in Spain, JUAN RUIZ, who died in 1350, and who is known as the Archpriest of Hita, wrote a ' Book of True Love ' (*Libro de buen amor*), for which critics compare him to Chaucer, and which is always famous for at least one character-study. This was a kind of feminine counterpart to Chaucer's ' pandar ' in *Troilus and Criseyde*. The ' Trota-conventos ' or convent-runner, whose well-understood business it was to act as go-between for naughty lovers in nunneries or monasteries, became the ' Nurse ' in Shakespeare's *Romeo and Juliet*, and

[1] In a book of that title, Cambridge, 1907.

has sundry other reappearances. Akin, too, both to Ruiz in his own country and to Froissart across the Pyrenees, is the great Spanish chronicler, PEDRO LOPEZ DE AYALA (1332–1407), who was for some years a prisoner in England and had experience of diplomacy and war. He translated into Spanish parts of Livy, Benoit de Sainte-Maure and Boccaccio ; he lived under four wild kings, Peter the Cruel, Henry II, John I and Henry III, and wrote a history of the events which he had helped to mould. He made experiments in modern verse-measures, and stands in the front of Spanish literature under the sign of the approaching Renaissance, which Spain led in Navigation and Discovery.

II. EUROPE AT SCHOOL

§ 1. GREEK TEACHERS.

THE 15th Century: *Ascendancy of Florence.* Petrarch, Boccaccio, Chaucer, the three stars in the dawn of modern Europe, were all dead by the end of 1400. Petrarch, by Chaucer's testimony, had 'enlumined all Itaille of poetrye,' and Chaucer had caught the light with a rapture of exhilaration. But it was not in Chaucer's troubled country, with royal uncles and nephews disputing the throne, that it shone steadiest in the 15th century. Edward III had died in 1377, leaving, like greater men before and since, several descendants but no successor. Richard II, son of the Black Prince, was eleven years old when his grandfather died, and was deposed in 1399. Between Edward's death in the jubilee of his reign and the accession of Henry VII in 1485 seven kings had worn the uneasy crown: Richard II, Henry IV, Henry V, Henry VI, Edward IV, Edward V, Richard III— truly a century of disaster, in which, as Shakespeare was to say through the mouth of the first of the seven, there might be told

> 'sad stories of the death of kings:
> How some have been deposed, some slain in war;
> Some haunted by the ghosts they have deposed;
> Some poison'd by their wives; some sleeping kill'd;
> All murder'd.'

Throughout that calamitous century, Europe, seeking the light, was still to turn to it in Italy, and in Italy Florence took the lead. There, in or about 1360, Leontius Pilatus, as we shall see[1], rendered service, fit if scant, to the first aspiring Homerists, and there, in 1494, Politian[2], 'Homericus juvenis,' died. The long century of 'the death of kings' in England was the century of the rebirth of learning in Italy. Dates are never much more than handles by which to hold a convenient

[1] Page 65 below.   [2] Page 17 above.

parcel of history, but these dates of Florentine ascendancy have real historical significance and should be remembered in the roll of fame. From the beginning to the end of an epoch corresponding roughly to the 15th century, Europe went to school at Florence, and the remainder of this section will be spent in the company of the schoolmasters. The brilliance of their achievement does not fade, and may indeed be compared with the record of the advancement of knowledge in the era now growing to a century since Darwin's *Origin of Species* in 1859.

Greek Teachers : *Pilatus and Chrysoloras.* The beginning and the end make a striking contrast. In or near 1360 was LEONTIUS PILATUS. Sir Richard Jebb, an eminent Hellenist of the 19th century, writes definitely of his contribution :

' Leontius evidently knew little or nothing beyond the Byzantine Greek of the day ; he was stupid and pretentious ; his temper appears to have been morose, and his personal habits were repulsive. Nevertheless, Boccaccio received him into his house at Florence. . . . He made for Boccaccio a bald and faulty translation of Homer into bad Latin prose, which was sent to Petrarch and received by him as an inestimable boon.'[1]

' A bald and faulty translation ' : this was the best that Petrarch could procure before he died in 1374, painfully annotating the *Odyssey* in his hand-made library in Arqua. He died twenty years too soon to see the fulfilment of his ambition. In 1396, MANUEL CHRYSOLORAS, a Greek of a very different stamp from Leontius, was invited by Florentine Hellenists to quit Constantinople for their city. There he resided till 1400, teaching, lecturing and inspiring, and he went on to similar posts in Milan and Pavia. He visited other Italian centres, as well as London and Rome, and died at Constance in 1415. Among his pupils was Leonardo Bruni, a scholar of eminent parts, who wrote of him : ' I gave myself to his lessons with such ardour that my dreams at night were filled with what I had learned from him by day,' and of whom

[1] *The Cambridge Modern History*, Vol. I, p. 541. It reminds us of Mr. Boffin and Silas Wegg.

it was written in his turn and inscribed on his tomb in Santa Croce :

> ' Postquam Leonardus e vita migravit, Historia luget, Eloquentia muta est, ferturque Musas, tum Græcas tum Latinas, lacrimas tenere non potuisse.'[1]

Demetrius Chalcondyles. The *Erotemata,* questions and answers, which Chrysoloras prepared for his Greek lessons, were printed at Florence in 1484, and were taken into use at Oxford and at Cambridge. Nor was it only new teachers whom Petrarch missed by so few years and of whom Leontius was so sorry a forerunner. Texts, too, began to pour into Italy. In 1389 COLUCCIO SALUTATI, who had already made some happy finds, and who as Chancellor of Florence had promoted the invitation to Chrysoloras, discovered Cicero's letters *Ad Familiares,* which Petrarch had long desired. POGGIO BRACCIOLINI brought from Cluny several of Cicero's speeches, and from St. Gallen in 1416 Quintilian's *Institutio Oratoria,* of which Petrarch had seen only an imperfect copy. But the biggest treasure-trove was made by GIOVANNI AURISPA (1370–1459), who was as keen a Hellenist as Poggio was a Latinist: He visited Constantinople in 1422 and brought back in the following year a precious cargo of 238 Greek MSS., of which he made a list for his friends in Florence. Another keen teacher was FRANCESCO FILELFO (1398–1481), and yet another DEMETRIUS CHALCONDYLES of Athens (1424–1511). It was this last-named successor to Leontius Pilatus whose record completes the contrast and rounds off the hundred years in Florence. In 1360 was Leontius's Latin *Iliad* received by Petrarch, burning for Hellenism, as ' an inestimable boon ' ; in 1396 came Chrysoloras's Greek grammar, which Linacre and Erasmus were to use ; in 1456, came Argyropoulos, afterwards tutor to Reuchlin at Rome and by that token Greek schoolmaster to the Reformation ; and finally from 1471 to 1492, covering the centenaries of Petrarch and Boccaccio, was the Greek lectureship at Florence of Chalcondyles, whose

---

[1] Since Leonardo has departed from life, History mourns, Eloquence is mute, and the Muses, Greek as well as Latin, are said not to have been able to refrain from tears.

editio princeps of the text of Homer, issued in 1488, was the first considerable book to be printed in Greek type in that city.

§ 2. THE MEDICI IN FLORENCE.

Let us rehearse it once more, the splendid tale of Homeric studies in Florence, marking the contrast between the beginning and the end. We may read it as typical of and in conjunction with the rest of the scholars' and critics' work. 1360 and 1488 ; Leontius Pilatus and Demetrius Chalcondyles ; a faulty manuscript in bad Latin prose and the first authentic text from a printing-press : truly a considerable record achieved in a hundred and thirty years in the leading city of the Renaissance in Italy. 'Dares and Dyte' are ousted at last ; Greek Homer is restored in his full stature to be the fount of new life in modern Europe.

The Medici Dynasty. All through this wonderful century the Medici family ruled in Florence. It was founded by a merchant-banker in the era of the emergence of a middle-class in various countries of the West, and its descendants intermarried with the old royal families of Europe. The two dynasties, Hellenism and the Medici, may be displayed in parallel columns :

1360–63 Leontius Pilatus at Florence.	1360–1418 Giovanni de' Medici.
1396–1400 Chrysoloras at Florence.	1389–1464 Cosimo de' Medici (son of above), ' Pater Patriæ.'
1453 Fall of Constantinople.	
1471–92 Chalcondyles at Florence.	1448–92 Lorenzo de' Medici (grandson of above), ' The Magnificent.'

We preferred to end the last Section with the triumph of Chalcondyles rather than with the death of Lorenzo, which was followed a year or two later by the French invasion of

Italy under Charles VIII, by the expulsion from Florence of Piero de' Medici, the feeble son of ' The Magnificent ', whose talents were transmitted to his younger son, Pope Leo X, and by the death in 1494 of two young and brilliant leaders of his Greek Academy, Angelo Poliziano (Politian) and Giovanni Pico della Mirandola. There are symbols enough of defeat and death. Deliberately we choose the sign of progress in the midst of these signs of gloom in Florence.

For the printing-press employed by Chalcondyles a hundred and fourteen years after Petrarch's death was destined from the close of the 15th century in every city and with accelerated speed to complete on the mechanical side the intellectual revolution of the Renaissance. It was the genius of Dutchmen and Germans which made the learning serviceable to life, and,

' while we gratefully recall the preservation of Latin MSS. in the medieval monasteries of the West, as well as the recovery of lost Classics by the Humanists of the 14th and 15th centuries, and the transference to Italy of the treasures of Greek literature from the libraries of the East, we are bound to remember that all this would have proved of little permanent avail but for the invention of the art of printing.'[1]

Lorenzo the Magnificent. Gratefully and hopefully, then, we close this parcel of history, when all Europe went to school in Florence and took Greek lessons in the art of life, at 1488. Lorenzo the Magnificent was still in power, with his seemingly bottomless exchequer, his endless occasions for pageantry, and his retinue of copyists and secretaries. No more fortunate combination could be devised for the fulfilment of the aims of the Humanists ; and Italian literature, presaging European literature, as it was reformed out of the broken dreams of Petrarch, owed its new birth to Lorenzo. By precept even more than by example, and with genuinely statesmanlike sagacity, this Florentine son of Latin Italy sought to fit to modern uses the forms of the old mother-tongue. By encouraging scholars to display their mastery of classic form and diction in carnival songs, dramatic interludes, and light verses of satire or love, all composed in the native Tuscan

[1] Sir John E. Sandys, *History of Classical Scholarship*, Vol. II, p. 95.

speech, and adapted to the taste of the populace, Lorenzo de' Medici broke down the last barriers remaining between the two greatest epochs of the Latin race, pagan Rome and humanistic Italy. In his reign, so justly termed magnificent, and largely by his personal efforts as a poet and a patron of poets, the seeds of Greek and Latin culture, sown by the scholars and the Humanists, were raised in his own Florence and beyond it to the fine flower of modern literature and learning. It was not that Latin was at once disused. Cicero's sedulous apes did not readily forego their practise of Cicero's tongue. They argued in Latin, they reasoned in Latin, they taught in Latin; but, gradually, Lorenzo the Magnificent, ably backed by his courtiers and associates, accustomed the literate world to sing in the soft Italian speech. The line between Latin and Italian was never very closely drawn; the point was that Lorenzo's example, building on Dante and Petrarch, restored the cultivation of the native language which the first zeal of classical study had deflected.

Lorenzo's life has been ably written by an English scholar, William Roscoe (1753–1831), whose pleasant pages should be consulted for the roll of illustrious men who were proud to throng Lorenzo's Court and to join the banquets at his Academy. Or a contemporary record may be sought in the not less pleasant pages of Vespasiano da Bisticci (1421–98), a Florentine bookseller, whose short *Lives of Illustrious Men of the Fifteenth Century* has been published in an English translation.[1] Best of all, perhaps, is the testimony of Politian (1454–95), who had acted as tutor to Lorenzo's children, and whose four Latin verse-declamations which he composed to accompany his lessons have been referred to above.[2] The last of them closed with a panegyric on the ruler, rendered by Roscoe in heroic couplets, from which we quote a few verses :

> ' And thou, Lorenzo, rushing forth to fame,
> Support of Cosimo's and of Piero's name !
> Endow'd with arts the list'ning throng to move,
> The senate's wonder, and the people's love,
> Chief of the tuneful train ! Thy praises hear,

[1] By W. G. and E. Waters, London, 1926.   [2] See page 18 above.

If praise of mine can charm thy cultured ear . . .
These the delights thy happiest moments share,
Thy dearest lenitive of public care ;
Blest in thy genius, thy capacious mind—
Not to one science nor one theme confin'd—
By gracious interchange fatigue beguiles,
In private studies and in public toils '.

On the whole, few princes in history have better merited such high praise, and it may be observed that Machiavelli, who was to write a guide to princedom[1]—the observation will fall into its due place—was a youth in Florence at this time.

The Printers. One word more about Chalcondyles's printing-press, at which we have made this pause. Vespasiano conservatively would not use it. He wrote out every book by hand for his patron, the Duke of Urbino, who, like a lover of horses in the first days of steam-transport, despised the new-fangled invention. But Gutenberg's victory needs no telling, and here we would only remark the swiftness of its achievement. Aldus Manutius (1449–1515), the printer-publisher of Venice, issued twenty-seven *editiones principes* of Greek writers before the end of his career, and Janus Lascaris printed five in Florence between 1494 and 1496. A pupil of his was Marcus Musurus, who was an assistant to Aldus Manutius in Venice, which he made, as was said, a ' new Athens '. William Caxton, our own first printer, lived at Bruges before settling at Westminster in 1477, and Froben and Erasmus at Basle, Thierry Martens at Louvain, and Christopher Plantin at Antwerp are among the pioneers of the art in this epoch. They ' did the work of giants,' says a modern writer,[2] ' and cannot but be counted as Humanist scholars.' Accordingly, we close with their names, however briefly and inadequately recorded, the story of Florence as the school of Europe between the death of Petrarch and the death of Lorenzo de' Medici, or, as we have preferred to count it, between the visit of Leontius Pilatus and that of Demetrius Chalcondyles.

---

[1] *Il Principe*; see page 81 below.   [2] Prof. Foster Watson.

III. HOME FROM SCHOOL

§ 1. THE ROAD ACROSS THE ALPS.

GREEK learning, humanizing medieval life, came back to Italy from Constantinople and the East, and its increased resources were distributed by the new art of printing. But this was not the whole of the matter. If this had been the whole, if there had been nothing more to it than a recovery of lost books, then the course of the Renaissance in Europe would have been marked by those possessions, and its roll of great men would have been composed of editors, grammarians and translators. It would have proved a useful and wholesome movement, even courageous and adventurous in certain aspects, but its value would have been limited. The chief benefit would have accrued to pure scholarship and letters.

Scholarship Was Not Enough. But consider again in this connection Chaucer's method with the tale which the Clerk of Oxenford told to his fellow-pilgrims. Scholarship was satisfied by his telling it. He had learned it, as he said, in Padua from another ' worthy clerk' (none other than Petrarch); and out of one of the old books which the Oxford man of learning took to bed with him every night he translated the story of Griselda. England should have its clerkly gloss; it should see life through the mirror of Italian books. But Chaucer deemed otherwise. He poked his sly and gentle fun at the Oxford manner as it existed even in those days and put a wedge between life and books. He applied the canon of conduct to the authority of the ancients, and pointed out that Griselda was dead and her patience should die with her. Learning was one thing, but life was another. Griselda was a dead woman in a dead book, but there was a wife in every English home, and let no clerk, he warned English wives, ' have cause or diligence to write of you' in the terms of patient Griselda. So, but not otherwise, interpreted, the old tale was to be read, and learning justified of its disciples. This, surely, was a big step forward. Life demanded more than the ' clerks ', however learned, could bring to it. Their gifts, won with so much pains, were to be welcomed with both hands open, but experience was to correct precept. Classical learning came back to Italy, and a blessing lay on its arrival, but its users and interpreters should determine what went out.

The Road Across the Alps. Foremost among the interpreters was the Greek, Johannes Argyropoulos, who lectured in Florence to Politian and in Rome to Johann Reuchlin. In 1482, when Reuchlin was twenty-seven and his Greek tutor was getting on for seventy, Argyropoulos bade him God-speed back to Germany with the ringing exclamation, *Ecce ! Græcia nostro exsilio transvolavit Alpes.*[1] What went out of Italy was ' Greece '—not Greek books, or Greek tales, or Greek grammar, but the communicable spirit of Hellenism, conveyed *nostro exsilio*, by the Greek scholar-exile, through his German disciple across the Alps. Those sundering mountains should unite one country of the Renaissance with another ; Greece herself should be spread abroad. Appropriately, too, an English disciple, Dr. Thomas Linacre, who was five years younger than Reuchlin, dedicated an altar to Italy on his homeward journey across the Alps. We cannot resist these appeals. The romance is there from the beginning, it is not imported by the sentiment of later times. For, surely it was a romantic salutation, like that of ' stepping westward ' in Wordsworth's poem, which the old Greek gave to the young German ; and, surely, it was a romantic act on the part of the young English physician, who had been Politian's pupil in Florence, to build a holy place to Italy before he climbed down the dividing slope. These keen aspiring youths of the new era, with their eyes turned to the light, were bringing out of Italy not learning only but learning lucid with life. Movements big with Renaissance and Reformation were to be unfolded from Tully (Cicero), (H) Omer, Stace (Statius), Ovid, Boece (Boethius), and the rest. A grand way in a great day was that scholars' road home across the Alps.

---

[1] Lo! Greece by my exile hath flown across the Alps.

§ 2.   ITALIAN   PUPILS.

Eight Italian Harvesters.   Some disciples, of course, were
Italian-born, missioners of culture to their own countrymen.
Politian himself, ANGELO AMBROGINI POLIZIANO (1454–94),
was Italian poet as well as classical tutor, and his *Orfeo*,
an operatic play, has its place in literary history between the
Tuscan poems of Petrarch in the 14th and of Tasso in the
16th century. BATTISTA SPAGNUOLI (1443–1516) wrote in
Latin, but his pastoral eclogues merit mention since they
were used as a reading-book in distant Tudor schools, among
others by William Shakespeare at Stratford-on-Avon.[1] The
' good old Mantuan ', as Shakespeare called him, derived his
name from Mantua, his birthplace, which he shared with the
greatest Mantuan, Virgil. LUIGI PULCI (1431–87) and MATTEO
MARIA BOIARDO (1434–94) forged a link which stood the
strain of a hundred years and which grapples them to Edmund
Spenser, who died in 1599. They are joined by the ' matière
de France,'[2] and particularly by the story of Count Roland in
the old heroic *roman* of Charlemagne. We shall come back to
Spenser's professed resolve to beat the Italians at their own
game. Here we observe that Pulci and Boiardo each wrote an
epic poem on the Roland theme, the former in his *Morgante
Maggiore* and the latter in his *Orlando Innamorato*.

JACOPO SANNAZARO (1458–1530) re-discovered Arcady,
joining Theocritus, the Sicilian Greek of the 3rd century B.C.,
to Montemayor, Cervantes and Sir Philip Sidney in Portugal,
Spain and England eighteen hundred years afterwards. He
recalled the rural muse to Europe by his *Arcadia* of 1504, and
greater writers than he followed him back to that land of bliss.
Sidney domiciled him in England as Sanazar. The Arcadian
countryside was conventional, like the fauna of heraldry. It
was always swept and garnished for townsmen's visits. It
admitted no noise from stricken fields where the peasantry
toiled in dust, but it was a land where, in the last words of
the first *Arcadia*, a man might ' live without envy of another's
greatness in modest contentment with his lot '. There its
lovers disported themselves as nymphs and swains, and

[1] See " Love's Labour Lost," IV, ii.   [2] See page 33 above.

innocence had not learnt to blush at the manners of sophisti-
cated society. A time was to come when the innocence faded,
and when real persons in pastoral disguises carried ribboned
crooks in the bosky glades. But at first the illusion was sincere,
and the 'happy melodist' of Keats, 'for ever piping songs
for ever new', goes right back through Sidney's 'shepherd-
boy, piping as though he should never be old', to the groves
of the fabled happy realm which Theocritus handed on to
Virgil and Sannazaro took from both.

An older Humanist was VITTORINO DA FELTRE (1378–
1446), whose boys' school at Mantua was the first of its kind
in modern Europe. He taught the Greek view of life, training
his pupils in an equal cultivation of the faculties of body and
mind, so that, when we write of Europe home from school
we must not omit the name of the first professional schoolmaster. In the next generation was LORENZO VALLA (1407–
57), a philologist who was not afraid of conclusions based
upon textual criticism, and whom Pope Nicholas V, converting
the critic into an ally, employed as an apostolic writer. His
Elegances of the Latin Language marks an epoch in linguistic
studies, and 'philology,' by the testimony of Hallam, 'seems
to owe quite as much to Valla as to anyone who has come
since.'

Lastly, in this short list of great men who extended the
school of the Renaissance on its native soil was GIOVANNI
PICO DELLA MIRANDOLA (1463–94), who shone like a star
in his brief lifetime, and who vividly impressed later Humanists
from Sir Thomas More in the 16th to Walter Pater in the 19th
century. Valla and Pico were both harbingers of the Reformation, the former by his handling of texts and charters, the
latter by his study of Hebrew as a first step to understanding
the Old Testament. If, as we shall shortly see, 'the event which
took the Old Testament out of the land of phantasy' and
'turned it into an instrument of reform'[1] was Reuchlin's
primer of Hebrew Grammar in 1506, then Pico, the mystical
scholar, filled with visions, half-Greek, half-Hebraic, of a
meeting-place for Plato and Christ, had his share in the sequel
to Luther.

[1] *The Cambridge Modern History*, Vol. II, p. 696.

The 15th Century In Italy. We have dealt very rapidly with eight men, Politian, the 'old Mantuan,' Pulci, Boiardo, 'Sanazar,' Vittorino, Valla, and Pico of Mirandola, who brought the harvest of Hellenism, sown by Greek scholars immigrant from the East, home to Italy itself. But the rapidity of our survey, though inadequate to their several gifts, and though it excludes the contributions of others hardly less generous than they, has a certain compensating quality. It corresponds to the briefness of the period in which all this glory was achieved. The harvest-home was a rich and brilliant festival, filling the city-States of Italy and particularly Medicean Florence with the amplest cultural resources. But there were no barriers to cultivation. The Latin language was a passport, love of learning levelled the Alps, and the harvesters who bore the grain abroad outran and outnumbered those at home. An Italian writer three hundred years afterwards described the 15th century in Italy as a 'solecism', and, indeed, in its strange and rapid course it has the effect of the unexpected and the unrepeatable. Guided by Petrarch into the ways of classical Latinity, which were likewise the ways of patriotism reanimate, Petrarch's countrymen at the Court of Lorenzo the Magnificent sought to conquer in one assault the forms of Cicero and Virgil and the spirit of the Grecians in their background. Always they feared the failure, not of their springs of inspiration, but of their tether of authority. Not 'Is this true?' but 'Is this permitted?' was their constant preoccupation; 'Does it conform with the canon of the ancients?' Even Sir Philip Sidney was to write that he 'dare not allow' Edmund Spenser to modify the pastoral conventions of Theocritus, Virgil and Sannazaro, whom he aligned as equal experts. This classical tradition in modern literature we shall find a formidable burthen. But the Italian Renaissance broke suddenly asunder. The last *quattrocentiste*, or 15th century men, made an illumination in a stormy sky. We have noted[1] the disastrous *fin de siècle*: the invasion of Italy by Charles VIII in 1494, and the death in that year of Politian, Pico and Boiardo, following Lorenzo's in 1492. The sack of Rome on May 6th, 1527, by German and Spanish troops

[1] See page 68 above.

completed the tale of Italian ruin. On May 17th the Florentine Republic drove out the restored Medici, and, in the words of the Oxford historians[1] :

'For over three hundred years Italy endured the chastisement of foreign rule. Yet in her darkest hour it was seen that she had really conquered Europe. Francis I carried the Renaissance back with him to France. Tudor England steeped itself in Italian literature, which it derived very largely from French sources. Italy was the great standard of appeal in matters intellectual and artistic.'

So, if these Italian men of letters, who, following Petrarch and Boccaccio, laid in re-Hellenized Europe the lines of the novel and the epic, of lyrical, pastoral and elegiac verse, of philology, criticism and history, and, summarily, of the arts and sciences, have been dealt with as types rather than as individuals, our defence is complete. The swift-moving 15th century in Italy founded types not only for the printing-presses of Chalcondyles in Florence and Aldus Manutius in Venice : it founded, too, the modern types by which great writers in all Europe were to express the increasing purpose of the human mind. The Genoese sailor, Christopher Columbus, who, in the service of the King of Spain, discovered America in 1492, the Florentine *savant*, Pico della Mirandola, who was reading Hebrew with a Jew in the same year, opened out a new earth for the physicists and a new heaven for the reformers : a new geography and a new theology. Italy's work did not end with the 15th century. Even out of the ruin of her polity eminent men were yet to arise, and the Renaissance, Italy's largesse, was fulfilled beyond the Alps, in France, Spain, Portugal, Germany, Holland, England. We turn now to some of the disciples who carried the harvest to farther homes.

§ 3.   DESIDERIUS ERASMUS (1466–1536).

ERASMUS, a love-child like Boccaccio, was the child of so romantic a love and a love so remote from modern cir-

[1] *Italy Medieval and Modern : A History*, Oxford, 1917 ; page 236.

cumstance that the story of Margaret and her priest was turned into a novel by Charles Reade.[1] Like Boccaccio in his birth, he was like Rabelais (1495–1553 : we shall come to him immediately) in his nurture ; for, loyal son of the Church though he was, he found the cloister too narrow to contain him. Brought up by the Brethren of the Common Lot at Deventer and Bois-le-Duc, he quitted the Augustinian Order and became a citizen of the world. And, like Boccaccio in his birth and Rabelais in his nurture, he was like Petrarch in his service to mankind. He, too, tried to look at human destiny with the clear, fearless uncorrupted vision of a man trained in the Greek (or ' pagan ') view. His constant object, in his own (Latin) words, was ' to arouse the rising generation from the feast of ignorance (*inscitia*) to purer studies,' and his bold way with ' the mysteries of Christ ', to which reference was made on page 21, has been called ' a literary Rubicon. The Middle Ages are on one side, the modern world is on the other.'[2] Finally, when he had built this bridge from medieval to modern modes of thinking, his love of, and labour on, the Bible made him a direct precursor of the Reformation. Its debt to him is pointed in the famous epigram that Erasmus laid the egg which Luther hatched.

Erasmus and Budé. All this is equivalent to saying that Erasmus of Rotterdam was an authentic son of his own times. The New Learning had crossed the Alps and was spreading West and North. Erasmus was brother to the great Frenchmen and Englishmen, the great Spaniards, Germans and Italians who had been at school in Italy. Franked with the scholar's passport of Latinity, he brought counsel to every company of wit. He visited Paris about 1497 in the train of the Bishop of Cambrai, and England in 1499 with Lord Mountjoy, one of his pupils. There he was warmly welcomed by the Oxford leaders, Sir Thomas More and Dean Colet, and, after visits to Italy and France again, he returned to England in 1509, staying with More in Bucklersbury, writing lesson-books for Colet's new St. Paul's School, and teaching divinity in

---

[1] *The Cloister and the Hearth*, 1861. It should be read as a companion to these pages.
[2] Prof. Foster Watson, *Nineteenth Century and After*, March, 1916.

Cambridge University. In 1514 he moved to Basle where Johannes Froben hǎd his printing-works, and which he made his headquarters till he died. From Basle he ruled literate Europe, exercising a kind of dictatorship not unlike that which, in a smaller sphere, Dr. Johnson was to exercise from Fleet Street. If he divided the throne, it was with GUILLAUME BUDÉ (1467–1540), the Hellenist in Paris. But their amity was as broad as their scholarship. Budé (Budæus) at the Court of King Francis I made Paris the Florence of the West, reproducing the conditions which had flourished under Lorenzo de' Medici, and the story is told of him that he was so much absorbed by learning as to wave away a servant sent to alarm him by the news of a fire in his house with the words, ' Go to my wife : I am not to be disturbed by domesticities.'

Writings of Erasmus. The personality and influence of Erasmus, the educator of Europe, as he has been called, were almost bigger than his writings. But these, too, are really big. The famous passage about the mysteries occurs in the *Paraclesis* (or introduction) to the *Novum Instrumentum* (or new tool) of learning, in which he treated the New Testament like an ancient classic, critically editing its text and furnishing it with a Latin translation. The sensation which this caused has been compared[1] with that provoked in the 17th century by the new methods in astronomy, and appropriately the fourth centenary of its publication was celebrated in 1916 as the founder's day of Biblical criticism. Nearer to common interest and full of literary meat are Erasmus's *Letters*, *Adages* and *Colloquies*. We have likened him to several men of his own times : in this connection he is comparable to Chaucer for the sake of his keenness in observation and his narrative skill. The parti-coloured life of the 15th century is richly illustrated in these Latin compositions, which were written with gusto and which may still be read with pleasure ; and novelists as eminent as Walter Scott went to them for scenes and characters. We should add, in special reference to the Latin language, that Erasmus, who did so much to promote it both by precept and example, warned scholars in 1528 by his treatise *Ciceronianus* against a too servile imitation of the Roman

[1] By Mark Pattison.

master. It lies outside our scope to note that the elder Scaliger (1484–1558) objected to this temperate protest, and that a scholars' controversy ensued in which the authority of Erasmus was disputed. It is more pertinent to observe how early in the history of modern Latin, used by Dante, Calvin, Thomas More, Francis Bacon, to some extent by Milton, and many others, this discussion of the propriety of its usage indicated that, after all, it was a dead language.

The Problem of Authority. We come back to Erasmus's pregnant aphorism about the ' mysteries of kings '. In 1516, it will be remembered, he deemed it ' safer to conceal ' them, though it was imperative, he held, in that dawn of the Reformation, to unveil the ' mysteries of Christ '. In the same year he wrote a Latin treatise ' on the training of a Christian prince ' (*Institutio Christiani Principis*), and he was only one among several writers who addressed themselves to the topic of State sovereignty. Dante had written *De Monarchia* and had been exiled from Florence in a political faction. Petrarch had jeopardised important friendships in order to support the pretentious ambition of Rienzi. Froissart had opposed the risen peasantry ; Langland had brought their quarrel to the King. Chaucer and Artevelde in their several capacities had served the economic policy of Edward III. Pope and Emperor —it is a commonplace of the age—involved all Europe in warfare, and Luther's defiance of both at the Diet of Worms in 1521 was at once an end and a beginning. It was prepared in Lorenzo de' Medici's Platonic Academy at Florence, since all ideal republics start from Plato ; it was promoted by the studies, practical and mystical, of Valla, Reuchlin and Pico della Mirandola ; and it issued in the religious wars which slid into territorial wars and which overwhelmed successively the Stuart, the Bourbon, the Hapsburg, and the Hohenzollern. The problem of the ruler and his authority was paramount in every stage of the pilgrim's progress, whether we think of him as Chaucer's pilgrim, resolute to live in the sun, or, as Bunyan's pilgrim, passing ' from this world to that which is to come '. The ruler's part in the human lot had to be accommodated to the progress of the human mind—a conservative principle to a progressive movement ; the ' divine

79

right' of kings had at last to be assorted with the people's will. We see in the theatre of Shakespeare (1564–1616), only a hundred years after Erasmus, the proof of this victory of Renaissance thought, reinforced by the activity of the Reformation. We hear, yet a few years later, the terrible accents of Milton (1608–74), 'proving that it is lawful, and hath been held so through all ages, to call to account a Tyrant, or Wicked King, and, after due conviction, to depose and put him to death, if the ordinary Magistrates have neglected to do so '[1]; and even now, while the Renaissance is in the making, and when Luther's egg is not yet hatched, we mark how men of letters home from school, Renaissance missioners fresh from their Greek books, dealt with the divine, the sheltered, the untouchable mysteries of kings.

§ 4. PUBLIC VIRTUE.

Renaissance Views on Government : Four Writers. Contemporary with Erasmus, the Dutchman, observing, comparing, preparing, were the Englishmen, SIR THOMAS MORE (1478–1535), the Italian, BALDASSARO CASTIGLIONE (1478–1528) and the Italian, NICCOLO DEI MACHIAVELLI (1469–1527). A little younger than these was the Frenchman, FRANÇOIS RABELAIS (1495–1553). We join the four in a single group, because, significant as they are in their separate contributions to European literature, they are even more significant in their concentration on the single topic of just governance. They wrote :

MORE—*Utopia* : an ideal republic founded on the travel-tales of a Portuguese seaman home from the new Atlantic voyage, whom More had met on the busy Antwerp quay. It was published at Louvain in Latin ; in French at Paris, with an introduction by Budé ; and in English, 1551.

CASTIGLIONE—*Il Cortegiano* (' The Courtier ') : a full-length figure of the Renaissance gentleman : the wits' Bible, as it has been called. It was translated into English by Sir Thomas Hoby, 1561.

[1] Sub-title of Milton's pamphlet, *Tenure of Kings and Magistrates*, 1649.

MACHIAVELLI—*Il Principe* ('The Prince'): an anatomy of the Renaissance ruler, written in the hope of uniting Italy under a powerful Medicean prince. The prince was not forthcoming, and the statesman's candid analysis of his psychology blackened its author as 'Old Nick' (Niccolo) and served political philosophers as an argument against absolute monarchy.

RABELAIS—the circus of giants, known summarily as *Gargantua*; a medley of adventure and fooling, which poured the liberties of young Europe, the wit and wine of the new thought, through a utopia derived partly from Lucian and Thomas More. 'Broad as ten thousand beeves at pasture,' George Meredith wrote of Shakespeare's laughter, and the verse exactly characterizes the comic spirit of Rabelais.

Common to all was this ichor of modernness, this sense of real things treading on the conventional, which makes Erasmus so companionable a writer four hundred years after his death.

Sir Thomas More. More's *Utopia* was more than Platonic; it was American as well, and was close to the first voyage of Amerigo Vespucci to the new world. For More's mariner

'took more thought and care for travelling than dying, having constantly in his mouth these sayings—He that hath no grave is covered with the sky; and, The way to heaven out of all places is of like length and distance.'

Sapit mare, it tastes of the sea. A salt breath from the new West road blew through its Latin leaves and caused the reforms which it recommended to seem, if not near, yet humanly possible.

Castiglione. Castiglione's *Courtier* was more than an Athenian acclimatized in Italy; he was the European Atticized. The scholar-gentleman was a European type, compounded of more ingredients than the two parts to his name; and the treatise was translated into Spanish even earlier than into English. As has been written by a scholar-gentleman of our own day:

' There was something profoundly sane, after all, in the ambitions that built New Place and Abbotsford. . . . It is time to remember our ancestry. Our proudest title is not that we are the contemporaries of Darwin, but that we are the descendants of Shakespeare ;. we, too, are men of the Renaissance, inheritors of that large and noble conception of humanity and art to which a monument is erected in The Book of the Courtier.'[1]

Machiavelli. Machiavelli's *Prince,* intended to establish stable government in the distracted Italy of his day, is said by Lord Acton, the historian, to be

' more rationally intelligible when illustrated by lights falling not only from the century he wrote in, but from our own.'[2]

The cruder conception of Machiavellism entered history on St. Bartholomew's Day, 1572, when the Huguenots were massacred in Paris. This crime of King Charles IX of France and his mother, Catherine de' Medici—this princely act for the safety of the State—was imputed by Gentillet, a French Protestant, to the direct influence of Machiavelli's *Principe.* Gentillet's treatise, *Anti-Machiavel,* was rendered into English in 1577 by a certain Simon Patericke, and enjoyed a wide vogue. In pure literature it introduced the Machiavellian hero on to the English stage. Marlowe's Prologue to the *Jew of Malta* (the soul of Machiavel flown across the Alps) was quoted on page 6, and now we are better able to measure the dire spiritual change which a brief hundred years had brought about. At the end of the 15th century Pico of Mirandola and Reuchlin were talking the stars to bed in Florentine nights with the philosophers ; at the end of the 16th century, the Reformation had been hardened out of the Renaissance, and a chief import from Florence was the political doctrine that might is right. The final ' anti-Machiavel' came at Whitehall in 1649, when Charles I paid the penalty for Machiavellian princes.

---

[1] *Some Authors,* by Walter Raleigh, Oxford, 1923 ; p. 121. New Place and Abbotsford, it will be recalled, were the country-houses acquired respectively by Shakespeare and Scott for their own residence.
[2] Introduction to *Il Principe,* edited by L. A. Burd.

Rabelais. Lastly, the giants' circus of François Rabelais. His great romance, famous in all languages, is a prose-epic of the quest for worldly knowledge. It is better known by its separate episodes and adventures than in its unwieldy whole, which was plainly written at different times and partly with different aims. The names ' Rabelaisian ' and ' Gargantuan ' both stand for something big and bold : the former denoting a style or an approach to experience—' le style, c'est l'homme même,' very signally—at once exuberant, unrestrained and imaginative, and the latter conveying a sense of immoderateness in appetite. Panurge, another character in the romance, a little like Mr. Hyde in R. L. Stevenson's well-known fable, was the precipitate of a wild desire for release from the shackles of conventional morality. Pantagruel, Gargantua, Panurge : through all the buffoonery of the episodes, through all the coarseness of the treatment, through all the turgidity of the language and the deliberate disguises of the thought, an increasing purpose ran. Rabelais clearly reveals himself as a philosopher and reformer, an original thinker in a changing world. He was often compelled to flee from the ecclesiastical authorities whom he constantly derided. But every flight was turned into a rearward action. He was a physician by training, and his fearless exploration of the science of his day counted against him as a heretic. Powerful friends did their best to protect him, King Francis I of France among them ; and partly to conciliate those patrons and partly from an instinct of self-defence Rabelais learnt to wrap-up his meaning in a cloud or a torrent of words. The words attracted him for their own sake. He became a master of rapid language, tearing round the corners of style with a retinue of epithets in motley at the tail of a cargo of new thought. The sound and noise of the words was irresistible, and the rebel in style and thought began to laugh, a little shamefacedly at first, while he fingered with gleeful curiosity the old, lewd, forbidden things; then more and more carelessly and loudly as the beauty of creation was unveiled and the joy of possession seized him. For ' le rire est le propre de l'homme '.

§ 5. AT THE COURTS OF PRINCES.

Queen Margaret of Navarre. More perfect and less wild things were written. The mention of King Francis, who, it will be recalled, ' carried the Renaissance back with him to France ', recalls his gallant sister, Queen MARGARET OF NAVARRE (1492–1549), who, like her brother, was a protector of Rabelais and other Humanistic writers, and who put her name to the ' Stories of Fortunate Lovers ', which a clever bookseller, Claude Gruget, called the *Heptameron* (1559). Partly by this suggestion of the *Decameron* and partly by its native merits, the French *Heptameron* became a best-seller, though the seven days' entertainments of the travellers stranded by flood are less brilliant than Boccaccio's tales of the fugitives from pestilence at Florence. More literate than the Queen was her secretary, CLEMENT MAROT (1497–1544), who made metrical renderings from the Psalms (always a red light to the watchful Church), and who founded a songful school of *Marotiques*. Margaret's Court, too, gave hospitality to LUIGI ALAMANNI (1495–1556), a Florentine exile from Florence, who was one of several Italian poets—FRANCESCO MOLZA (1489–1544) was another—to make experiments in *versi sciolti*, or loose (unrhymed) verse. Molza's blank verse translation of the *Æneid* passed into the tradition of Tudor poetry in England, and Queen Margaret at Lyons is rememberable as a patron in that Italian-French-English community of the modern muse.

The Lurking Terror. Germany, too, was to claim her part, when Johann Reuchlin, the pupil of Greece in Italy, brought the harvest of the new learning to Saxony, where Martin Luther, the monk, was awaiting it. But the spacious days were still to come. The free and full expatiation of the mind of Europe, when Shakespeare was to crowd his stage with all kinds and conditions of men and women, and Cervantes was to prove in *Don Quixote* that manners, not codes, make the gentleman, was still postponed for a while. A sense of terror in the background oppressed men of culture in the 16th century. The fate of Sir Thomas More, who was beheaded, 1535, for a scruple of conscience against his king ;

the fate of Stephen Dolet, a French printer, who was executed, 1546, for too much speculation about Plato's doctrine of immortality ; the fate of the Huguenots in Paris, who were massacred in 1572 : these facts discouraged free thought and placed an embargo on open speech. Writers on controversial topics wrote what they might, not what they would, and the range of controversy was almost endlessly extended. Theology, politics, lay learning, were all included in its ambit, and these, the last, especially, in the eyes of censors and spies, spread fairly comprehensive nets. The least originality was unorthodox. It was dangerous to translate the Psalms, to discuss the governance of the State, or even to comment on Plato, the father of political philosophy.

Effects on Literature. We are bound to take account of these facts. Students of literature would gladly ignore them, and, as far as possible, we shall do so. But we cannot do so all the way. They produced two marked effects on literature, neither of which can safely be neglected. The first was the tendency of advanced writers to cultivate an expedient wariness. They went slow, showing obscured lights. They circumnavigated their capes perilous by all kinds of tacks and ambiguity. And the next was the common resort, as prudent as it was polite, to the patronage of princes. A writer was freer in the shelter of a Court than he was in the shadow of a cloister, still more than in the open market. Thus it happened that Court-songs, Court-tales, Court-treatises on morals and education—even Castiglione's for example—formed the staple literature of the first half of the 16th century. The greater men will arrive, the apprentices' work will be done. The straits will broaden into the stream. One country, as we shall see, will be left dry for many years. The searing ordeal of the Reformation, which applied the new learning to the old faith, will be found to devastate Germany, just as France, two hundred and seventy years afterwards, was devastated by her experiment of Revolution. Before following Reuchlin, therefore, and his harvest of the Renaissance on German soil, we may conclude the present section by a brief reference to two writers, the one of whom by revolt and the other of whom by compliance illustrated the force of authority. The rebel is

FRANÇOIS VILLON, a Frenchman, who was born in 1431 ; the complaisant poet is LUDOVICO ARIOSTO, an Italian, 1474-1533.

(1) VILLON. Villon ' walked off ' at an unrecorded date ' into the unknown '. Yet he belongs to the modern world by virtue of a few great ballads which defy the oblivion that he chose. How and where he lived does not matter. It was always a hand-to-mouth existence—from another's hand to his own mouth. But somehow his lyric note rang true. Somehow, he touched the hem of truth, through all ignoble works and days. He thieved, and drank, and brawled. He was familiar with a felon's prison, he was even sentenced to be hanged. He haunted the stews of Paris till his final sentence of banishment ; but, as Swinburne royally acknowledged,

> ' From thy feet now death hath washed the mire,
> Love reads out first, at head of all our quire,
> Villon, our sad, bad, glad, mad brother's name '.

For Villon saw the light in darkness. In a sense, it is even true to say of him, and of his passionate, impotent aims, that ' there has been no greater artist in French verse, as there has been no greater poet ; and the main part of the history of poetry in France is the record of a long forgetting of all that Villon found out for himself '.[1] Dante Gabriel Rossetti, himself a poet, translated several of Villon's ballads, and the refrain of the *Ballade des Dames du Temps Jadis*,

> ' Mais où sont les neiges d'antan ? '

' But where are the snows of yester-year ? ' is among the permanent things of poesy.

(2) ARIOSTO. Ariosto lived at a Court and never sought any outside experience. His headquarters was Ferrara, where he built himself a house, which he inscribed with the famous couplet :

> ' Parva, sed apta mihi, sed nulli obnoxia, sed non
> Sordida, parta meo sed tamen ære domus.'

He wrote in matchless stanzas of *ottava rima* a re-fake of

[1] Arthur Symons, *Figures of Several Centuries*.

Boiardo's Roland poem[1] under the name of *Orlando Furioso*, which may be read in English in Harington's Tudor version. It was not only translated but imitated, for it exactly satisfied the Court-poets' longing for a national epic in a modern tongue which should bring Virgil home out of the shades. Art, not conduct, was Ariosto's aim—a fact which will derive importance when we find Spenser seeking to ' overgo ' him ; and Hallam, the historian of European literature, expounds his three virtues as ' purity of taste ', ' grace of language ' and ' harmony of versification '. A fourth virtue is ingenuity of invention. So at last Petrarch's vision was fulfilled : a new Virgil had arisen in modern Italy ; not speaking the Latin tongue, nor revolving the Latin theme, but making a native *Æneid* out of a local hero, and singing in the new octave stanzas, swept by a master's hand into undulating waves of correct rhythm and cadence, the romantic love which drove to madness Roland, paladin of Charlemagne.

This was Ariosto's boon, his largess to poets to be. He left for the emulation of modern Europe the perfect model of romance-epic. The Courts of Renaissance princes had protected their poets to this end. And from that fine achievement, which marked the completion of one part of the Renaissance aim, we pass at once, with deliberate abruptness, to the German portion of Court-defiance, with its sequel of war and woe.

[1] See page 73 above.

IV. THE SECOND PHASE

§ 1. Two Schools of History.

THEY came home from school on many fronts. Ariosto and Castiglione at Ferrara and Urbino, respectively, cultivated beauty in tranquillity and expounded the ideals of their Greek teachers at the Courts of princes of the Renaissance. A yet remoter and more unruffled ease was found by Sannazaro in Arcady, and Sir Thomas More in Utopia extended its borders to the New World. So doing, he touched the grosser things, by contact with which, as Lord Chancellor to King Henry VIII, he lost his wise and learned head.

Across the Alps. Those contacts were unavoidable across the Alps. Rabelais roamed unquiet between the real and the ideal, trailing angel's wings in heavy mire. Villon went down in the mud. Vittorino at Mantua and Colet in London at intervals of nearly a hundred years founded boys' schools filled with the modern spirit; and Erasmus, the educator of Europe, moving his genial *aura* from one home of learning to another, in France, England and the Low Countries, made each habitation a *schole*, or place of leisure, a *giocosa*, or place of pleasure, as Vittorino had named his house in Mantua. Only Machiavelli in Florence, investigating the science of rule, displayed ' the mysteries of kings ' to a social order jealous of their authority. So the 15th century slid into the 16th, and with more perfectness went more revolt. The growing perception of beauty increased the demand for reform.

Views of the Reformation. We come to the reformers. It grew harder and more positive, the soul of ' Greece ' across the Alps, when JOHANN REUCHLIN (1455–1522), sped by Argyropoulos, brought back to Germany from Rome the applied culture of the ancient world. There are two main views of these happenings. There are those who regard the Reformation as ' a mighty process which destroyed the

common culture of Europe,'[1] and who deplore its course
accordingly. There are those who characterise it more
acceptably as 'part of a mightier movement than itself—the
manifestation upon religious ground of the intellectual forces
which inspire the speculation and have given us the science
of to-day,'[2] and who would not reverse the way of history.
We cannot compose this quarrel, but in a history of European
literature we may follow the latter school by treating the
Reformation as a part of the Renaissance and regarding the
whole as beneficial to humankind. The German experience
involved its participants in long years of literary infertility.
The wars which swept across Europe in the wake of the
Reformation swept its first home bare of culture till well on
in the 18th century, and the historian of letters, writing without
reference to politics, must record a debt of gratitude to
Germany for the sacrifices entailed by her fearless extension
of the new learning. True, all the sequel was not foreseen :
neither Germany's barren centuries nor the blame she was to
bear for the later wars that issued from her experiment.
But even if it had been foreseen, even if MARTIN LUTHER
(1483–1546), standing at Worms in April, 1521, had foreseen
the Thirty Years' War of 1618–48 and the last war of 1914–19,
both of which, at the ultimate bar of history, may be found
to have been wrapt up in his challenge to the Emperor
Charles V, is it certain that he would have been turned from
his purpose ?

The Continuity of History. A tentative answer, useful in
computing the above debt, may be constructed out of the
aphorisms of trustworthy historians. 'The War of 1870,' it
has been written,[3] 'was needed to efface completely the
consequences of the Treaty of Westphalia' (1648), which
closed the Thirty Years' War. We know now that the war
of the present century was needed to efface the consequences
of the Treaty of 1871, so that here at the beginning of that
long warfare from 1618 to 1919, to which Luther's protest
directly led, we see what dread and strange results are said

[1] Hilaire Belloc, *How the Reformation Happened*, London, 1928 ; p. 277.
[2] Charles Beard, *The Reformation* (1883) ; new impression by Prof. Ernest
Barker, London, 1927 ; p. 34.
[3] By Sir Stanley Leathes.

to have ensued from the Latin musings and Greek lessons of the Italian scholars who went before the Renaissance. The German Reformation and the French Revolution both belong to them : we have already associated these events with what Erasmus wrote in the *Novum Instrumentum* about the mysteries of Christ and of kings. Take now a principle of deep import, which was ratified by the Truce of Augsburg (1555), within twenty years of Erasmus's death. *Cujus regio, ejus religio,* ran the formula of those early treaty-makers, who, designing to settle a dispute of creeds, sowed the seeds of the territorial warfare which was to persist till 1919. Seldom, if ever, has future history been written in letters so plain, and we select now three further texts, each from an authority of repute, in order to illustrate our theme. They point to the close connection between the scholars and the statesmen, between those who thrust back the barriers of knowledge, secular and religious successively, and those who in consequence had to adjust the frontiers of kings—between the reformers of *religio* and the defenders of *regio*. Our first is from Sir John Sandys :

' Petrarch's efforts to return to the Old World of the Latin classics led to his discovery of the New World of the Italian Renaissance.'

This brings us from the 14th to the 15th century. Our second is from Sir Richard Jebb :

' So far as concerns the main current of intellectual and literary interests, the German Renaissance is the Reformation.'

This brings us from the 15th to the 16th. And our third, bringing us to the 17th, is from John Neville Figgis, a well-known disciple of Lord Acton :

' Had there been no Luther, there could never have been a Louis XIV.'

We might pursue it further in both directions, forwards to the death of Louis XIV in 1715 and the fate of his Bourbon successors, and backwards behind Petrarch to the antiquity which he explored ; for ' the Renaissance itself,' we have read,

' was the work of Cicero's spirit '. But enough has been said to prove the truth of the dictum of Bryce, author of *The Holy Roman Empire* : ' In history there is nothing isolated '. History, we see, is continuous from Cicero and his Greek masters through the Renaissance and Reformation to the French Revolution and the present day. Let that truism prevail. No theory of any school of historians can contract out of any chapter or part of the smaller or the larger series. Whether foreseen or not in Worms or elsewhere, every link in the chain was truly made.

§ 2. REUCHLIN AND LUTHER.

1506, 1806. Reuchlin, at any rate, to come back to him, was in no doubt where he stood. He had come home to Germany as a Hellenist, as a pupil of the Italian Renaissance, and, carrying its fruits to his own countrymen, he extended the Hellenic method to the Bible. With no irreverence to the contents of that Book—on the contrary, with intentional reverence—he resolved to treat it with the same attention as was being applied by the Humanists of the new printing-presses to the texts of Greek and Roman Classics. The Old Testament, like Homer, should be translated. Boccaccio had learnt Greek from Leontius Pilatus, Reuchlin would learn Hebrew from Jacob Loans ; and except that Loans, physician to Emperor Frederick III, was in every respect superior to Pilatus, the parallel is exact. Boccaccio took Greek lessons in 1360, Reuchlin took Hebrew lessons in 1492. The Renaissance started from the one, it spread into the Reformation with the other. Luther was still to translate the Bible into homely vernacular German in accordance with the reforming zeal of Erasmus, but the tool which prised open that treasury was Reuchlin's *Rudimenta Hebraica*, his Hebrew grammar of 1506. Just three hundred years afterwards the Holy Roman Empire came to an end.

Defenders of the Breach. That doom, inevitable, yet in-conceivable—for all the sequel could not be foreseen—was resisted almost instinctively from the start. Hardly had

91

Reuchlin got to work before the dogs of the Empire set upon him. They denounced him for studying Hebrew books, and, led by a renegade Jew,[1] who may have regretted his desertion of a rising market, they carried the quarrel to Rome. They drew down on their own diminished heads the one lively squib in the whole proceedings, the satire of the young dons of Erfurt against the old monks of Cologne. These were represented as contributing to the controversy two series of ' Letters of Obscure Men ' (*Epistolæ Obscurorum Virorum*[2]), in reply to Reuchlin's testimonials from ' illustrious men,' and the epistles thus fathered upon the monks added obscenity to obscurantism. The satire lives as a piece of literature, and this rally of Reuchlin's learned friends helped to save him from the full wrath of Rome.

The German Renaissance. The Reformation—the German Renaissance—filled Europe with story and song. Across the land of ' folkbook ' and ' folly ', with their shrewd, homely, mediocre entertainment, broke the light of the Bible as a native *Volksbuch*, adorned by Luther himself with native hymns. This was what learning could do, the new learning home from Italian schools : Latin learning, to decode the Vulgate ; Greek learning, to edit the New Testament ; Hebrew learning, to edit the Old. Let Pope Leo build St. Peter's in Rome, and his agents hawk Indulgences in Saxony in order to defray the heavy cost[3] : this was not enough for forward minds in Germany. ' Folkbook ' and ' folly ' were not enough. HANS SACHS (1494-1576), the cobbler-poet on the sunny side of an old street in Nuremberg, where he plied his last and his lyre and brought up a large family by two wives, could not satisfy the new German aim. He wrote more

---

[1] Johann Pfefferkorn, a man of otherwise no importance.
[2] Edited with an English translation, Notes, Introduction, etc., by Francis Griffin Stokes ; London, 1909.
[3] 'What provoked Luther and many others was not only the abuses which prevailed in the use of Indulgences, about which there was much grumbling and the constantly recurring collections which were a burden both to the rulers and to their people, but also the tales current regarding the behaviour of the monk acting as Indulgence-preacher. Tetzel did not exactly shine as an example of virtue. . . . He was, as impartial historians have established, forward and audacious and given to exaggeration. . . . He even employed phrases of a repulsive nature in his attempts to extol the power of the Indulgence preached by him.' H. Grisar, S.J., *Luther*, E.T., London, 1913 ; Vol. I, p. 329.

than 4,000 songs and more than 1,700 tales and fables drawn from the Bible and other quarries, and much miscellaneous stuff besides. He made a poem out of everything but nothing into a poem, said a German critic in an unkind epigram; and, indeed, though amiable and entertaining, Sachs is a second-rate figure by the side of such contemporaries as Rabelais and Ariosto. SEBASTIAN BRANDT (1458–1521), by his shipload of fools (*das Narrenschiff*), 1494, gave an impetus to folly-literature, and Erasmus enhanced it in 1509 with his *Encomium Moriæ* (' Praise of Folly ') which was dedicated to Sir Thomas More, and, later, illustrated by Dürer. The woodcuts, indeed, made half the fun of those popular emblem-books of vice and virtue, in which most things new were wrong and most things old-fashioned were good ; and Brandt's ' Ship ' sailed into England in a translation by ALEXANDER BARCLAY (*c.* 1475–1552), a Scottish satirist.

But these, too, were not enough, nor the native legends of Dr. Faust, Tyll Eulenspiegel, the Wandering Jew, Paster Kahlenberg and others, the first of which, as is well-known, found its supreme poet in Goethe. For the German genius, turning to the light which scholar-missioners were bringing home from Italy, demanded greater and nobler things.

The demand was met by Luther. A peasant by birth, he communicated the light to men bred in poverty like himself. He appealed to men of his own class by speaking to them in German, not in Latin. The classical Latin of More and Erasmus would have served his purpose no better than the kennel-Latin of the monks which had been parodied in Reuchlin's cause by the *Epistolæ Obscurorum Virorum*. He required a German equivalent to the Hebrew Bible.

' The language of the Hebrews,' Reuchlin had written in the little book whence this controversy started, ' is simple, uncorrupted, holy, terse and vigorous. God confers in it direct with men, and men with angels, face to face, as one friend converses with another ' ;

and so it should be with the Bible of the Germans. God should talk in it German to Germans, face to face, as one friend with another. So Luther *biblicised* German : he made it the literary language of the Church. Where he found two dialects of Teuton speech, *platt* and *hoch*, the low and the high, he left the model of a single language, the *Neuhochdeutsch* of German literature among the nations. The Lutheran Bible became a German Classic—a Homer, a Cicero, in its own kind— fulfilling the aspiration of Erasmus that the husbandman should sing it at his plough, the weaver hum it to the loom, and the traveller con it at his journey's end. In every German inn for many centuries, as in many humble ones to-day, a Bible was put in every bedroom.

Biblical Song and Story. The people's Bible was also the scholars' Bible. The authority of priests was shaken by the labours of comparative critics, who collated the Latin Vulgate with the Greek and Hebrew texts, and emended while they translated. And then came the German songs, the *Volkslieder* recommending the *Volksbuch*. Read what Ranke, the German historian of the Reformation, writes of Luther's hymn, ' Ein' feste Burg ist unser Gott ' :

' It professes to be a paraphrase of the 46th Psalm, but is in fact merely suggested by it ; it is completely the product of the moment in which Luther, engaged in a conflict with a world of foes, sought strength in a consciousness that he was defending a divine cause that could never perish. He seems to lay down his arms, but it was in fact the manliest renunciation of a momentary success, with the certainty of that which is eternal. How triumphant and animated is the melody ! How simple and steady, how devout and elevated ! It is identical with the words ; they arose together in those stormy days.'

What a weapon was placed at the disposal of militant reform, when the poorest peasant from the fields could approach the throne of Omnipotence by these simple words and tunes, without recourse to the Latin tongue. Finally, in this special context, so closely set with the thorns of controversy, we would cite the testimony of a modern student, Lord Ernle (R. E. Prothero), who writes in Chapter VI of his *The Psalms in Human Life* :

' The Psalms in Latin, as well as hymns and anthems in the same tongue, had been consecrated by centuries of use in public worship. But they were chanted by priests or choristers, and to the people they were for the most part unintelligible. Church hymns to be sung by the whole congregation in the vulgar tongue were the special creation of the Lutherans. To Luther the German people owed not only the Catechism and the Bible, translated into forcible, racy, idiomatic language, but also a hymn-book.'

Germany's Boon to Civilization. Measuring the Renaissance to-day by its contribution to human happiness, or to the intellectual liberty and spiritual welfare of mankind, the increase of which increases happiness, can it be said that the German Renaissance was less fruitful than the Italian ? Wars, long and bitter, came out of it : the War of 1914, we have seen, was a sequel to the Peace of 1648. But, whatever Germany's share in war-guilt—and from first to last she has not been exonerated—the value of her contribution still remains. If Petrarch had not wanted Hellenism . . . If Reuchlin had not wanted Hebraism . . . History had not been written under these hypotheses, and the historian of literature need not dispute which part brought more to the whole. He observes that by immense pains antiquity now has been rifled of its treasures. The legacies of Israel, Greece and Rome have been recovered for common use. The 16th century has implemented the 15th. The rest may be summarised in advance in the words of a recent humanist, S. H. Butcher :

' Henceforth it is in the confluence of the Hellenic stream of thought with the waters that flow from Hebrew sources that the main direction of the world's progress is to be sought. The two tendencies summed up in the words Hebraism and Hellenism are often regarded as opposing and irreconcilable forces : and, indeed, it is only in a few rarely gifted individuals that these principles have been perfectly harmonised. Yet harmonised they can and must be. How to do so is one of the problems of modern civilisation '.[1]

How to extract them from the mystery-keepers of the Middle Ages was the contribution of the Renaissance and the Reformation.

[1] *Some Aspects of the Greek Genius*, London, 3rd edition, 1904 ; pp. 45-46.

BOOK III
THE AGE OF SHAKESPEARE

FOREWORD TO BOOK III

IT is sometimes less than fully realized how closely in time the achievement of Shakespeare followed the experiments of the Humanists. The two centuries, 1321 to 1521, from the death of Dante to the Diet of Worms, which have been covered, hurriedly but fairly adequately, in the previous Book, were the time of the making of the Renaissance and Reformation. In a time of experimentation nothing perfect is made, and, though many great books were written in the course of those two hundred years in Italy, France, Spain, England, and, less greatly, in Germany, the perfect work of Dante, as the supreme representative of his age, was not repeated in European literature till the production of the perfect work of Shakespeare, the supreme representative of the new age built on the ruin of some of Dante's certainties. Shakespeare's ' victory ', writes Professor Dover Wilson,[1] to quote another serviceable aphorism by a modern scholar, ' was a victory for the whole human race. *King Lear* is a piece of exploration, more dearly won and far more significant than that of a Shackleton or an Einstein ; for, while they have enlarged the bounds of human knowledge, *Lear* has revealed the human spirit as of greater sublimity than we could otherwise have dreamed.' It is the aim of the present Book to make this aphorism valid.

[1] *The Essential Shakespeare*, Cambridge, 1932 ; p. 124.

§ 1. GROUPS AND SINGLETONS.

LUTHER died in 1546, after winning a sure 'victory for the whole human race.' The translation of that victory and of the cognate triumphs of Humanists and Discoverers into the terms of their own art of literature was the task of men of letters in the 16th century. The first thing, then, is to enumerate them, and, while enumerating them, we shall conveniently sort some of them into groups.

Schools of Wit. A chief group of formative influence may be described compendiously as the schools of wit. They flourished in Spain, France and England, where the writers concerned were moved by a like resolve to turn their native tongues into literary languages. They were ambitious of laureation, if we may use the word, of crowning with wreaths of poets' laurel the speech of peoples content hitherto with literary forms and measures not developed *al Italico modo*,— not passed after the manner of the Italians, taught by Petrarch and his heirs, through the discipline of Hellenic standards. The schools of wit included :

In *Spain* : ANTONIO DE GUEVARA (*c.* 1490–1544).
JUAN BOSCAN (*c.* 1490–1542).
GARCILASSO DE LA VEGA (1503–36).
In *England* : THOMAS WYATT (1503–42).
EARL OF SURREY (*c.* 1517–47).
In *France* : JACQUES AMYOT (1513–93).
PIERRE DE RONSARD (1524–85), and six other members of a group famous as the PLEIAD.

And a little apart but not far from them :

In *Germany* : CONRAD GESNER (1516–65).

They are all, as we see now, and as learned books—sometimes too learned—have been written to prove, on the way to and tributary to Shakespeare. But, of course, they did not know that he was coming. Only two or three of them

H

lived into his lifetime, and with none of them was there any question of subserving his objects. They were men who stood on their own feet, spending their lives, short or long—and it will be observed that many of them were short-lived—in the pursuit of beauty as they saw it. They were working in twilight with imperfect tools, but they wrought to the best of their ability.

Politicians. We remarked above the close connection between writers on the training of the Renaissance gentleman (Castiglione, for example) and writers on the Renaissance State—Sir Thomas More and Machiavelli, for example—in which the virtue (*virtù*) of the gentleman should be displayed. The ideas fostered by the statesmen would facilitate, if put into practice, the intellectual freedom aimed at by the schools of wit; and we may now mention among such political writers :—

FRANÇOIS HOTMAN (1524–90), whose *Franco-Gallia*, 1573, was a reasoned plea for liberal institutions.

' ERASTUS ' (1524–83), a Swiss theologian, whose name was grecized out of his patronymic Lüber (or Lieber), and whose Latin controversial pamphlets, we are assured,[1] were designed ' not to magnify the State nor to enslave the Church, but to secure the liberty of the subject.' The Erastianism derived from his teaching ranked in Scotland particularly as a kind of heresy, though the question has been asked, Was Erastus an Erastian ?

JEAN BODIN (1530–96), a French Huguenot, and

JUAN DE MARIANA (1535–1624), a Spanish Jesuit, both of whom discussed the problem of tyrannicide, the former in his *La République*, 1577, and the latter in his *De Rege et Regis Institutione*. The crux in the *De Rege* occurs in Book I, Chapter vi, where the assassin of King Henry III of France is termed *æternum Galliæ decus*. The Society of Jesus repudiated this work in 1606 and it was burnt by the common hangman in Paris before Ravaillac's assassination of King Henry IV of France in 1610. The interest of these speculations to Milton and Cromwell is obvious.

[1] By J. N. Figgis, in *The Divine Right of Kings*.

PHILIP MARNIX (1538–98), French by birth and Dutch by adoption in exile. He was poet as well as pamphleteer, and wrote the 'Marseillaise' of Holland, *William of Nassau*, 1568, and a brilliant Protestant satire known as the *Bienkorf* or 'Beehive of the Holy Roman Church', 1569 (translated into English and German, and many times reprinted).

Other names might be mentioned in this group, but their *literary* interest is to-day so remote that they are chiefly to be remembered as champions, not without pain and suffering, of the civil liberty so congenial to great literature.

Scholars. Even more remote from present literary interest, yet not justly to be omitted from a history of letters, are the middlemen of culture, whose devotion to learning made a powerful contribution to the growth of the mind of Europe in the 16th century. They flitted to Switzerland, England and the Netherlands, calling, perhaps, at Lyons on the way, from less hospitable or liberal climes. They founded presses and wrote dictionaries, translated, edited and compiled, and lived lives adventurous by circumstance and noble by zest of adventure. A few names may be commemorated *honoris causa*; Sandys's *History of Classical Scholarship* should be consulted for more detailed information :

JOHANN STURM (1507–89), and

ROGER ASCHAM (1515–68), German and English school-masters respectively and founders of educational method.

JUAN DE VALDES (d. 1541), Spanish moralist, who wrote a valuable 'Dialogue on Language,' 1535, which had great influence on prose-style.

JOHN PALSGRAVE (d. 1554), English tutor to Princess (Queen) Mary. His *Éclaircissement de la Langue Française*, 1530, was immensely useful to French students in Tudor times.

THOMAS WILSON, whose *Arte of Rhetorique* is said to have been used by Shakespeare.

NICOLAI CLEYNAERTS (1495–1542), whose Greek grammar (Louvain, 1530) was a pioneer in its class.

J. J. SCALIGER (1540–1609), 'the founder of historical criticism'; JUSTUS LIPSIUS (1547–1606), the Leyden historian; and ISAAC CASAUBON (1559–1614), the Huguenot, who found a refuge and a welcome in England, a grave in Westminster Abbey, and an English biographer (1875) in Mark Pattison. Their names are typical of many more.

Individuals. Outside these groups, which, of course, have been assembled merely for convenience of classification, are the individual writers in various countries who lead up the hillside to Shakespeare :

JORGE DE MONTEMAYOR (*c.* 1521–61), Portuguese pastoral poet, whose *Diana Enamorada* enjoyed immense popularity.

LUIS DE CAMOENS (1524–80), Portuguese sea-poet, whose ' Lusiads ' (*Os Lusiadas*) in octave stanzas are the national epic of Portugal in her era of the Navigators.

LUIS PONCE DE LEON (*c.* 1528–91), Spanish sacred poet of exquisite musical notation.

MONTAIGNE (1533–92 ; Michel Eyquem, Sieur de Montaigne), the famous French essayist, whose unfaded renown leads directly to the men of the golden twenty years, 1544–64, in which were born DU BARTAS, TASSO, CERVANTES, SPENSER, SIDNEY, LYLY, BACON, LOPE DE VEGA, CHRISTOPHER MARLOWE and WILLIAM SHAKESPEARE.

The light travelled more slowly to other countries. In the Netherlands, the fruits of the Renaissance were gathered by a group of writers who made a centre in Amsterdam, and among whom the names of HOOFT, GROTIUS and VONDEL will recur in a later Section of the present Book. Mention, too, here is due in advance to MARTIN OPITZ (1597–1639), their German contemporary, who ranked as the Ronsard of his own country, more backward than England, France and Spain perforce of its greater sacrifice in the cause of religious reform.

§ 2. THE SCHOOLS OF WIT.

Lists of names, though the material of history, are not history itself. If we can construct a short paragraph of history out of the lists of names in the foregoing Section we should say that the combined efforts of minor poets, grammarians, scholars, statecraftsmen and reformers in various kinds were all directed to the one object of improving the tools of the mind. The human mind between Dante and Luther had been immensely expanded by discovery and experiment in various fields, but the means and even the right of expression had not kept pace with that expansion. What was wanted were more books and booksellers, quicker ships, better roads, more light and water; and, apart from such equipment of the robot, so lavishly furnished now, above all, a sense of secure possession. What the mind had won slipped from hand and tongue : the roving mind was held in leash by those tamer members.

The Pleiad. If the atmosphere of the epoch be at all clearer for this brief exposition, the aim of the wits in their several countries—a ' wit ' is simply a man of learning who can talk or write—will be much more readily understood. They sought first to release the tongue, to give it words and the right to use them, in order to enlarge the freedom of the kingdom of the mind. A concerted effort in this direction was made by a French group known as the Pleiad, to which, therefore, we first address ourselves.

The Pleiad, or seven stars, who took their name from a Greek group in Alexandria, appointed themselves as a kind of Commission to report on poetry and poetics. Their terms of reference were briefly : How to make French poetry the equal of Latin and Greek. Not the echo, but the equal. ' Are we inferior to the Greeks and Romans ? ' asked JOACHIM DU BELLAY (1524–60) in the chief manifesto of the group, called *La Défense et Illustration de la Langue française* (1549) : *la Langue*, the halting and backward tongue; and he answered his own question in a tone of eager, imperative affirmation. French satire was to be lifted out of its cradle of medieval allegory. French drama was to be freed from its baby-clothes of the mystery-play. French long poems were to be composed on topics consecrated by French history. French sonnets were to rival Petrarch's; French odes were to be Pindaric, and a new Greek MS., just found in France and ascribed to Anacreon, was to furnish new French lyric measures. It was all very gay and shining. If new words were wanted, French Hellenists should invent them. A plentiful supply of words— Rabelais had shown the way in this respect—was the surest sign of creative strength.

Of the Commission's main recommendations for French master-poets to be, PIERRE RONSARD, the brightest star of the Pleiad, attempted at least three : the ode, the sonnet and the long poem (or epopee). In the two first he succeeded brilliantly, and his *Franciad* was at least a brave experiment in the third towards an *Iliad* or *Æneid* of France. When Ronsard struck his lyre a new note rippled through all Europe. For he relied on his own ears and eyes. He marked April's tears and laughter. He *heard* the song of the lark rise leaping to the sky, and *saw* the bird's fall back to earth. Thus observing, noting, expressing, and finding French words for what he heard and saw, Ronsard became du Bellay's final argument. In the year after the *Défense* he published four books of *Odes*, which proved the case for the defence. French poetry had been written in the French language. A French poet had equalled the Greeks. Take one poem only of his writings :

'Mignonne, allons voir si la Rose . . .'

It will be found in any anthology, and the fast-fading rose of youth may be traced backward through Florentine voices to Greek ode and Roman elegy and forward to Meredith's *Love in the Valley*. In that long line of human-garden verse— maidens gathering the rose and time gathering the maidens— Ronsard's 'Mignonne' is the first pure flower of native European cultivation. In his stanzas we reach at last a set of verses responsive to pagan sentiment yet trailing no fetters of pagan make ; sincere, delicate, musical, as a song by Catullus, yet modern in every phrase. We shall come to a reaction from Ronsard, and shall find in its due place that the criticism of his 'learned brigade' was not altogether un- deserved. They imported more than they could carry. They were too certain of immortality, and lived too lavishly on one another's applause. But, when all is said and done, their solid achievement in French poetry is comparable to nothing in history, except, perhaps, to the invasion of Roman literature by Greek, which Nævius, the old Latin poet, confessed his inability to stem. Not till Rossetti and the pre-Raphaelites, and not in their instance with similarly wide results, were the charm and confidence of young men combined to such effective vigour. Further, the Pleiad acted as a clearing-house of the Italian Renaissance. All that Petrarch had aimed at in his Italian poems passed through Ronsard and his company into the currency of European tongues.

Ronsard's six satellite-stars may be briefly enumerated. (1) Du Bellay's short lead we have noticed, as author of the *Défense et Illustration*. He wrote, too, a little book of sonnets, inscribed to Mlle. de Viole, and entitled anagrammatically, *Olive*; sonnets on the 'Antiquities of Rome', which Spenser rendered into English and several other little volumes. (2) Remi Belleau (1528–77) translated the newly-found 'Anacreon', and helped to sing April into fashion in a lyric *Bergerie*. (3) Etienne Jodelle (1532–73) was the dramatist of the Pleiad. He revived Greek tragedy so thoroughly that he was accused of the impiety of sacrificing a goat to Dionysus. Alike in temperament and achievement, Jodelle was the Marlowe of the French stage, and his *Cléopâtre* and *Didon* are still noteworthy to-day. The founder of the Pleiad's Academy was (4) Jean Antoine de Baïf (1532–89). It had as its object ' de renouveler l'ancienne façon de composer des vers mesurés pour y accommoder le chant pareillement mesuré selon l'art métrique '. These ancient quantitative metres were so foreign to the genius of French speech that the principles and the Academy proved short-lived. But de Baïf's creed had a purging effect, and his example was repeated in the Areopagus, founded in London, 1579, by Gabriel Harvey, who sought to impose similar rules on English poets. Finally, the two remaining stars were (5) Pontus de Tyard (1521–1603), who quickly exhausted a not powerful vein, and (6) Jean Dorat or Daurat (1508–88), who had taught Ronsard Greek.

Amyot and Gesner. Similar service to that of the Pleiad was rendered by JACQUES AMYOT, Bishop of Auxerre, who was called the prince of translators as Ronsard was called the prince of poets. The learned Bishop earned this distinction by his renderings of Greek novels by Longus and Heliodorus, and particularly by his noble versions of the *Parallel Lives* and *Morals* of Plutarch, the Greek historian in Alexandria, who died A.D. 125. These were issued respectively in 1554 and 1572, and we have contemporary evidence to their value and vogue. Montaigne, to whom we come immediately, wrote in an easy passage of his essays :

' Je donne avec grande raison, ce me semble, la palme à Jacques Amiot sur tous nos ecrivains françois, non seulement pour la naïfveté et pureté du language, en quoy il surpasse tous autres, ny pour la constance d'un si long travail, ny pour la profondeur de son sçavoir, ayant pu développer si heureusement un autheur se espineux et ferré ; . . . mais sur tout je lui sçay bon gré d'avoir sçeu trier un livre si digne et si à propos, pour en faire present a son pays. Nous autres ignorans estions perdus, si ce livre ne nous eust relevez du bourbier : sa mercy, nous osons à cett' heure et parler et escrire ; les dames en regentent les maistres d'escole ; c'est nostre breviaire.'

Note, first, the epithet ' our breviary '. It is the same confession of delight in discovery, of a kind of virginal joy, which Petrarch acknowledged to Cicero and Chaucer to the *Roman de la Rose* ; and when Sir Thomas North in 1579 had translated Amyot's Plutarch's *Lives* into Tudor English, the book became a breviary to Shakespeare. It was a very close corporation, for Plutarch, dead more than sixteen hundred years, was a new writer to Montaigne and Shakespeare. Note, next, Montaigne's praise of the naïveté and purity of Amyot's language. The instrument of speech was being perfected for use, and Amyot helped to enlarge the French vocabulary and to make it equal to the Greek by finding native equivalents for Greek terms such as ' enthusiasm ' and ' panegyric ', which had been current in Europe hitherto only in Latin forms. The technical vocabulary of arts and crafts, we may add, owed much in the same period to another Frenchman, Bernard Palissy (*c.* 1510–89), a Huguenot potter.

In Germany, CONRAD GESNER was a naturalist, with a garden of botanical specimens at Zurich. He was the first scientific student of comparative philology, and the first compiler of an ' every man's library ' of Greek, Latin, and Hebrew books, with critical notices of the entries. Gesner, too, was a pioneer of mountain-travel, in the line from Petrarch to Rousseau and Leslie Stephen. He climbed the Alps once a year, ' partly to study the flora, partly to refresh my mind ', and enhanced modern resources in both capacities. His ' prodigious erudition ' is duly notified by Hallam.

Closer akin to the service of the Pleiad was the contribution of MARTIN OPITZ, who, though so late in time (1597–1639), achieved in his few, busy years some real reforms in German prose and verse. It was an ill time for such labours, in the midst of the cruel devastation wrought by the Thirty Years' War (1618–48) ; but Opitz, in his Latin treatise on poetics (*Aristarchus*) and in his German *Buch der deutschen Poeterey*, showed that he had the heart of the matter, and in a happier age he might have achieved more striking success.

Spanish Writers. The same aim at articulate learning— the kind of aim which Huxley brought to ' evolution ' and which Sir James Jeans brings to astronomy—moved the makers of the Renaissance in Spain, and the first name which occurs is that of another learned Bishop, who, like Amyot, found his translator in Sir Thomas North. Bishop GUEVARA was confessor to the King of Spain who was also the Emperor Charles V, and his chief work, published in 1529 and translated by North in 1557, was the *Relox de Principes*, known in English as the ' Dial of Princes, with which is incorporated the Very Famous Book of Marcus Aurelius '. It was part-history and part-romance, though the historical part was written down rather severely by later critics. Guevara set before the King of Spain, and, through various versions, before other princes, a final model of knightly virtue, and he employed all the resources of an elegant style to recommend his Greek wisdom to modern practice. North's translation was not direct but through the French, and much that was exquisite was lost in the double passage, so that the influence of Guevara on John Lyly and the English ' euphuistic ' style[1] is not rated as highly as it used to be. But the diminution of the debt increases the significance of the likeness between stylists in two countries alike devoted to the enhancement of their native languages.

BOSCAN is his own witness to the urgency of this reform in Spain. In 1526 a certain Andrea Navagero was Venetian Ambassador at the Court of Charles V. He was a minor poet of the Italian Renaissance, and, when he met Boscan in Granada, the talk turned to ' matters of wit and letters He asked me,' Boscan himself tells us,

' why I did not make an attempt in Castilian at the sonnets and their poetic forms employed by good Italian authors. . . . A few days afterwards I travelled home and on the long and solitary journey I had an opportunity of thinking over what Navagero had said. So I began to practise this kind of poetry.'

The seed fell on fruitful soil, and in this detail of biography we see the Spanish Renaissance in the making. Boscan illumined it like a Pleiad, borrowing his light from Navagero. He and his fellow *Petrarquistas*, as the writers in Petrarchan measures came to be styled, encountered attack in the old ways from eminent anti-Italianates, who tried to laugh the new stylists out of court—literally, out of the Spanish Court to which Navagero was accredited. The old guard of Spanish letters was known as the Salamanca School, and the new poets were known as the Sevilians, after the city of Seville. Thus Navagero's disciples in Spain, starting with Juan Boscan, set new lines for Spanish poetry. To their contemporaries, doubtless, they seemed futurists and iconoclasts with a taste for breaking images, as the Italianizers seemed to Roger Ascham in England. But, ' seen at a distance, in the perspective of literary history, Boscan appears to us as the founder of a new poetic dynasty, the head of an irresistible advance-guard '.[2]

The first irresistible assault upon old-time metres and

[1] See page 135 below.   [2] J. Fitzmaurice Kelly, *Litterature espagnole*.

diction in Spain was made by ' the famous poet ' (we owe the epithet to Cervantes), GARCILASSO DE LA VEGA, who was a kind of Aaron to Boscan's Moses. He turned to full harmonies of Spanish poesy Boscan's less expressive music. He was master where Boscan was apprentice ; master of the Italian Renaissance in Spain, where Boscan had been apprentice to Navagero.

Garcilasso died young, as his dates show ; and this, too, was a part of his fame.

> ' Tomando ora la espada, ora la pluma,'

' Wielding at one time the sword, at another the pen,' he wrote of his activity as a soldier-poet, and the verse, which is equally applicable to Sir Philip Sidney and Rupert Brooke in our annals, has justly become proverbial. A very Virgil of the West, he founded the School of Seville. He caught the undertones of Virgil, the allusive, melancholy music, best described as *morbidezza*, which gave him his patent as a poet apart from his derivative debt to Boscan and his foreign models.

In England. Lastly, in this inspection of the workshops of wit, we pass from Spain to England, from the rivals in arms to the brothers in art. The two countries drew near as they drew apart. King Philip of Spain, son of the Emperor Charles V, became the husband of Mary, Queen of England, and Queen Elizabeth, Mary's half-sister, was Admiral of the Fleet which defeated him. But throughout these policies of bed and war, which streak the annals of the 16th century, men of letters followed the same star. Quixote and Hamlet, twin sons of the Renaissance, survive the Habsburg and the Tudor and the Holy Roman Empire itself.

(1) *Sir Thomas Wyatt.* Three generations of the Wyatt family—Sir Henry, Sir Thomas the poet, and Sir Thomas the younger—achieved the honour of Knighthood and the suspicion of treason, for which the third was tried, convicted and executed in 1554. He had conspired to prevent the marriage of Queen Mary and King Philip ; his grandfather had been joint-constable with Sir Thomas Boleyn of Norwich Castle ; and his father, with whom only we are concerned,

had been a lover of Anne, the other constable's daughter, before her marriage with Henry VIII, to whom she bore the future Queen Elizabeth.

These royal contacts are interesting, not so much for their tales of gallantry as for the evidence they afford to the class from which poets were drawn. In England, as in Italy, France and Spain, in the first half of the 16th century, it was at the Courts of princes that the labour of verse-formation and language-extension was almost professionally performed. Courtier-poets, following the tradition set at Florence in the reign of The Magnificent, and illustrated by Castiglione at Urbino, who called his book exactly *The Courtier*, show that the idea of a poet-laureate, though conventional to-day, was originally essential to a princely ménage, and show, too, that the direction of poetics proceeded normally from that fount. It was entirely proper to his station that Wyatt should study the writings of Alamanni, Marot and the rest, and should be zealous to introduce to England the elegances of his foreign models. The Earl of Surrey, to whom we come immediately, and who survived Wyatt by five years, praised him in an elegy for

' A tongue that served in foreign realms his king ;
 Whose courteous talk to virtue did inflame
 Each noble heart ; a worthy guide to bring
 Our English youth by travail unto fame.'

It was a true Renaissance portrait : the ' courteous talk ' was the wit's quality ; ' virtue ' (*virtù*) was the mark of the gentleman ; and Wyatt was justly said to have been a pioneer in England of the labour—the real hard work at words, metres and so forth—required to make our native poesy equal to that of Greece and Rome. The Pleiad of English poetry was the Wyatt-Surrey constellation, or Sir Thomas Wyatt was England's Boscan and her Garcilasso de la Vega was Lord Surrey.

(1) *Henry Howard, Earl of Surrey.* Between them they articulated and strengthened English verse-style. They introduced the sonnet as a native measure, though Surrey, who was the better Italianate of the two, proved more careful of the

genius of his own language[1]. He was notable, too, for his introduction, after the pattern of Italian poets, of the stately measure of blank verse, which he used in his version of Books II and IV of Virgil's *Æneid*. Thus, he rendered more permanent service to English poetry than was rendered by Ronsard in France when he sought to match the *Æneid* by a *Franciad*.

Surrey, again, was of the courtly class; but he lost more than he gained by that dangerous privilege, and ended his soldier-life on the scaffold.

A Contemporary Witness. It was well-made, this highway of the Renaissance, well-laid, well-watered, well-rolled, by the poet-adepts, grammarians and philologists who had learned their trade from Italian pioneers. The greater writers are now very close: Du Bartas, who wrote the French epic, was born in 1544, Cervantes in 1547, Spenser in 1552. The aims of the Pleiad, Boscan, Wyatt and the other wits were as near to fruition as they dared to hope. For their belief in their own course was a powerful part of their success in it. We would quote in this context, not any of the learned historians who look back to the 16th century from the 20th, but a critic in that century itself, whose treatise on *The Art of English Poesy* was published in 1589. In the course of his remarks he rendered honour to those who had

'by their thankful studies so much beautified our English tongue that at this day it will be found our nation is in nothing inferior to the French or Italian for copy of language, subtlety of device, good method or proportion in any form of poem.'

Looking back across the few years from Queen Elizabeth to King Henry VIII,

'In the latter part of the same King's reign,' he went on, 'sprang up a new company of courtly makers, of whom Sir Thomas Wyat the elder and Henry Earl of Surrey were the two chieftains, who having travelled into Italy and there tasted the sweet and stately measures and style of the Italian poesy

[1] 'Any superiority that Surrey had over Wyatt was largely that Surrey was able to mould his English to the sonnet-form where Wyatt could only cramp his.' W. L. Renwick, *Edmund Spenser*, London, 1925; p. 70.

as novices newly crept out of the schools of Dante, Ariosto and Petrarch, they greatly polished our rude and homely manner of vulgar poesy, from what it had been before, and for that cause may justly be said the first reformers of our English metre and style.'

Next, he mentioned very properly some of the great Tudor translators: Thomas Phaer and Thomas Twyne who translated Virgil, and Arthur Golding, whose Ovid was used by Shakespeare; and, retracing his footsteps:

'Henry Earl of Surrey and Sir Thomas Wyat between whom I find very little difference,[1] I repute them (as before) for the two chief lanterns of light to all others that have since employed their pens upon English Poesy. Their conceits were lofty, their styles stately, their conveyance cleanly, their terms proper, their metre sweet and well-proportioned, in all imitating very naturally and studiously their Master, Francis Petrarch.'

Petrarch died, we remember, in 1374. It had taken two hundred years to spread his sweetness and strength through Italy to France, Spain and England. But Puttenham at the close of the 16th century is justified in his claim. The stream of Renaissance and Reformation is now in full flood.

§ 3. Epic Poetry.

We come to the greater writers, to the men whose greater work could be done because the smaller men had gone before them. The powers of modern languages had been supplied by constant emulation of Greek and Latin, and the increasing liberation of modern institutions had partly proceeded from

[1] Prof. Renwick found more in 1925. See page 113, note [1]. The conclusion to Puttenham's treatise is worth quoting, just to show the change of taste in Royal addresses. After enumerating the poets of his own day: 'But last in recital and first in degree,' he declared, 'is the Queen our sovereign Lady, whose learned, delicate, noble muse easily surmounteth all the rest that have written before her time or since, for sense, sweetness and subtlety, be it in Ode, Elegy, Epigram, or any other kind of poem Heroic or Lyric, wherein it shall please her Majesty to employ her pen, even by as much odds as her own excellent estate and degree exceedeth all the rest of her most humble vassals.'

and partly stimulated the study of classical literature for its æsthetic values. The more sensuous enjoyment of earthly beauty, the more final sense of its mortality, and the stronger aim at glory and achievement within the brief limits of human endeavour, which were at once a heritage from Antiquity and an inference from the New Learning in its various aspects of observation, experiment and discovery, commanded now more perfect instruments of literary expression. The forms of expression were of old, according to the precepts of the writers on poetics, but the clamps of the workshop were knocked off them, the poets flew out of the schoolmaster's nest, and the spirit rose more freely and without trammels.

Four Poets. It will be recalled that the long, ' heroic ' poem, the *Iliad* or *Æneid* of the modern nation, was one of the chief diploma-pieces which Ronsard desiderated for France. It would be an unmistakable specimen of the laureation—the formal crowning with the poet's wreath—which was to satisfy the ambition of the Pleiad by equating French poetry with Greek. That his own *Franciad* was inadequate to this design was no cause why it should not be improved, and in fact, almost simultaneously in four countries, Ronsard's invocation was repeated. In Portugal LUIS DE CAMOENS (1524–80), in France itself GUILLAUME DU BARTAS (1544–90), in Italy TORQUATO TASSO (1544–95), and in England EDMUND SPENSER (*c*. 1552–99), working separately on the same models though meditating different themes, wrote poems which have challenged comparison with the masterpieces of Homer and Virgil. The *Lusiadas* were published in 1572 ; the seven Books of *La Semaine* in 1578 ; the correct version of *Gerusalemme Liberata* appeared in 1581, and the *Faery Queen* in 1589. They were a prompt complement (and, indeed, a direct compliment) to the *Franciad* of 1572. Milton's *Paradise Lost* is the last masterpiece in this epic school.

(1) *Camoens.* The dates preclude the hypothesis of an imitation of the *Franciad* in the *Lusiads.* But both writers were working in the same *genre* ; each was equally affected by the common movement towards national epos, and Camoens anticipated in Portugal what later and greater poets wrought elsewhere. He had the advantage of being a countryman of

Vasco da Gama, who had made his first voyage to India in
1497-99, and whom Camoens celebrated as the hero of his
poem. He had the ocean in his blood, and he possessed the
poet's qualification that he had learnt in suffering what he
taught in song. He was unhappy in love, unfortunate in war,
and a victim of exile, shipwreck and plague—an accumulation
of disaster which may have made him a more than commonly
romantic figure to the early generations of his readers at home.
He has been much translated, too, into English, and, as the
maritime poet of Lusitania (Portugal), using his own travel-
memories for the decoration of his verse, and inventing his
epic mould and measure, he has real staying-power in literary
history. Whether this interest is mainly historical and whether
we miss much by not reading him are questions which have
been answered in a sense adverse to his literary fame.

Indeed, it is idle to pretend that a taste for epic poetry is
either native to, or growing in, modern Europe. The conditions
which produced it in antiquity do not exist to-day and were
not even quite the same in the days of the *chansons de geste*.
We cannot pause here to defend this view : it may suggest
a topic for debate or for an essay ; but we would quote from
Dr. Mackail's Introduction to his edition of the *Æneid*[1] the
supporting statement :

'Lyrical instinct is so grounded in the English genius
that it gives to the whole body of English poetry a quality
of its own ; the epic as such is to some degree foreign to the
English mode of creation ; and still more is it foreign to the
movement which now runs so strongly towards disintegrating
and demoralizing all art.'

And we recall in this direction that, when Tennyson tackled
the Arthuriad in the dawn of that democratic movement,
he broke up the big epic canvas into little pictures or *Idylls
of the King*.

(2) *Du Bartas*. This change of taste, or failure to acquire
a taste, despite the force of classical example and the precepts
of the Pleiad and other schoolmasters, goes some way to
explain the swift decline from popularity of Du Bartas,

[1] Oxford, 1930 ; p. lxxv.

author of the epic tale of ' The (Sacred) Week ' (*La Semaine*).
There were in fact other causes. One was personal and another
political. The personal cause was Ronsard's jealousy of a star
so near to his own orbit and shining with stronger epic beams.
The political cause was derived from the fact that Du Bartas
was a Huguenot (they called him the ' Protestant Ronsard ').
The Massacre of St. Bartholomew in 1572 quickened French
interest in Huguenot writers, but a reaction ensued, and it
was in Protestant England that the influence of Du Bartas
was most felt. King James VI of Scotland translated one of
his poems and procured the translation of another. He
invited Du Bartas to his court, and the visit, paid in 1587,
included a reception by Queen Elizabeth and a warm welcome
by Sir Philip Sidney. The version of *La Semaine* by Joshua
Sylvester followed these visits at a short interval, and Milton's
choice of topic for *Paradise Lost* as well as touches in his style
are properly associated with the seven books of the seven
days (' la semaine ') of the Creation. Goethe, too, was his
ardent admirer. Still, we have to reckon with the slump in
epic : it was the chief cause of the fall from esteem which
overtook this best-seller of the third quarter of the 16th
century. Thirty editions of *La Semaine* are said to have been
sold between 1578 and its author's death at the Battle of Ivry
in 1590, but ' who is there,' asked Wordsworth, poet and
critic, ' that now reads the *Creation* of Du Bartas ? ' And we
echo the cry. ' Yet all Europe,' he went on, ' once resounded
with his praise ; he was caressed by kings ; and, when his
poem was translated into our language, the *Faery Queen* faded
before it.' The century and a half since Wordsworth wrote
have brought no revival to Du Bartas.

(3) *Tasso*. The caged song-bird has fared better than the
fighting Huguenot, a fate which suggests, if readers are just,
that the tame Italian was a better poet than the militant
Frenchman. Perhaps he was. Duke Alfonso II shut him up
at Ferrara and required him to sing. It was the right of the
Renaissance prince to have a laureate, to clip his wings if he
proved restive, and, if he sang too loud to a mistress out of
his reach, to quiet him in an alienist prison. This was Tasso's
lot for lifting his eyes to Alfonso's sister, the Princess Leonora ;

and, in the presence of that major terror, which lasted for seven unhappy years (1579–86), we need not pause at the jealousy of rival poets, the suspicions of the Church, the cabals of the courtiers, or Leonora's fitful favours. To all these Tasso was over-sensitive ; together, they broke him at the age of fifty-one.

But they did not break his epic mould. The prince got his poet in his own way, and Duke Alfonso d'Este of Ferrara is duly remembered as the patron of Torquato Tasso, author of *Gerusalemme Liberata*. The tragedy of the thing appealed to Goethe at the Court of the Grand Duke of Weimar (as it had appealed to Goldoni, the Italian playwright, thirty years before him), and in 1790 he published his *Torquato Tasso*, of which he said to Eckermann :

' I had Tasso's life, I had my own life, and in combining two such strange figures, the conception of *Tasso* arose in my mind. . . . As for the other circumstances of a court, in love and life, they were to be found in Weimar as well as in Ferrara ; and I can say with justice that the drama is bone of my bone and flesh of my flesh.'

He wrote, too, of Tasso :

' 'Twas thou alone who from a life of limits
    Didst raise me to a splendid liberty ;
    Who tookest off my shoulders every load,
    And gav'st me freedom, that my soul might grow
    And spend itself in undistracted song ;
    Aye, all the merit that my labour earns
    Is due to·thee, and thine be all the thanks '.

This aims beyond Ronsard and the *Franciad*. It leaves the teachers' craft behind it, and touches the heart of great poetry, the constructive music of the world.

The ' Christian *Iliad* ', as Tasso called his epic, was drawn from the old heroic tales, part-Greek, part-færy, part-crusaders', of the siege of Antioch and the road to Jerusalem.

' The sacred armies and the goodly knight
    That the great sepulchre of Christ did free
    I sing.'

Arma virumque cano, but the battles were of the Lord.   Tasso,
like Milton after him, invoked the Muse of Heaven as well as
the Muse of Helicon :

> ' O heavenly Muse, that not with fading bays
>   Deckest thy brow by th' Heliconian spring,
>   But sittest, crown'd with stars' immortal rays
>   In Heaven, where legions of bright angels sing,
>   Inspire life in my wit, my thoughts upraise,
>   My verse ennoble, and forgive the thing,
>   If fiction light I mix with truth divine,
>   And fill these lines with others' praise than thine.'

So, in this epic of the First Crusade, historical and fictitious
characters, with Godfrey of Boulogne (Bouillon) at their head,
are combined in varied adventures of love, war, magic and
Christian zeal.   There is much that modern taste rejects : the
invention of a d'Este among the crusaders out of compliment
to the living patron-duke, some heavy incense, and some
Homeric fights.   But no detailed criticism affects the loveliness
and the majesty of the poem, which moves through its octave
stanzas, made perfect after the pattern of Ariosto, Boiardo and
their predecessors, with a smoothness hitherto unmatched.
Voltaire, an excellent judge, declared it to be ' astonishing
how Tasso impresses a new character upon the soft Italian
tongue, enhancing it by stateliness, and reforming it with
strength.'   Hallam described the poem as ' the theme, not of
a single people, but of Europe,' and so it found its way into
every language, including Arabic and Chinese. Its tales are
said to have been chanted by peasants in their huts and galley-
slaves at their oars; and if their response to Tasso exceeds
his merits to-day, open the Tudor translations (*Godfrey of
Bulloigne* ; *or The Recoverie of Jerusalem*) by R. C(arew ; 1594)
and Edw(ard) Fairfax (1600) where we will, and the sheer
beauty of his achievement will compel instant admiration.

(4) *Edmund Spenser*. It compelled Spenser's on the spot.
We shall come to the story of Keats and Spenser, how he
went through the *Faery Queen*, like 'a young horse through a
spring meadow ramping.'   As Keats with Spenser, so Spenser
with Tasso.   To the poet of the coming age great poetry is

always a spring meadow, a *prima vera*. Spenser was but eight years younger than Tasso and survived him only four years, but he was younger enough and sufficiently a disciple to greet the author of the *Gerusalemme Liberata* among

'the antique Poets historicall; first Homere, who in the Person of Agamemnon and Ulysses hath ensampled a good governour and a vertuous man, the one in his *Ilias*, the other in his *Odysseis*: then Virgil, whose like intention was to doe in the person of Aeneas: after him Ariosto comprised them both in his Orlando; and lately Tasso dissevered them againe, and formed both parts in two persons, namely that part which they in Philosophy call *Ethice*, or vertues of a private man, coloured in his Rinaldo; the other named *Politice* in his Godfredo. By example of which excellente Poets I labour to pourtraict in Arthure, before he was king, the image of a brave Knight. . . .'

This passage from the Preface contains the whole purpose of the *Faery Queen*. It was a Renaissance document in the sense that it included good governance with virtuous conduct; Machiavelli's object with Castligione's.[1] True again to Renaissance methods was its foundation on the common base of the epic examples which had gone before it: Homer, Virgil, Ariosto, Tasso, ranked as masters of equal authority.[2] Of the essence of the Renaissance, too, is Spenser's pre-occupation with language. His laureation of rustic talk in the *Shepherd's Calendar* was an experiment made in the spirit of the reforms counselled by the Pleiad in France. It offended the taste of Gabriel Harvey, a critic and poetaster of the age, who took the lead at the little club of 'pure English' which met at Leicester House and called itself the Areopagus. But Spenser was unperturbed in innovation. Alike in metre and in language he belonged, like Chaucer before him—and between the two there was no English poet of equal standing—to the forward school of Italian wit and Renaissance learning.

[1] See page 102 above.
[2] So, Sir Philip Sidney, as noted on page 194, rebuked the licence of rustic talk which Spenser permitted himself in his *Shepherd's Calendar*, on the ground that the equal authorities 'neither Theocritus in Greek, Virgil in Latin, nor Sanazar in Italian did affect it.' It is naïf but it is also attractive, this faithful homage to the modern masters among the old.

Belonging to this, he belonged to the school of beauty. For beautiful writing, when all is said and done—the *bello stile* which Dante learned from Virgil—was the final aim of poets in every country who used their 'illustrious native tongue', in preference to, though in fee to, scholars' Latin. Spenser went for his topic to the third of the 'trois matières à nul homme entendant',[1] that of Bretagne, or the Arthuriad, and designed to portray Arthur as perfect 'in the xii private moral virtues, as Aristotle hath devised.' He sought, too, to 'overgo' Ariosto, in at least one aspect of that master, declaring in the closing line of his first stanza :

'Fierce warres and faithful loves shall moralize my song.'

Of war and love and ferocity and faith there had been plenty in his epical exemplars, but the added, extra *moral* purpose was Spenser's bounty to his countrymen. Or was it his countrymen's to him? We must not be too precise about what he gave and what he took in that busy, brilliant Elizabethan age. Few of us read the *Faery Queen* to-day for the sake of the Arthuriad or of Aristotle or of the moral underlying love and war. We do not read it, though it is worth studying, for what Spenser learned at large from France and Italy, and particularly from Ronsard and Du Bellay, as to how to emulate Ariosto and Tasso. All these features have critical interest and increase appreciation of the poem, at least in an historical sense. But it is for its beauty that we value it : for the long, languorous stanzas which wind their music through wonderland and dreamland ; for that stanza itself, wrought to finer metal on the Italian anvil and adding a ninth verse of twelve syllables to the *canzone* of eight decasyllabic lines (the rhymescheme is *a b a b b c b c c*[2]) ; and for the images, idylls and

---

[1] See page 33 above.
[2] Canto I, Stanza 1, may serve as example :

'A gentle knight was pricking on the plain,	*a*
Y-clad in mighty arms and silver shield,	*v*
Wherein old dints of deep wounds did remain,	*a*
The cruel marks of many a bloody field ;	*b*
Yet arms till that time did he never wield.	*b*
His angry steed did chide his foaming bit,	*c*
As much disdaining to the curb to yield :	*b*
Full jolly knight he seemed, and fair did sit,	*c*
As one for knightly jousts and fierce encounters fit.'	*c*

Note that, out of the 12 Books contemplated, 1–3 were published in 1589,

episodes which have made him for ever a poets' poet, a touchstone of perfect poetic art. For Spenser, too, raised poetry under our fogs, and even merriment among our marshes. He, too, though taught by foreign masters, transferred his exemplars into the English heritage. He, too, though a language-reformer, like those to whom he owed allegiance, was the master, not the servant, of his words, sitting on no lonely Areopagus but descending into the fields and vales of men. So he left in the *Faery Queen*, or in such parts of it as he completed, a book which is a constant delight and a new refreshment of the wells of English poetry. The young read it for its romantic story of the adventures of the Knight of the Red Cross, the discerning for its abundant charm, and all alike for its high faith in courtesy and gentlehood, and the discipline which inspires a noble life and has power to irradiate a noble death.

The Dutch Renaissance. To (5) MILTON we shall return in the concluding section of the present Book. Here, in considering the spread of the light cast by the Pleiad in Portugal, Spain and England, we may note that in the Netherlands, as in Germany, it arrived at a rather late date. Three names, as indicated above, particularly call for mention, the equal stars of the Dutch Renaissance :

PIETER CORNELIS HOOFT, 1581–1648,
HUGO GROTIUS (de Groot), 1583–1645, and
JOOST VAN DEN VONDEL, 1587–1679.

Hooft's *Muiderkring*, or circle at Muiden, where he was Governor in 1609, formed a centre for cultivated Dutchmen, comparable to the *salons* in Paris which showed the way to the French Academy of 1637. His *History of the Netherlands* has earned him the title of the Dutch Tacitus, and he wrote, too, lyric verse and plays.

Grotius, the erudite jurist, is one of the fixed lights of European scholarship. His book-learning stood him in strange

---

4–6 in 1590 : 7–12 were not completed. Among other of Spenser's writings were *The Shepherd's Calendar* (12 eclogues for the 12 months), 1579 ; *Colin Clout's Come Home Again* (including *Astrophel*, his lament for Sidney), 1595 ; *Four Hymns*, 1596 ; and a prose *View of the State of Ireland*, where he spent some months as a provincial governor, issued posthumously in 1633.

stead on one occasion, when, in a political *émeute*, he was assisted by a colleague to escape in one of the big boxes in which his books habitually accompanied him. He wrote a Latin sacred play, *Adamus Exsul*, 1601, which became well known to the future author of *Paradise Lost*, and his final title to renown, due to his treatise *De jure Belli ac Pacis*, has been stated by Sir William Rattigan, an Anglo-Indian jurist of the 19th century, in the following terms :

' Grotius was the first to discover a principle of right and a basis of society which was not derived from the Church or the Bible, nor in the insulated experience of the individual, but in the social relations of men.'

Vondel we shall meet again in § 8, for the sake of his Biblical plays, chiefly *Lucifer*, 1654. The Dutch painters of this epoch are more famous than the writers, but the history of the literary Renaissance in the North is incomplete without these three supreme names.

INTERSECTION I

We pause for a moment to reflect on the knights of the 16th century, gentle in courtesy, punctilious in honour, valiant in adventure, ardent in love, some of whom were mentioned in § 3. Climbing the hill of fame to the topmost peak of passion, they are romantic in fact as in fiction, and worshipful in real life as in heroic verse. Spenser's famous exordium is familiar :

> ' A gentle Knight was pricking on the plain,
> Y-clad in mighty arms and silver shield,
> Wherein old dints of deep wounds did remain. . . .
> Upon a great adventure he was bound,
> That greatest Gloriana to him gave, . . .
> To win him worship and her grace to have'.

The ideal was not confined to one country. Camoens, the sailor-poet, lost an eye in a sea-fight against the Moors. Garcilasso de la Vega was fatally wounded at the assault of

Muy. Lord Surrey, the soldier-poet, perished at the scaffold
on Tower Hill. Tasso languished for love of a princess. Sir
Philip Sidney, amiable in life and death, fell in action at
Zutphen. Cervantes lost his left hand (' for the greater glory
of the right ') in the Battle of the Gulf of Lepanto and was
captured by Algerian pirates. Of Ponce de Leon, the Spanish
poet-saint, Spenser's further verses might have been written :

> ' on his breast a bloody Cross he bore,
> The dear remembrance of his dying Lord,
> For whose sweet sake that glorious badge he wore,
> And dead, as living, ever him ador'd.'

But the flame was consumed in ecstasy. ' Gloriana ' not in
England only grew old and even ugly in the shadow of
chivalry's decline. They could not enlarge the narrow foothold ; the air of the summit was too rare. They climbed down
the hill of anti-chivalry from the passionate height of steep
desïre : Don Quixote, lovable but foolish ; Sir John Falstaff,
fond and fat; even the image of the White Knight by Lewis
Carroll. It is all, of course, written in Shakespeare, to whom
we presently come :

> ' I have ventured,
> Like little wanton boys that swim on bladders,
> This many summers in a sea of glory,
> But far beyond my depth. . . .
> Vain pomp and glory of this world, I hate ye :
> I feel my heart new open'd. O how wretched
> Is that poor man that hangs on princes' favours ! '

Such was the final cry of the courtier to the prince, of *il
cortegiano* to *il principe*, in the very century of the text-books
of those names by Castiglione and Machiavelli : Castiglione,
whose day-star was Sir Philip Sidney ; Machiavelli, who
peopled Marlowe's stage. The way of life recovered by
Petrarch—'the first modern man', as Renan called him—from
his musings with Cicero and other ' dead authors ', was
brought to a splendid effectiveness during the two hundred
years after his death. It was the way, we recall, of the
' stranger, a man well stricken in age, with a black sun-burned
face, a long beard, and a cloak cast homely about his shoulders',

whom Sir Thomas More met in 1575 on the crowded quay at Antwerp and immortalized in his *Utopia*. Do we want present pictures of the Elizabethan seamen? Charles Kingsley's *Westward Ho!* and Tennyson's ballad of *The Revenge* are readily accessible. It did not fade, the Humanists' ideal, the living legacy of the scholar-gentlemen of the 16th century. The Industrial Revolution did not destroy it, nor did French *égalité* stamp it out. Robert Scott in the Antarctic in 1912 travelled the equal way to heaven, and knights of the air in war and peace have proved as worshipful as knights of the plain. 'We too,' as we were reminded above, 'are men of the Renaissance, inheritors of that large and noble conception of humanity and art', and it will be an ill day for our successors if the heritage is ever misprized or mislaid.

But we administer it with a difference. Our softer days do not make softer virtues. Perhaps those harder days made harder vices. The fall of Bacon, the fate of Essex—to name but two men out of many—illustrate the moral conflict, the fight of good and evil, in their time. We find this, too, of course, in Shakespeare, who wrote in Sonnet cxliv of his 'worser spirit', how it

> 'Tempteth my better angel from my side,
> And would corrupt my saint to be a devil.'

The new psychology would re-state the moral problem, and the new ethics, which have revised the values of war and even of religion (the fate of More, among others, is not conceivable to-day), confuse exact comparison with the 16th century. But a great poet made the attempt in the 19th, and even his partial failure, which will be shown in its due place, may help us to conclude this intersection, brief and halting though it be. Tennyson in his *Idylls of the King*—and we suggested above why they are broken pictures—returned to the Arthuriad which was the theme of the *Faery Queen*. He, too, like Spenser before him, and, indeed, like Malory of old, sought to 'ensample a good governor and a virtuous man' and to 'portray the image of a brave knight' for the emulation of little Arthurs to be. In verses of matchless eloquence he unrolled the standard of chivalry:

> ' To reverence the King, as if he were
> Their conscience, and their conscience as the King,
> To break the heathen and uphold the Christ,
> To ride abroad redressing human wrongs,
> To speak no slander, no, nor listen to it,
> To honour his own word as if his God's,
> To live sweet lives in purest chastity,
> To love one maiden only, cleave to her,
> And worship her by years of noble deeds,
> Until they won her; for indeed I know
> Of no more subtle master under heaven
> Than is the maiden passion for a maid,
> Not only to keep down the base in man,
> But teach high thought, and amiable words,
> And courtliness, and the desire of fame,
> And love of truth, and all that makes a man.

Tennyson's Arthur declared that he failed by the sin of Guinevere:

> ' And all this throve before I wedded thee '.

But is there not more of Victorian marriage-law than of Arthurian knights'-law in his analysis? Did Arthur well to be angry with Guinevere, or Tennyson to put all the blame on her, remembering how the last of the knights-errant had tilted at knight-errantry itself? Cervantes at the end of the 16th century had faced the problem more courageously. He depicted chivalry *fin de siècle*, quixotism disembodied out of courtliness, the cloak woven by Castiglione for Sir Philip Sidney—and the rents hidden behind its seams. ' Like little wanton boys that swim on bladders,' said Wolsey in the hour of disillusion which preceded the break of the new day: ' I feel my heart new open'd.' But Tennyson's Arthur shut his heart:

> ' Thou hast not made my life so sweet to me
> That I the King should greatly care to live '. . . .

Yet life had to be made sweet when the 16th century turned into the 17th, and men took stock of the fruits of the Renaissance, sown with such lavish ambition. It is the new conduct of life in philosophy and example which will occupy us in the remaining sections of the present Book.

§ 4. GUIDES, PHILOSOPHERS AND FRIENDS.

Seven writers, though individual and distinct, may be grouped conveniently under the above heading. In order of birth they are :

c. 1521–61,   JORGE DE MONTEMAYOR, Portuguese pastoral-novelist and poet.

c. 1528–91,   LUIS PONCE DE LEON, Spanish lyric poet.

1533–92,   MICHEL EYQUEM DE MONTAIGNE, French essayist.

1547–*c.* 1614,   MATEO ALEMAN, Spanish picaresque novelist.

1554–86,   PHILIP SIDNEY, English pastoral-novelist and poet.

c. 1554–1606,   JOHN LYLY, English writer of plays and romances.

1561–1626,   FRANCIS BACON, English essayist, philosopher and lawyer.

Their lifetime covers, roughly, a century, from 1521 (the year of fate) to 1626. Technically they are contemporary in the sense that the youngest was born in the year in which the eldest died (at the early age of forty); the bulk of their work falls in the second half of the 16th century ; and ideally they are coeval by community of inspiration and achievement. It may be observed, though without emphasis, that the three Englishmen are at the tail of the list : we are aware that the Renaissance crossed to England from the Continent. More significantly we observe the occurrence of two pairs in the list : Montemayor and Sidney as pastoral-novelists, Montaigne and Bacon as essayists. Thus the English dependence on foreign models is twice exemplified. More significant still in literary history is the occurrence of two new names : the ' essays ' written by Montaigne and the ' picaresque ' novel by Mateo Aleman. These kinds of writing are new ; they are of indigenous growth in modern Europe ; and the invention of new kinds is a proof that the makers of literature have passed out of their apprenticeship in classical workshops.

Montaigne. ' Je suis moi-même la matière de mon livre,' said Montaigne in the Preface to his first series of Essays, dated June 1588 ; and ' moi-même ' is a notable departure from the ' matières a nul homme entendant ' which had furnished so many writers with abundant copy. It is not, of course, a new topic. Cicero in his prose letters, Horace in his poetic epistles, and many another in former times had taken the world into his confidence and told us his opinions on all and sundry :

' Nullius addictus jurare in verba magistri '.

Perhaps the best and most recent example of the genial philosopher in undress was Erasmus in his colloquies and travel-notes, which are essays in everything but name : he was a kind of Robert Louis Stevenson of the 16th century. Petrarch, too, though a little more self-consciously, had employed ' moi-même ' as his ' matière'.

What is the difference, then, in Montaigne as the author of several series of *Essais* ? First, there is a more deliberate design, a direct aim at capturing his readers' interest by no procedure more elaborate than talking to them about himself. Thus—Chapter 2 of Book I treats ' De la Tristesse ', and Montaigne opens his discussion with the remark : *Je suis des plus exempts de cette passion.* ' No one is more exempt from this feeling than I am ' : Moi, Montaigne, I am broadcasting to the world. This, first; and, next, and more novel, is the employment of the French language on his design. Cicero and Horace were protected by their shield of Latin from the harshness or ridicule of listeners-in ; Petrarch, the ardent Latinist, was a Ciceronian, and Erasmus, the Dutchman, had used the same privileged tongue. Montaigne boldly threw away the shield, and exposed his heart to his fellow-countrymen. Availing himself fully of the resources which Rabelais had introduced into his native language, but avoiding the extravagance of that word-tamer, Montaigne applied the principles of the Pleiad not to any known kind of literary product—the long poem, the drama, and so forth—but to the common, everyday topics which occurred to him in his library on his small estate. Without stiffness and without luxuriance he wrote what he wanted to say on themes as diverse, to select a few titles, as ' Liars ', ' Fear ', ' The Force of Imagination', ' The Profit of One is the Loss of Another ', ' Pedantry ', ' The Education of Children', ' Cannibals ', ' Sleep ', ' Sumptuary Laws ', ' The Parsimony of the Ancients', and he said it admirably in French. It is the first time in the history of European literature that this attempt, this ' essay ', had been made.

The Eyquem in Montaigne's patronymic is said and was claimed by him to be English in origin, representing Egham or Ockham, and his mother, a Lopez by birth, was descended from Spanish Jews. These non-Latin blood-ties may have helped him to formulate a philosophy of life and death—for, like Shakespeare, he wrote much about dying—a little in advance in some respects of the experience of his own times. He took as his emblem a balance, and as his motto ' Que sais-je ? ', and this habit of suspended judgment, quickened so magnificently by Shakespeare when the fires of the Renaissance began to wane, proved stimulating and attractive. Direct debts have been traced almost too exactly[1] : the clearest example, which every reader can consult, is the derivation of *The Tempest*, Act II, Scene i, at ' Had I plantation of this isle.', from *Essais*, Book I, Chapter 30, at ' It is a nation (would I answer Plato)'. The indirect debt, if less obvious, is more important, and lies in Montaigne's permanent contribution to the problem of the conduct of life. We are told a good deal about ' mon père ', for whose methods and opinions his Michel had a huge respect. We are introduced to one authority after another in the ample and pleasant range of Montaigne's reading in that library designed to his own taste and decorated with short aphorisms from favourite writers. But first and last Montaigne thought for himself, and, so thinking, all his questions did not find ready answers. ' If philosophizing is doubting ', he wrote in Book II, Chapter 3,

' Si philosopher c'est douter, comme ils disent, à plus forte

[1] By J. M. Robertson, for instance, in *Montaigne and Shakspere*, London, 1897.

raison niaiser et fantastiquer, comme je fais, doit estre douter :
car c'est aux apprentifs à enquerir et à debatre, et au cathedrant
de resoudre. Mon cathedrant, c'est l'authorité de la volonté
divine, qui nous reigle sans contredit et qui a son rang au
dessus de ces humaines et vaines contestations '.

And then he related two tales from the annals of antiquity
in order to illustrate his proposition—

' Il y a en la vie plusieurs choses pires a souffrir que la
mort mesme '.

' Hamlet ' in the near future, Voltaire in the more remote,
some of the conclusions of the French Revolutionaries and
some of the ideas of the Russian novelists were contained in
solution in Montaigne's creed.

Francis Bacon. The essay caught on. We owe to the
erudition of Sir Sidney Lee[1] the proof of a personal link
between Bacon and Montaigne. Anthony Bacon, his elder
brother, was at Bordeaux in 1583–91 and formed a close
friendship with Montaigne, who was Mayor of the city during
a part of that period. But even without this link the little
treatises, or sketches, or *obiter dicta*—throws-off from his main
work as they were—which the great English jurist, who
became Lord Chancellor and Viscount St. Albans, issued as
Essays in 1597, confess their obligation to the Frenchman
whom his brother knew so well. The opening essay ' On
Truth ' contains a quotation from Montaigne ; the second
essay is ' On Death ', which, as we have seen, was a favourite
topic of Montaigne's ; and, though Bacon's essays for the
most part are briefer and more pithy than his, and though
they were not the chief occupation of their author's busy
days, yet Bacon learnt the art of them from Montaigne, whose
fame in England was hardly smaller than in France, and whose
writings were circulated in an English version, familiar
probably to Shakespeare, a year or two before the issue of
John Florio's translation in 1603. Bacon himself called his

---

[1] *The French Renaissance in England, Oxford*, 1910 ; pp. 169 ff. Lee points out,
too, as noted here, how closely ' French literary effort was watched in Elizabethan
England '. A licence for an English translation of the *Essais* was issued by the
Stationers' Company in London in the very year of their appearance in Paris.
A like close watchfulness for new French books is observable to-day.

essays 'civil and moral counsels' and declared that they 'came home to men's business and bosoms'. It is an exact description of Montaigne's prior aim, and it illustrates the extension of the reading public and the growing interest in popular philosophy.

Bacon's bigger work as philosopher lies outside the scope of the present survey. It is contained in his part-Latin, part-English *Instauratio Magna*, 1620, which formed Part II of the *Novum Organum* (New Instrument), Part I of which was *The Advancement of Learning*, 1605, and Part III the *De Augmentis*, 1623. Hallam tells us that no one hitherto had ' carried mankind so far on the way to truth ', or had ' obtained so thorough a triumph over arrogant usurpation without seeking to substitute another '. We learn that Bacon founded the inductive method, and exposed the fallacies (*idola*) of reason, distributing them into four classes, those of common consent (*tribus*), of personal obscurantism (*specus*), of vulgar language (*fori*), and of false systems (*theatri*). The immenseness of his design, so different from the specialization of modern scientists and comparable only with that of his early namesake, Roger Bacon, fills us with reverent astonishment, and, in contemplating the majesty of his brain, we condone the meanness of his hand, which consented to accept bribes. King James I remitted the penalty and posterity forgets the crime.

Mateo Aleman. Akin to this extension by the essay was the extension by the novel.

' There are more things in heaven and earth, Horatio,
Than are dreamt of in your philosophy.'

So Shakespeare was to write in *Hamlet* before the century's end, and a philosophy of life in the course of it was not the prerogative solely of learned men. Horatio's even-tempered sanity, his acceptance of heaven and earth as they are, had to be shaken by inquiry—by the ' philosophy ' which was ' doubt ' and which might lead, as a later poet said, to ' endless dole '. But the spirit of inquiry was abroad, and the Horatios of this world could not evade it. There were more things in chronicle and story than old Froissart had dreamt of, when he followed the fortunes of valiant knights and ignored the

churls whom they rode down. There were more things in
story and song than Boccaccio and Chaucer had dreamt of—
though Chaucer may have had a shrewd suspicion of them—
when they preferred the tales to the tellers in the garden at
Fiesole and at the Tabard Inn. There were life and death :
such lots of life ; so many ways of dying ; and who knows
what comes after, 'when we have shuffled off this mortal
coil' ; and some things in life worse than death, *pires à
souffrir que la mort même.* So Montaigne and Shakespeare
wrote around it, pricking the mystery which could not be
pierced, weighing the evidence which defied judgment in the
balance with the emblem of *que sais-je* ? And the soldiers came
home from the wars and exposed the seamy side of chivalry,
as it was exposed in plays and novels—*Journey's End* and the
like—after the Great War of 1914–19. The one-armed or
one-eyed fighters, the unemployed and the unwilling-to-be-
employed, the adventurers deprived of adventure, the jolly
shipmen paid off from their ships, these helped to create a
social problem new in the experience of statesmen and men
of letters.

The social problem took to the road, particularly in Spain
after the defeat of her Armada, and it is responsible for the
Acts which comprise the Elizabethan Poor Law. That of 1571
included in the class of vagabonds 'able-bodied persons
having no land or master, practising no trade or craft, and
unable to account for the way in which they earn their living',
'able-bodied labourers, loitering and refusing to work at
such reasonable wages as is commonly given in such parts
where such persons happen to dwell,' 'shipmen pretending
losses by sea,' and 'discharged prisoners begging without
licence from two justices.' And the new vagabond of the
social problem, who made the Poor Law of Elizabeth, became the hero of the picaresque novel, the Spanish name for a
rogue being *pícaro*.

So the novel was extended, first in Spain, to include this
romantic *pícaro*, this rogue or vagabond of the road, whose
emergence into the social complex was a new phenomenon
of the age—one of the ' more things ' on earth not dreamt
of in the philosophy of moderate men. It began, so far as we

know, with an anonymous life of *Lazarillo de Tormes*, and this little Lazarus of 1554 ascended through various phases to the characters created by Lesage, Fielding, Dickens, and to Gogol's Chichikov in *Dead Souls* : a distinguished, even a splendid company. The first rung in that ladder was built by Aleman, Part I of whose *Guzman de Alfarache* was on the market in 1599, and had run through twenty-six editions before 1605. That it hit the popular taste is obvious : indeed, it became known simply as *Pícaro*, thus taking the name which it gave. The English edition by James Mabbe, 1622, had a prefatory poem by Ben Jonson, who called don Guzman 'the Spanish Proteus.' His quick-change talents added plausibleness to his roguery. For it deeply consoled every new-made *chevalier d'industrie* to cite Aleman as his authority that he was a better fellow than he seemed, as much sinned against as sinning, and a parasite for which society was to blame. Meaner rogues have repeated it less wittily.

Montemayor, Sidney, Lyly. We may treat more briefly three writers, who, in Spain and England—divided by religion, disputing the New World, fighting at sea, yet united more firmly by Renaissance strivings than by the brittle bond of a Royal alliance—helped the novel to grow to its later form.

JORGE DE MONTEMAYOR was a Portuguese who wrote in Spanish, and the six Books of his Arcadian prose-romance, *Diana Enamorada*, were interspersed with admirable verses. Published between 1542–49, they were rendered into English by Bartholomew Yonge in 1598 and contained the story of the shepherdess, Filismena which reappeared in Shakespeare's *Two Gentlemen of Verona*.

More direct is the contribution of SIR PHILIP SIDNEY, whose *Arcadia* (printed 1590), like Montemayor's, eschewed magic and faëry and relied most fully for its effect on the interplay of character and an extension of the story-interest. It contained the first Pamela in English fiction, showing the way to Samuel Richardson and Maria Edgeworth, and the plot, though confused and hard to follow, unravelled threads of real human conflict which were utilized by the playwrights of the morrow. Sidney commanded, too, resources of colour which relieved the monotony of conventional dwellers in Arcadia.

133

K

But there is more to his *Arcadia* than this, and more to Sidney than his *Arcadia*. Written by a fastidious scholar at the country-seat of Mary Countess of Pembroke, his sister, this *Arcadia* took shape as a pastoral romance with a practical aim. It was designed to show forth in prose the native resources of the English language as fitting speech for princes and their courtiers; and since, as schoolmasters know, there is always a subtle connection between language and conduct, between the utterance of the lips and the manners of the man, courtiers trained to niceness in speech would be likely to live on a level of high endeavour. In other words (and this is important), if a worthy language could be invented for the new ways of commerce, conquest, and exploration, to all of which Sidney was drawn by every fibre of his adventurous being, these new ways would be consecrated to the old ideals of chivalry and honour. Sidney, following Castiglione, was a kind of schoolmaster at Court, eager to teach the new industrialism the culture of the old feudalism. At somewhat tedious length and with conscious artifice, learnt from Montemayor, he aimed at new conduct-values, and sought to prove, however tentatively, that Arcady, like heaven, lies within us.

He wrote, too, a sonnet-sequence, *Astrophel and Stella*, which is not therefore less sincere because the form was common to many poets. We still go a-courting when we woo, and the courtier's way with his mistress may be as true as that of a man with a maid. Certain phrases recur in such sonnets and the metre itself imposes restraints in its own kind. But for purposes of enjoyment, at any rate, which, after all, is the chief aim of literature, it is as just, or nearly so, to read the lyric love-verse of Sidney and Shakespeare and the rest of the Pleiad and Tudor poets with the same detachment from their sources as the sonnet-sequence called *Modern Love* by George Meredith in the 19th century. None has been disproved to express certain modes of personal experience and an individual point of view.

Reference has been made to Sidney's *Apologie for Poetrie*, which may be compared with Shelley's *Defence*, and final reference in this context is due to him as a type of the Renaissance gentleman. Dying young on the field of battle, Sir

Philip Sidney was acclaimed as ' the world's delight ' and ' the wonder of our age ' in terms of eulogy which did not sound excessive. Kings, statesmen and artists met him on equal terms. William of Orange's proverbial silence yielded to his charm. The Italian painters, Veronese and Tintoretto, Giordano Bruno, the philosopher, Frobisher, the voyager, Hakluyt, the voyagers' historian, Languet, the French bishop-humanist, were all included in his circle. His tastes and character had crowned him with a reputation for gentleness and courtesy unique in a life so short. Great books were dedicated to him in his lifetime, and, when he died, the fluent writers of his age, headed by Fulke Greville, Lord Brooke, his biographer, inscribed more than two hundred poems to his memory. He was the type of Castiglione's ideal courtier, and he surpassed that ideal by a certain inflexibility of moral temper native to the Renaissance in the North.

JOHN LYLY was a conscious stylist, who invented an Oxford manner for the Court, and whose *Euphues, or The Anatomy of Wit*, 1579, gave its name to the antithetical, alliterative and epigrammatic style of writing, with profuse allusions and illustrations from natural history, which, however easy to parody (as by Shakespeare in 1 *King Henry IV*, ii, 4), and however tiresome in excess, did confer permanent benefit on English prose. The formal vogue of Euphuism was short-lived. Lyly's animals returned to their ark, his birds and flowers to the medieval volucraries and herbaries from which he had fetched them for the purposes of decorative art. But the influence of his reforms remained. There is Euphuism in Macaulay and Ruskin, though neither writer consciously euphuized. There is Euphuism in Walter Pater and, perhaps, in James Joyce. Whenever a writer aims at a logic of style, at a co-ordination of thought, at a rhythmical disposal of words, at graphic and striking images, at evenly balanced sentences, at a harmonious use of ornament, he aims in the spirit of Lyly's *Euphues*.

Luis de Leon. We shall come back to Lyly as a playwright. Here, lastly, our praise is due to the Spanish singer, whose translation of *The Song of Songs* from the original Hebrew into Castilian verse formed the basis of a charge of sympathy with

Reform learning which kept him in the prisons of the Inquisition from March, 1572, to December, 1576. Acquitted at last, but admonished, he returned to the University of Salamanca, and is said to have resumed his lectures on Biblical study with the words, ' As we were saying the other day ' (*Dicebamus hesterna die*). Whether genuine or not, the story is typical of the spirit in which the guides, philosophers and friends of progress and humanism in the 16th century endured opposition, and overbore it when they might. This gentle poet and scholar had a lion's heart as well as name, and was as devoted an adventurer and discoverer as any navigator who sailed to the New World. He is remembered to-day, not for his contributions to theology, but for a few odes and hymns, which reveal in places, it is written, ' a majestic and serene simplicity not found again till Wordsworth '.[1] The epithets recall particularly his poem *Noche Serena*, ' The Serene Night ', and a briefer illustration of the genius, as confident in prose as in verse, which saw eternity in an hour, may be found in his lyric lines, ' On Leaving Prison '. Perhaps, in concluding this Section, we may associate them with the larger view of an escape ' out of the prison-house of theological system ' into ' the homely disorder of our familiar world ' which we quoted from Sir W. Raleigh on page 25, and to which we shall come back yet once more :

> ' Falsehood and hatred here
> Held me in prison pent :
> Happy whose life is spent
> In learning's humble sphere,
> Far from the world malevolent ;
> He with poor house and fare,
> Communing with God alone,
> Doth in the country fair
> Dwell solitary, there
> By none envied, envying none '.[2]

---

[1] Kelly, *Litterature espagnole*, p. 57. A monograph, *Luis de Leon : A Study of the Spanish Renaissance*, by Aubrey F. G. Bell, was issued at Oxford, 1925.

[2] Compare the verses written by Ariosto on the lintel of his house at Ferrara, which we quoted on page 86.

§ 5. DRAMA.

' The play's the thing,' as Shakespeare said, and when we read or see a play by Shakespeare we do not insist on an account of dramatic art. Yet some such account must be rendered, when we are writing not an essay in appreciation but a history of literature. For the historian, too, may be useful to the reader or spectator, and may increase enjoyment of ' the play ' by a brief review of the playwrights and their theatres. He may at least show why ' the thing ' which Shakespeare made before the end of the 16th century was so much bigger than could have been foretold from its origins.

The Background. It is not necessary to begin very far back. There is, of course, a background to modern drama as there is to every literary kind ; and we are fortunate in finding in Shakespeare, our chief dramatic practitioner, a sure signpost to that background. In the players' scene (*Hamlet*, ii, 2), just quoted, we read :

' Seneca cannot be too heavy, nor Plautus too light. For the law of writ and the liberty, these are the only men.'

Seneca for tragedy, Plautus for comedy, and to Plautus Terence must be added, and behind them both the Greek comic dramatist Menander, whose plays are only fragments to-day. Their dates are :

> Menander, 342–291 B.C.
> Plautus, 254–184 B.C.
> Terence, 194–159 B.C.
> Seneca, 4 B.C.–A.D. 65.

Menander was much admired in antiquity, and the Romans paid him the tribute of imitation. His stock character seems to have been the foundling, a fate of childhood commoner then than now, though it forms the sub-title to Fielding's picaresque novel, *Tom Jones*, and it is rich with opportunities for the fun of recognition and restitution. It is for these comic characters and situations that Menander became famous, and they descended through Plautus and Terence to Spanish, English and French drama, in the last of which we shall find

Molière (1622–73) supreme. It was said by Ovid in ancient Rome :

> ' So long as fathers bully, servants lie,
> And women smile, Menander cannot die,'

and the clash of generations, classes and sexes is the ever-renewed ' liberty ' of the comic stage, for which Plautus (with Menander behind and Terence in front) is the only man.

Seneca's ' law of writ ' is another story. Seneca, a Roman born at Cordova, was a moral philosopher as well as playwright and was tutor to the Emperor Nero. Part of Nero's crimes have been attributed to the lax discipline of Seneca, who paid the penalty of a favourite and practised his Stoic philosophy by committing suicide at his tyrant-pupil's bidding. All this is outside our story. Within it are the nine tragic dramas, founded on topics in Greek myth—*Hercules* (2), *Troades*, *Phœnissæ*, *Medea*, *Phædra*, *Agamemnon*, *Œdipus* and *Thyestes*—by which Seneca entertained the literary leisure of Nero. There was plainly no ' liberty ' in their production. They were Court-plays, probably never acted, and written to measure. They were learned in the sense that the moralist used the vocabulary of the *Stoa*, or porch, from which the title of his school was derived, and it was suitable to Nero's taste that they were bathed in blood. The last scene of *Hamlet* is Senecan ; the ghost is a Senecan stock-character ; violence, tending to grossness, and rhetoric to ranting, are Senecan legacies to later drama ; and in its origins at any rate, and even a little way into the theatre of Shakespeare, Corneille and Racine, we have to accept the Senecan tradition. Addington Symonds, in a book[1] to which we shall refer again, says that—

> ' Every tragic scene which the Italians of the Renaissance set forth upon the boards of Rome or Florence or Ferrara was a transcript from Seneca. Following this lead, our English scholars went to school with Seneca beneath the ferule of Italian ushers '.

We need not linger among the ushers—Giovanni Rucellai

Shakespeare's Predecessors in the English Drama. New Edition, London, 1900, p. 175.

(1475–1525), Giovanni Trissino (1478–1550), and the rest. For the dead hand of Seneca has been lifted from the modern stage. His reign was long, probably longer than he ever dreamed when he wrote those vehement plays for the distraction of the Roman tyrant in the 1st century of the Christian era. It is really a remarkable fact that a dramatic method and tragic features derived from him and called by his name should still have been pleasing playgoers after more than fifteen hundred years. But he is dead to-day. Ibsen, who did so much to reform the stage of Europe in the 19th century, did not use this ' only man ', and we look for him in vain and without regret in the work of modern playwrights.

School Plays, ' *Autos* ', etc.   There we may leave the matter. But on the road through Italy to Shakespeare from the background of antiquity there are one or two other milestones at which a brief pause must be made. There were the Latin University-plays—original ' Westminster Plays ' by Reformation schoolmasters—which flourished chiefly in the North. They rang variations on the theme of the Prodigal Son, and there was the welcome rough humour of the whipping scenes. The *Stylpho*, 1470, of JAKOB WIMPHELING was one of the first in this kind ; the *Rebelles* of GEORG LANGVELDT (*c*. 1475–1558), a Dutchman commonly known as Macropedius, was among the most amusing; and the *Acolastus* (Unchastised) of WILLEM VOLDER (1493–1558), another Dutchman, was among the most famous and was rendered into English by John Palsgrave.

The Italian Biblical plays (*sacre rappresentazioni*) form another class, rather in the nature of a pageant tied to a Lord Mayor's Show, but in a southern June instead of a northern November; and the German Shrovetide-plays (*Fastnachtspiele*) and the religious jollity of the French *Confrérie de la Passion* likewise flourished in the first half of the 16th century.

More permanent, though in the same kind, was the *Auto* (=*actum*, or Act of the Sacrament) in Spain, which persisted till 1765 when it was suppressed by royal decree. Briefly, the *Auto* took shape as a one-act dramatisation of the mystery of the Holy Eucharist and was played in the open air on Corpus Christi day. It ranged from the rude performances furnished by pious village folk to the most magnificent masques which Church and State could organise in Madrid. Calderon, as we shall see, gave new life to the *Auto* in the 17th century, and on the road to Calderon may be mentioned JUAN ESCRIVA (*fl.* 1500) of Valencia, JUAN DEL ENZINA (1469–*c.*1530), and, chiefly, BARTOLOME DE TORRES NAHARRO (1480–1531). Naharro worked out for his own guidance a complete theory of his craft. He adopted from Horace the division of a play into five parts (he called them days, *jornadas*, not acts), and he limited his personages to not less than six or more than twelve. He was a skilful, even an elaborate metrist, and a like elaboration is observed in his employment of appropriate dialects. He classified plays into comedies *a noticia* (founded on knowledge) and comedies *a fantasia* (founded on fancy) : a distinction pointed in Milton's verses—

> ' If Jonson's learned sock be on,
> Or sweetest Shakespeare, Fancy's child,
> Warble his native wood-notes wild ',

and corresponding, too, to the distinction between ' the law of writ ' and ' the liberty ' which we noted above. The *punctilio*, or point of honour, and the *gracioso*, or gentleman's gentleman, are also Naharro's inventions, or were at any rate first clearly defined by him. GIL VICENTE (*c.* 1465–1536) founded the Portuguese theatre on the Enzina-Naharro model.

Two Famous Comedies. In France *Maître Pierre Pathelin*, revived in the 17th century as *L'Avocat Pathelin*, dates from 1485, and in Spain *Calisto and Melibea*, later famous as *Celestina*, dates from about 1490. Both are important to dramatic origins and each enjoyed a long vogue. *Pathelin* is written in verse, and its plot turns on a practical joke. A country lawyer advises his client to try bleating like a sheep when at a loss for a better answer, and the jest is turned against the lawyer when he comes for his fee. The judge's ' revenons à nos moutons ' is a familiar tag from this old play. *Celestina*, a ' tragi-comedy ', is in prose. Its authorship is obscure, and several countries added to its features. The standard English version by James Mabbe, 1631, was made from the Italian. But its Spanish descent is clear. Calisto and Melibea, tragic lovers, were own children to Juan Ruiz[1], and own parents, we may say, to Romeo and Juliet, who, like this play, came to England through Italy. The comic part was sustained chiefly by an ' old bawd ', the descendant of Ruiz's convent-runner, who reappears in Juliet's nurse. Her racy idioms tickled the ears of a public, indulgent, as in Menander's day, to the stratagems in vogue against a bullying father.

Actor-Managers.   A few words are due to the actor-managers, the journeymen-promoters of popular plays, who carved their own way to the stage perforce of their insight into spectators' needs. They worked *a fantasia*, by the light of nature (' sweetest Shakespeare, Fancy's child ') rather than *a noticia*, by wit and learning (' Jonson's learned sock '), and were at once fecund and ingenious. Their fame belongs to the history of the theatre more strictly than to that of literature, and of one of them, LOPE DE RUEDA, who died about 1565, we have the advantage of a contemporary notice by no smaller an authority than Cervantes, his fellow-countryman.

' In the time of this celebrated Spaniard ', he writes, ' the whole apparatus of a manager was contained in a large sack, and consisted of four white shepherd's jackets, four beards and wigs, and four shepherd's crooks. The plays were dialogues, like eclogues, between two or three shepherds and a shepherdess, filled up with two or three interludes played by a negress, a bully, a fool, or a Biscayan. In all these four parts and others Rueda used to act with the utmost possible skill '.

The primitiveness of the proceedings may be judged from a direction to the spectators in Rueda's comedy *Eufemia*—

' O audience, go now and dine ! Then return to the market-place, if ye wish to see a traitor's head cut off and a just man set at liberty '.

Those for whom the play was not the thing did not return, it may be assumed, from dining. Rueda took his booth round the towns, to Segovia, Toledo, Seville, Madrid ; and behind

[1] See page 62 above.

a blanket pulled by a cord he amused and thrilled countless audiences.

In the same class, though later in date and higher in technical skill, was the Frenchman, ALEXANDRE HARDY (*c.* 1570–1631). He is said to have written or manhandled between six and seven hundred plays, any of which might have been called ' As You Like It ', so confidently did he cut them to the measure of his stage out of the miscellaneous material at his disposal, which he had taken over from the *Confrérie de la Passion* above. Morality or mystery-play, it was all grist to Hardy's mill. His business was to fill the theatre, and this exacting business he performed through thirty assiduous years. Rough and ready though his stagecraft was, he cast out the stones for his successors.

On the Highway. We omit those successors. We possess what they prepared—the stage of Marlowe and Shakespeare in England, of Lope de Vega and Calderon in Spain, of Molière, Corneille and Racine in France. Yet one or two names should be recorded for the sake of their influence on the masters to be, and in illustration of the kind of influence which they exerted. But it must be a very summary illustration. Thus, LUIGI PASQUALIGO in Italy wrote a prose-comedy, *Il Fidele*, which PIERRE LARIVEY rendered into French (*La Fidelle*) and ANTHONY MUNDAY into English (*The Comedy of Two Italian Gentlemen*). All that is best in it is extant in Shakespeare's *Two Gentlemen of Verona*. Thus, ROBERT GARNIER, a Frenchman, wrote Greek and Roman tragedies, taken, like Shakespeare's, from Plutarch's *Lives*. MARY, COUNTESS OF PEMBROKE rendered his *Mark Antony* into English blank verse, and he anticipated the greater French dramatists by employing the Alexandrine metre for his plays. Thus, too, ETIENNE JODELLE, whom we met as the dramatic star of the Pleiad, laid the foundation in France alike of tragedy and comedy. We must leave to specialists the task of assessing the debt of Shakespeare's *Antony and Cleopatra* to Jodelle's *Cléopâtre*. Thus, too, JUAN DE LA CUEVA wrote a Spanish play, *Infamador* (' The Slanderer '), which invented the type of comedy known as *de Capa y Espada*, or of Cloak and Sword, associated in the great age with the plays of

LOPE DE VEGA. Further, he introduced the character of the typical libertine, later fashionable in Spain and England as Don Juan.

So we pass through the straits to the stream. All roads of drama and story converge at last on the greater names of Cervantes (born 1547), Lope de Vega (1562), Marlowe and Shakespeare (1564), Calderon (1600), Corneille (1606), Molière (1622) and Racine (1639). We shall observe the distinction, artificial though it be, between the 16th and 17th centuries, and shall not include the three Frenchmen in the present Book, which will close the annals of the stage with its supreme enhancer, Shakespeare. But because Calderon belongs to the grand age of Spain, and because his fame was so much akin to Lope de Vega's, we shall cross our boundary in his instance and consider him with his fellow-countrymen in the next Section.

§ 6. THE GLORY OF SPAIN.

MIGUEL DE CERVANTES SAAVEDRA (1547–1616), though he wrote plays like the rest, and was much reputed for them in his lifetime, does not live in literary history as a playwright. He made a contract at Seville to supply the manager of a theatre with six comedies at thirty ducats apiece, but whether he wrote them or was paid for them we do not know. His *Numancia*, a drama on Petrarch's theme of Scipio Africanus, was praised by Goethe for its art and by Fichte for its sentiment. His renown, however, is by story-books. He wrote a *Galatea* in the pastoral vein, and he wrote *Exemplary Tales* which would have made the reputation of a smaller man. Above all, he wrote *The History of the Valorous and Witty Knight-errant, Don Quixote de la Mancha*. ' With one foot in the stirrup ', as he said, adapting the words of an old play to the still older joust with death, he put the last touches to that book on April 19, 1616. Four days afterwards he died. His wife died a few years later ; ' but no one knows where they lie. Spain had nothing to give, not even the vain honours of the grave, to her greatest son '.[1]

[1] *Cervantes*, by Mrs. Oliphant ; a charming little book.

Life and Reputation. Posterity was to give more. Take April 23, 1916, which was celebrated as the tercentenary of Shakespeare's death and his. Their countries had been at war in their lifetime, and England was at war again. But Spain now was benevolently neutral, and the Kings of England and Spain exchanged greetings, the cordiality of which was increased by the dissensions of the time. We like to think that the genius of the Renaissance, represented by its two great sons, met above the memory of old warfare and lit a torch in the darkness of the new.

Cervantes, unlike Shakespeare, had his bellyful of fighting. He fought at Lepanto, Navarino, Tunis, lost his left hand, was captured by pirates, and spent ten years in the ' hell ' of Algiers, where the record of his patience and of his noble aid to his fellow-prisoners may be read between the lines of the Preface to his *Tales*. But his homecoming did not spell prosperity. He depended for a precarious livelihood on miscellaneous literary work, and he held a deputy-collectorship in the Department of Naval Stores. It was no sinecure, however. The loss of the Armada did not make it easy to gather taxes for the King's Navy, and a long term of petty misery was broken by only one bright event, his happy marriage, on December 12, 1584, to Catalina de Salazar de Palacios. So the lean years went by, till, at last, at Valladolid, ' in calle del Rastro, on the first floor, in the year 1603, and at the rate of a chapter or two a week, with but the stump of a left hand to hold down the leaves of his note-book, this middle-aged, silver-bearded, weather-beaten soldier and collector wrote the first part of *Don Quixote*, and made himself immortal '.[1]

' *Don Quixote* '. What was the motive of *Don Quixote* ? How and why should the idea occur to this ' middle-aged soldier and collector ' ?—and what do *Don Quixote* and quixotism mean when the fun of the road is exhausted ?

First, the time had come to take stock, to put off the shining armour and to face the realities of life. Anti-Empire and anti-Chivalry had propaganda-values. In this sense Cervantes

[1] *Don Quixote* (2nd edn., London, 1914), with a *Life* of Cervantes, by Robinson Smith.

in Spain was the antitype to Sir Walter Scott in Britain. Scott's purpose was to revive romance ; Cervantes' was to estop the flood of feigned ardour and fictitious sentiment. We can cite text and verse for this aspect from the opening of his book. Don Quixote was bemused with romantic dreaming. He

' passed his nights from twilight to dawn and his days from dawn to twilight entangled in his books, till from little rest and much reading he muddled his wits, which were filled with the fantasy of all that he had read, whether of enchantments, broils, battles, challenges, wounds, wooings, amours, hurricanes, or of other the wildest absurdities.'

Recall here the opening words of Ariosto's *Orlando Furioso* in Harington's Tudor translation—

' Of Dames, of Knights, of arms, of love's delight,
    Of courtesies, of high attempts I speak,'—

and one source of Quixote's ' muddlement.' is obvious. Recall again, the epithet *furioso* (' mad ') by which Ariosto characterized his hero, and read how Quixote (1, 25) resolves to pursue his Dulcinea in the very manner of Count Roland. His faithful squire, Sancho, cannot see the *reason* for it ; Dulcinea had not erred like Angelica ; but ' just there lies the *beauty* of it,' retorts Quixote,

' for no thanks or value attaches to a Knight when actually driven to insanity. The thing is to go mad of yourself, making a lady wonder, if I so act when dry, what will I do when drenched ? '

In an age when the chivalric romances were so familiar that nearly every reference was recognized, this allusive method was used with immense effect. More than a hundred and thirty romantic writers were laid under contribution by Cervantes, even outside Book I, Chapter 6, where the famous bonfire of the romantics occurs. And more remarkable than the wide reading was the quick writing. This happy hunting-ground for scholars, this mosaic of romantic antiquaries, was transformed by the genius of Cervantes into the grandest story - book for men and boys which has yet been composed.

Nor is this the whole of the matter. *Don Quixote* is very much more than a travesty or transfer of chivalric romances, which, like the 'penny-dreadfuls' of yesterday or the 'sex-films' of to-day, were becoming a nuisance to the authorities. Immortality is not built on censure, and the anti-chivalry of Quixote is the negative aspect of his teaching. It was easy enough to be anti-chivalrous. The rogue-heroes and pot-house bullies of Spanish picaresque novelists had proved that adventure is to the crafty and success to the unscrupulous. But 'the famous history of the errant knight' was not merely a warning, but an inspiration. It was a call to conduct as well as to renouncement, to action no less than to abstention from it. The proof of this is more difficult, since it is contained in all the history of the knightly Quixote and his squire. Quixote's heroic temper emerged unscathed from trial and tribulation. Though all which he attempted failed, though all which he imagined proved vain, though he was but a poor, mad visionary in a generation of positivists and opportunists, he preserved a higher reason and a nobler sanity than theirs. Don Quixote, Falstaff, Gil Blas, Parson Adams, Colonel Newcome, Chichikov are among the makers of a new mind attuned to a new society in Western Europe. And of these Quixote was the first. His humility, his vision, his humanity survived the ruin of his world and helped to base philosophy on the new things (Hamlet's 'more things') instead of the old. Hence the common acceptance of his wisdom, con-currently with the enjoyment of his adventures, and the penetration of our intellect with his teaching. In every epoch of reconstruction, we are all apt to tilt at windmills, to mistake a new inn for an old castle, and natural phenomena for enchanters' magic. By such mistakes progress is made. We have to accustom ourselves to our environment. We all go better armed with the sure shield, persisting through disillusion and disappointment, which Quixote fashioned out of his ideals, and never a philosopher or dramatist has wrought more for humankind than Cervantes.

Lope and Calderon. First of all, they are yoked as a tandem, and not, like Marlowe and Shakespeare, as a pair. The dates are :—

1562–1625	1564–1593
Lope Felix de Vega Carpio.	Christopher Marlowe.
1600–1681	1564–1616
Pedro Calderon de la Barca.	William Shakespeare.

Secondly, when Calderon died Spanish literature itself passed away. It burned brightly for two hundred years—1492 to 1681. In 1492 the Spanish Main was opened, Columbus sailed to the New World, and proud Spain, ignoring her debt to Moorish and Hebrew culture, asserted the national principle of ' Spain for the Spanish ' by her overthrow of the Moors and her expulsion of the Jews. Calderon's death, 1681, was followed in 1700 by the death of Charles II, the last of the Habsburg kings of Spain, and the accession of Philip of Anjou, grandson of the *roi Soleil*, King Louis XIV of France. In 1713 came the Treaty of Utrecht and the diminished heritage of King Philip, and in 1714 the new Spanish Academy was founded on the model of *l'Académie française*. At the beginning of the two centuries Spain had looked forward across the Atlantic ; at the end she was looking backward across the Pyrenees. The glory of Spain stretched out to the end of Calderon's long and active life, and then broke with the fallen Empire. The links are not disjoined in order to start a new chain in a new century. There was no successor to Calderon : no Milton, born in 1608, no Dryden in 1631, no Swift in 1667, no Pope in 1688, to prolong the glory of Spain and to renew it. The lifetime of Cervantes, Lope de Vega and Calderon, 1547 to 1681, is an epoch which came to a full stop. Lope was greeted by Cervantes in 1614 as *el monstruo de naturaleza*, the ' prodigy of nature ', and he greeted young Calderon in his turn in 1622 as the appointed wearer of his own mantle. Shakespeare died in 1616 at fifty-two ; if he had lived till seventy-five and had seen the end of Milton's first poetic period his greeting to the young new poet would have been differently worded. He would have marked a difference, not a likeness.

' *The Prodigy of Nature.*' Prodigal as well as prodigious

is an epithet appropriate to Lope's work. He is said to have
written twenty-one million verses, and he acknowledged the
authorship of 219 plays in 1603 and 1,500 in 1632. The total
number is an impressive quantity. Like Hardy in France, he
wrote what the public wanted ; like Shakespeare, he raised
the level of taste ; like both, he wrote to please himself. In
this immensity of output a list of his writings would be
wearisome. He has been partly absorbed by foreign creditors.
The French dramatists of the *grand siècle*, to whom we shall
come in Book IV, drew generously on his provision : even
Molière's *Médecin malgré lui* owed a big debt to Lope's *Acero
de Madrid*. But he still has a name of his own, not only in
Spain but in Europe. He wrote an *Arcadia*, when Arcady was
fashionable, and a *Dragontea* in 1598, celebrating the death of
Sir Francis Drake, in six cantos of patriotic verse. Drake had
singed the Spanish king's beard ; Lope twisted the English
dragon's tail. More famous were his *capa y espada* (cloak and
sword) plays, which turned on a point of honour (*punctilio*) :

' Two ladies, a gallant and his friend, their lovers, a jealous
brother or a difficult father, with the attendant servants of all
parties ; mistake, accident, intrigue and involvement, honour
touched and honour righted—such is the universal recipe '.[1]

It was a recipe which, as Ticknor remarks, excluded on the
one hand those dramas in which royal personages appear, and,
on the other, those devoted to common people. A time was
to come when the gallant would lose his swagger and his
glitter, when his cloak and sword would be worn less easily
than the broadcloth of a merchant or even a maid-servant's
cotton gown, and when Gulliver would travel to a country
where the very horses were superior to their cavaliers. So, a
Quarterly Reviewer could write in 1894, when horse-sense had
become proverbial :

' To us, perhaps, Lope remains as great a wonder as he was
to his contemporaries and fellow-countrymen ; but we can
hardly be expected to share in their profound veneration for

[1] C. Whibley, in *Cambridge History of English Literature*, Vol. VIII. The *graciose*,
or confidential servant, reappears in French drama and English fiction (*e.g.*
Major Pendennis's Mr. Morgan).

gifts that in our eyes belong more properly to the mechanic than to the artist. To them Lope was the greatest of all poets ; to us it is a question whether he was a poet at all '.

' Mechanic ' is too strong a term, however far we have moved from Lope's standards, and we should recall what Robert Southey, writing in the *Quarterly* in 1817, quoted from the Lord Holland of his day :

' So associated was the idea of excellence with Lope's name that it grew in common conversation to signify anything perfect in its kind ; and a Lope diamond, a Lope day, or a Lope woman, became fashionable and familiar modes of expressing their good qualities '.

This Lope died in Spain. But his countrymen did not willingly let him die. His funeral rites lasted for a fortnight, and, when they had buried him at last, Pedro Calderon was working in his lines.

The Perfect Playwright. It was Goethe, a competent judge, who said of Calderon that ' his plays are thoroughly stage-perfect ', and, though he said at another time that Calderon's characters ' are as alike as tin-soldiers ', the praise may be taken with the blame. Probably the tin-soldier effect is increased by the stage-perfectness : Calderon is at once same and unusual, and, while we admire without reserve, we do not—at least, not many of us outside Spain—yearn to come back to him again and again. The story is told of a guardsman in his audience who sprang up, sword in hand, to prevent the sale of the Spanish heroine to the Moorish infidel in Act III of Calderon's *Gomez Arias*. It is a high tribute to the dramatist's life-illusion : the more so, since he was as careless as Shakespeare about the details of history and geography. But his Castilian pride and Catholic faith limited the range of his sympathy, and he borrowed from Lope de Vega as freely as he was put under contribution by Corneille and others. He was the regular purveyor of *autos* to Madrid ; of the 70 or 80 which are known to be his the best is said to be *The Divine Orpheus*. Among his tragedies, *No Monster Like Jealousy*, from the Josephan story of Herod and Mariamne,

149

L

captured the taste of the French theatre right away down to Voltaire. *The Physician of his own Honour* burns the convention of the *punctilio* on our consciousness, and play after play might be named which achieved success in its own day and which has won the admiration and even the imitation of writers as supreme as Shelley, Schiller and Schlegel.

The Renaissance in Spain. This Section, closing with the death of Calderon and the decline of the star of Spain, has carried us to the edge of the 17th century, nearly a hundred years after the Age of Shakespeare, which is the topic and the title of the present Book. But Calderon's dates do not agree with his times. He is of the same generation as Lope de Vega, and there is no real but merely an apparent discrepancy in ignoring the fact, that, when Calderon died in 1681, Milton had been dead for seven years and Boileau was forty-five years of age. For ' in Spain ' we read,[1] ' the Renaissance met something on which it could secure no hold ' ; and, though, with praiseworthy tenacity, it prolonged its hold tandem-wise by stretching out the Lope–Calderon dramatic triumphs to the extreme limit of their temporal capacity, it could not establish a succession : ' a strong national character ', we read on, ' unchanging, and so close in the fibre that it never really admits a foreign influence, could not well do more than express itself once. The time came when it had said its say— and nothing then remained except, first mere juggling with words, and then silence—Gongorism[2] and Decadence. In England and in France there was the hope, and even the assurance of far more to come. . . . Englishmen and French-men had learnt their lesson from the Renaissance, and were to use their own knowledge.'

We come back, then, to England and France.

---

[1] *The Later Renaissance*, by David Hannay, Edinburgh, 1898 ; pp. 375, 377–78.

[2] *Note on Gongorism.*—LUIS DE GONGORA Y ARGOTE (1561–1627) was a Spanish poet in the Italianate School founded by Boscan and adorned by Garcilasso (see p. 111 above). He had two poetic periods, the first pure and unaffected, the second, which started about 1609, possibly under the stimulus of an essay on ' poetic erudition ' by Luis Carrillo y Sotomayor (1583–1610), a disciple of Marini (below), displaying the anxious desire to cause surprise by unexpectedness, which, as a device of style, was known in Spain as *cultismo* (high-browism) and in Italy as *conceptista*, or the pursuit of *concetti* (conceits), Critics call the Spanish variety Gongorism and the Italian variety Marinism.

§ 7. SHAKESPEARE SHAKE-SCENE.

The above name was thrown at him by Robert Greene, a rival playwright, who was his senior by a few years. Dying young in 1592, disappointed, beaten, resentful, in *A Groatsworth of Wit bought with a Million of Repentance*—too late, and on a pauper's death-bed—Greene warned ' his quondam acquaintance' against ' those puppets that speak from our mouths, those anticks garnisht in our colours '. Particularly he indicated

' an upstart Crow, beautified with our feathers, that with his *Tygers heart wrapt in a Players hide* supposes he is as well able to bumbast out a blank verse as the best of you ; and being an absolute *Johannes factotum* is, in his own conceit, the only Shake-scene in a countrie '.

The occasion was the presentation of Shakespeare's *Third Part of King Henry VI*, in Act I, Scene iv, of which occurred the verse (137) :

' O tiger's heart wrapp'd in a woman's hide '.

Whether Greene had written the whole speech in which the phrase which he parodied occurs, or whether the contrast

---

after their respective founders, Gongora and GIOVANNI BATTISTA MARINI (1569–1625). The English equivalent is Euphuism (see p. 135 above), after the title of the chief book of JOHN LYLY (*c.* 1554–1606). It will be seen that they are contemporary movements, and it may be said at once that no poet in any country or any century would be worrying words as a vicious dog worries sheep. The longer purpose of Gongorism, Marinism, Euphuism, was to extend and enlarge the native language. It introduced Grecisms, Latinisms, and foreign locutions, frequently, let it be admitted, solecisms, inversions, and obscure allusions, but its object was an improved speech. In a sense, Robert Browning and George Meredith used to gongorise, like Pirandello, Proust, James Joyce and others in our own day. Lope de Vega used to say that he could train a *culto* poet in twenty-four hours ; and without offence to the dead, Sir Lewis Morris might have made the same offer with the same contempt. But it is much easier for a conventional writer to pick out the marks of a futurist's style than for a reformer to invent them, and Lyly, Gongora and Marini all suffered from easy criticism at home. Theirs is a style, too, which, cultivated for its own sake, leads to word-play, empty sounds and autumn tints. Therefore, Mr. Hannay is justified in yoking Gongorism with Decadence. But they are not identic terms. Word-experiments are necessary to a growing language, and these reformers did their appointed work. In a history on the present scale but brief reference can be made to those who sat cross-legged in word-bazaars manipulating the jewels of language, but this tribute to their fine service is seemly.

of his fate with that of the 'upstart crow' made the parody seem to him appropriate, we shall never know. Certainly, more than one hand went to the production of the three parts of *King Henry VI*, and certainly, too, Greene himself, and George Peele, and Christopher Marlowe, and Thomas Nash,[1] who are most probably the 'quondam acquaintance' addressed in his dying outburst, were all University men of noisy habits and short lives. Greene, the 'ape of Euphues', as he had been dubbed, had spent his substance and his talents in the green-rooms, and was jealous of the superior success and, it may be, the more wholesome bearing of the brilliant, young, provincial actor, who seemed to know so well what the public wanted. It was a kind of class-hatred to which he gave utterance—the gentlemen *versus* the players.

300 *Years After*. Turn now from this violent utterance, written in 1592, to a later testimony to the 'scene-shaker,' written in 1883. John Addington Symonds,[2] in whose feeble frame the fires of the Renaissance glowed with passionate vitality, was not less convinced than Robert Greene that Shakespeare had revolutionized the English theatre. He, too, discussed 'the only Shake-scene', but with how different a vehemence. Looking back across the centuries he wrote :

'What a future lay before this country lass—the bride-elect of Shakespeare's genius.'

Greene's closing eyes could not see this future. He could not guess that the 'native wood-notes wild' of the open-eyed playwright from Warwickshire would substitute 'the liberty' for 'the law of writ', and would be combined to produce an English romantic drama, as secure in its canons and its fame as that formed according to Aristotle's rules.

'For her'—the country lass with her native wood-notes— 'there was preparing empire over the whole world of man :—

[1] 1567–1601 ; author of *The Unfortunate Traveller, or The Life of Jack Wilton*, 1594, a pioneer adventure-novel in England ; literary and religious controversialist ; to be distinguished from his namesake Thomas Nash, 1593–1647, who married, 1626, Shakespeare's granddaughter, Elizabeth Hall, later the heiress of New Place, Stratford-on-Avon.
[2] 1840–93.

over the height and breadth and depth of heaven and earth
and hell; over facts of nature and fables of romance; over
histories of nations and of households; over heroes of past
and present times, and airy beings of all poets' brains'.

Need we annotate this eloquent apostrophe? The 'fables,'
'histories', 'heroes', and 'airy beings' are familiar to
readers of Shakespeare's plays, and 'the whole world of man'
and woman, is surely represented on his stage. Take the
famous passage from *Hamlet*:

'What a piece of work is a man! how noble in reason!
how infinite in faculty! in form and moving how express
and admirable! in action how like an angel! in apprehension
how like a god! the beauty of the world! the paragon of
animals!'

The creed of the Humanists is contained in it, and the long
aim of the makers of the Renaissance : their fearless confidence
in the liberty of man, studied in all his manifestations, from
the undeveloped mutterings of Caliban to the subtlest utterance
of Wolsey or Mark Antony. On Shakespeare's stage medieval
woman was transformed and recast. Dante's Madonna-like
Beatrice and Tasso's languishing Leonora were changed for
quick types of living femininity, from Dame Quickly up to
Desdemona, all 'express and admirable' with tears and
laughter. He mixed high and low in his *dramatis personæ*, and
shifted his times and places with the practical manager's
contempt for the rules of critics and pedants. He was always
free to go his own way, from Warwickshire to London, and
home again, when he had rung the curtain down, to the civic
neighbourliness of Stratford-on-Avon.

Shakespeare's Predecessors. We return to the passage from
Symonds. The 'country lass', for whom this 'empire' was
reserved, inherited all that went before :

'Hers were Greene's meadows, watered by an English
stream. Hers, Heywood's moss-grown manor-houses, Peele's
goddess-haunted lawns were hers, and hers the palace-
bordered, paved ways of Verona. Hers was the darkness of
the grave, the charnel-house of Webster. She walked the

air-built loggie of Lyly's dreams, and paced the clouds of
Jonson's Masques. She donned that ponderous sock, and trod
the measures of Volpone. She mouthed the mighty line of
Marlowe. Chapman's massy periods and Marston's pointed
sentences were hers by heart. She went abroad through
primrose paths with Fletcher, and learned Shirley's lambent
wit. She wandered amid dark dry places of the outcast soul
with Ford. " Hamlet " was hers. " Antony and Cleopatra " was
hers. And hers too was " The Tempest ". Then, after many
years, her children mated with famed poets in far distant
lands. " Faust " and " Wallenstein ", " Lucrezia Borgia " and
" Marion Delorme " are hers.'

We must not pause, tempting though it be, at the allusions
in this paragraph. Would GREENE be appeased by the first ?
Perhaps not, but is there much more to him than the Tombland
reaches of Norwich, where he was born, now that his grievance
is forgotten ? THOMAS HEYWOOD, the Lincolnshire dramatist,
knew best the country gentleman in his manor-house. GEORGE
PEELE wrote pastorals and masques. Juliet loved in a palace
in Verona. JOHN WEBSTER's Duchess of Malfi challenged her
murderer to explain ' this talk, fit for a charnel.' JOHN LYLY
was a master of court-comedy, a blithe lyrist and a writer of
plays for children, apart from his ' Anatomy of Wit ' in the
Euphues volumes. THOMAS KYD, author of *the Spanish Tragedie*
and of a ' Hamlet ' play (since lost) before *Hamlet*, should be
added to Symonds's list. BEN JONSON (*c.* 1573–1637), literary
dictator and a great man at the Mermaid Tavern, where he
met Shakespeare in wit-combats and lyric feasts, wrote
comedies, *Every Man in* and *out of his Humour*, in the former
of which Shakespeare acted at the Globe Theatre, 1598. The
comedy of ' humours ', a medical metaphor, took its name
from those plays. In his second period he wrote character-
plays, of which *Volpone, or The Fox* is the best-known, and,
like most Tudor playwrights, he was a skilled song-smith.
A big, burly, bibulous man, his place among his contemporaries is comparable to that of the later Johnson. The
' learned sock ' is from Milton's *L'Allegro*, where Jonson is
matched with ' sweetest Shakespeare, Fancy's child ', an echo

as noted before, of the distinction between plays *a noticia* and *a fantasia*. MARLOWE'S 'mighty line' is a quotation from Ben Jonson. For Marlowe first, in his vehement tragedies, *Dr. Faustus*, *Tamburlaine*, *The Jew of Malta*, displayed the full powers of blank verse as a vehicle for dramatic speech. He found it a succession of even lines, and left it in paragraphs of music, showing the way which Shakespeare followed. The Marlowe touch in drama is as distinct as the 'Nelson touch' in seamanship. Of his mighty desire we spoke on page 6 ; ' might is right ' was his rule for stage-kings, a doctrine which he imported from Machiavelli in Italy. It enjoyed but short shrift on the English stage (as, indeed, in the practice of England's kings), and Shakespeare's ' Within the hollow crown ', etc., of *King Richard II*, Act III, Scene ii, deflated the might of the prince. But the magic of the mighty line remained.

Of GEORGE CHAPMAN, whose ' Homer ' ravished Keats, JOHN MARSTON, PHINEAS FLETCHER, JAMES SHIRLEY and JOHN FORD we must forego even these brief notes, and the marriage of Shakespeare's genius with that of playwrights and poets in later centuries will be celebrated at the due time. Here we have tried to show, with the help of Robert Greene and J. A. Symonds, how at once, when Shakespeare was a new writer, but lately arrived in London, he was recognized, however grudgingly, as ' the only Shake-scene in a country ', and how his unique fame as the supreme dramatist was confirmed after three hundred years.

In the Cold. But not always during the three centuries. Greene's grudge was fulfilled in his own despite. There was a period, short and not important, when a sort of darkness, not very deep, was drawn across the essential Shakespeare, and when an attempt was made, by critics consulting his own interests, to conform him to the prevailing taste for classical drama. We shall come in the next Book to this conflict between ' Classic ' and ' Romantic '. But we do not propose to dwell upon it long. Obviously, it is a critics' arena. The names have been invented since the fight, so far as the protagonists may be said to have fought consciously, and no one in the 16th century, and Shakespeare least of all, or, at any rate, as little as Alexandre Hardy, set out to be a classicist or romanticist. True, as Sir Sidney Lee says, Shakespeare ' defied at every stage in his career the laws of the classical drama '. But he defied them—this is the point—as an outlaw much more than as a lawbreaker. ' He rode roughshod ', Lee goes on, ' over the unities '.[1] But he rode without knowing how his steed was shod. Probably he had not heard of the ' unities '. Certainly, he could not have quoted the authority for them ; and though he was aware, as we have seen, of a distinction between ' the liberty ' and ' the law of writ ', his sole concern was to make good, acting plays. If he could get improbabilities of place and time across the primitive conventions of the Tudor stage, so much the better for the display of action. His rules were made in the green-room of the people's theatre, not the *chambre bleue* of French hostesses to Cardinal Richelieu.

But this expediency did not suit academic sticklers. They drew their screen of classicism across the stage, and through it Shakespeare was discerned as a rude fellow ignorant of Aristotle. Many of his plays, accordingly, as Lee tells us,

' were deemed to need drastic revision . . . in order to satisfy the alteration alike in theatrical taste and machinery. No disrespect was intended to Shakespeare's memory by those who engaged in these acts of vandalism '.

They ' worked arbitrarily ', we are told :

' They endeavoured without much method to re-cast Shakespeare's plays in a Gallicised rather than a strictly classical mould. . . . In the French spirit, they viewed love as the dominant passion of tragedy, they gave tragedies happy endings, and they qualified the wickedness of hero and heroine. . . . Shakespeare's language was modernised or simplified, passages which were reckoned to be difficult were rewritten, and the calls of intelligibility were deemed to warrant the occasional transfer of a speech from one character to another, or even from one play to another '.

An odd business, it will be seen, and plainly of no permanent significance, despite the occurrence of a name as great

[1] Of time, place and action in a regular ' classical ' play. See page 187 below.

as Dryden's among Shakespeare's revisers. Their chief significance is due to the reaction from them—to the full flood of Shakespeare-worship in the era of Romantic revivalism, associated largely, as we shall see, with Lessing (1729–81) and the Schlegels in Germany. On a long view, the appreciation of Shakespeare, extorted reluctantly from Greene and freely accorded by Ben Jonson, has increased steadily down to the present day; and if we may take a little man as typical of the extremer Classicists, we shall mention only Thomas Rymer (1641–1713), whom Saintsbury characterises, in his *History of Criticism*, as

'a man of remarkable learning for his age and country, but intensely stupid to begin with, and Puck-led by the *Zeitgeist* into a charcoal-burner's faith in "the rules",'

and of whom he quoted with approval Macaulay's verdict: 'I never came across a worse critic'. Except for the influence of the *Zeitgeist*, we should have left poor Tom in the cold.

The Praise of Shakespeare. In a single section of a short history of a great subject it is not possible to summarize the causes which readers in every era and in every country of the Old World and the New have discovered for praising Shakespeare. To act the chief parts which he created has been and is to-day the highest ambition of members of the profession to which he belonged. Have you seen so-and-so's Juliet or Lady Macbeth, so-and-so's Mark Antony or Iago, is the question of which every actress and actor longs openly or secretly to be the object. And the playwright who can make players' triumphs is the enduring inspiration of poets. This hardly needs illustration. The last speech of Cleopatra has been described as 'a passage surpassed in poetry, *if at all*, only by the final speech of Othello',[1] and the three little words which we have underlined are characteristic of a sober man's enthusiasm. They are not extravagant, but of common acceptation. Shakespeare as a poet is only self-surpassed. So we shall not repeat the world's praises: space forbids and the exercise is superfluous.

His Humanism. But consistently with the course of this

[1] Prof. A. C. Bradley, *Oxford Lectures on Poetry*, London, 1909; p. 303.

history there is a road of approach to Shakespeare's greatness which may be followed very briefly, and which will illumine some places still in darkness. We referred just now to his deflation of the Renaissance prince, puffed-up with the pride of ' divine right ', and we were thinking particularly of King Richard II's speech, how Death, keeping his Court in the hollow crown,

> ' Comes at the last and with a little pin
> Bores through his castle wall, and farewell King !
> Cover your heads and mock not flesh and blood
> With solemn reverence ; throw away respect,
> Tradition, form and ceremonious duty,
> For ye have but mistook me all this while :
> I live with bread like you, feel want,
> Taste grief, need friends : subjected thus,
> How can ye say to me, I am a King ? '

So, too, Shylock, the prince of avarice, the Machiavellian usurer handed on to Shakespeare out of medieval legend and story-book, broke his framework of tradition, in Act 3, Scene i, of *The Merchant of Venice*. The lust of gold, like the the lust of power, was not absolute. The absolute was graded by degree :

' I am a Jew. Hath not a Jew eyes ? Hath not a Jew hands, organs, dimensions, senses, affections, passions ? Fed with the same food, hurt with the same weapons, subject to the same diseases, healed by the same means, warmed and cooled by the same summer and winter, as a Christian is ? '

These subject-kings—a new conception—of the Shakespearean stage differed from Marlowe's heroes by their profound consciousness of the subjected in the kingly state. Barabbas, Faustus, Tamburlaine, no one could possibly have ' mistook ' them. They were consistent absolutists in every act and word :

> ' I will, with engines never exercised,
> Conquer, sack, and utterly consume
> Your cities and your golden palaces . . .
> I will persist a terror to the world . . .
> And weary Death with bearing souls to Hell ',

cried Tamburlaine, conscious of his might. But Shakespeare tempered these excesses. ' Take but degree away ', he wrote in a famous passage of *Troilus and Cressida*, ' and hark what discord follows ! '

> ' Force should be right ; or rather, right and wrong,
> Between whose endless jar justice resides,
> Should lose their names, and so should justice too ;
> Then everything includes itself in power,
> Power into will, will into appetite ;
> And appetite, an universal wolf,
> So doubly seconded with will and power,
> Must make perforce an universal prey,
> And last eat up himself '.[1]

These verses might have been written—perhaps they were—in direct contravention to Marlowe's doctrine. The will-to-power degenerates into the wolf, and at last destroys himself. Certainly, negatively stated, we may say that, by as much as Shakespeare departed from the lead given to Marlowe by Machiavelli, by so much the England of the Stuarts never became as the France of the Bourbons. English literature—we shall come to it—derived immense benefit from French models in the 17th century, but England in 1649[2] was not as France in 1789. Shakespeare, a saner genius than Marlowe, reinterpreted policy to princes and conduct to common men. When he redeemed English drama from the exceeding blood-and-thunder tradition of the elder playwrights, bred and trained in the Senecan tradition, he moderated in England the full heritage of the Italian Renaissance. He humanized its supermen, and caught the conscience of mankind. He broke Wolsey, Richard, Lear, and, breaking them, remade them. The great *Moi*, which, as we shall see, was so resonant a note in Corneille (1606–84), was compelled by Shakespeare's psychology to strange aberrations and unexpectednesses, and the stage-conventions had to accommodate themselves to

---

[1] Compare this warning with the speech by Wolsey (*King Henry VIII*, Act III, Scene ii), quoted on page 124 above.
[2] Execution of Charles I ; 1789, the French Revolution.

dramatic truth. How can ye say to me, I am I? cried his heroes. ' I live with bread like you,' said Richard ; ' Fed with the same food' as a Christian, said Shylock; ' If Hamlet from himself be ta'en away, . . . Then Hamlet does it not '. Then a King is not always a King nor a Jew always a Jew. There is room for God's mercy and forgiveness of sins. Lear reveals the human spirit as of greater sublimity than we had dreamed.

We have left out the loveliness of Shakespeare : his flowers, his fairies, his lovers ; these joys are for every man to find. What we have tried to make clear in this account of the greatest of the writers of European literature is his culminating, out-topping (Matthew Arnold's epithet) quality as the heir of the Humanists of the 15th century. They passionately, painfully sought to recover the ' pagan view ', and to reconcile it with Christian civilization. ' A human Calvary ' is Dr. Dover Wilson's description of the final scene in *King Lear*, and in its humanism lies its convincing power. Much has been written about Shakespeare : there is hardly a critic in any country who has not made Shakespeare his mark ; the critics have been as ambitious as the actors. Perhaps the best conclusion here is to refer readers back to Shakespeare's works, which, after all, are the ultimate source of all the criticism. But one writer of an older fashion may be cited. He is not much consulted to-day, yet in his *Introduction to the Literature of Europe in the 15th, 16th and 17th Centuries*, now about a hundred years old, Henry Hallam (1777–1859), before Acton and Saintsbury, took all Europe as his province and brought to it a wide survey and a tranquil sceptre. What he wrote about Shakespeare in Part III, Chapter vi, of that History is the more valuable, perhaps, because, while he knew the writings of Coleridge and Lamb, he preceded Lee, Dowden, Raleigh, Sir Edmund Chambers, C. H. Herford, A. C. Bradley, and the rest of the brilliant band of Shakespearean critics who have illumined the topic since his death. With his words, accordingly, we close the present Section :

' The name of Shakespeare is the greatest in our literature— it is the greatest in all literature. No man ever came near to him in the creative powers of the mind ; no man ever had such strength at once and such variety of imagination. Coleridge has most felicitously applied to him a Greek epithet, given before to I know not whom, certainly none so deserving of it, *myrionous*, the thousand-souled Shakespeare. The number of characters in his plays is astonishingly great without including those, who, although transient, have often their individuality, all distinct, all types of human life in well defined differences. Yet he never takes an abstract quality to embody it, scarcely perhaps a definite condition of manners, as Jonson does. . . . Compare with him Homer, the tragedians of Greece, the poets of Italy, Plautus, Cervantes, Molière, Addison, Le Sage, Fielding, Richardson, Scott, the romancers of the elder or later schools—one man has far more than surpassed them all. . . . The philosophy of Shakespeare, his intimate searching out of the human heart, whether in the gnomic form of sentence, or in the dramatic exhibition of character, is a gift peculiarly his own '.

§ 8. MILTON.

The Age of Shakespeare, literally interpreted, ran from 1564 to 1616, the years of his birth and death. But he died at fifty-two, probably of a fever due to bad drains, and his ' age ', even literally interpreted, might be extended for another thirty years. Then it would include the birth of Molière, 1622, Pascal, 1623, Bunyan, 1628, Dryden, 1631, Boileau, 1636, and Racine, 1639—the last three of a very different generation. If Shakespeare had been living in 1639 as a septuagenarian at Stratford, would any greeting have reached him from the ' Immortals ' in the newly-founded French Academy ?

Two Movements in the 17th Century. Probably not. For, rearranging the men of this age by affinity instead of chronology, we are aware of an imaginary line dividing them into two groups. They sort themselves in order of birth as follows :

1552	Spenser	1555	Malherbe
1562	Lope de Vega	1606	Corneille
1564	Marlowe	1622	Molière
1564	Shakespeare	1623	Pascal
1600	Calderon	1631	Dryden
1608	Milton	1636	Boileau
1628	Bunyan	1639	Racine, and
			l'Académie (1637).

The imaginary line was drawn by Boileau, who exclaimed of Malherbe, the eldest in his group, ' Enfin Malherbe vint ', as if his advent had been awaited all through the century, and who went on to say even less exactly, ' Tout reconnut ses lois '. But everyone, or everything, did *not* recognize the laws of this first founder of ' the French rule ' to which we shall come in the next Book. The Spenser-Bunyan group did not acknowledge them. Corneille, as we shall see, tried to refuse them, and Dryden modified them for English practice and theory. Still, they directed French taste through the curtains of the *chambre bleue* in the famous Hôtel de Rambouillet to the portals of Richelieu's Academy, and Europe in general followed where Paris led. There were two movements in the 17th century, simultaneous and partly—but only partly— consciously opposed : the wildling movement of which Ronsard (1524–85) had been the chief inaugurator, and the orderly movement initiated by Malherbe (1555–1628) to correct its irregularities and excesses and to standardize French language and metres. To that second group we shall come in Book IV. Here we note that Boileau's *enfin* measured the interval between Du Bellay's *Défense et Illustration de la Langue française* (1549) and Malherbe's arrival with his pruning-hook, and we may recall the remark, most helpful in our present context, that ' Du Bellay preached what Shakespeare prac- tised '.[1] So, postponing the contrary practice recommended by Malherbe to his successors, we conclude this Section of our history with the contribution of Milton to the age in which Shakespeare was the leading figure.

[1] Saintsbury, *History of Criticism*, Vol. II, p. 115. For Ronsard and Du Bellay *see* §1 above.

Milton and the Renaissance. There is external as well as internal evidence to the close association of JOHN MILTON (1608–74) with the literary movement introduced by the Pleiad out of Italy into France—with the Renaissance in solution, as we may call it.

First of all, there was the long-poem ambition, attempted by Ronsard in his *Franciad* and achieved by Du Bartas in *La Semaine.* We need not return to these forgotten epics, but there is no doubt that, whatever the degree of Milton's direct obligation to Du Bartas, his choice of the Fall of Man as an epical topic was influenced by that example. Something, too, was due—though they both owed more in common to Du Bartas—to the Dutch poet, Joost Van Den Vondel, who was twenty-one years senior to Milton, and whose drama, *Lucifer,* treated the same theme. As we saw at the end of § 3, Vondel shares with Hooft and Grotius the primacy of literary renown in the oceanic age of Holland, when Amsterdam was a true world-metropolis. Grotius's famous treatise on 'War and Peace' focused attention on international law in the times of Barneveldt and Cromwell, whom Milton served as Latin Secretary, and Milton and Vondel alike drew inspiration for their counsels of government in heaven from those juridical writings.

Another Renaissance contact is Milton's reverence for Tasso (1554–95), Spenser's acknowledged model in romantic epos. It was at the house of the Marquis Manso that Tasso completed his 'Jerusalem Delivered', and Manso painted his portrait and wrote his life. Years afterwards Milton visited Manso, then a very old man, and confided to him his poetic dreams. He was pondering then the exploits of King Arthur, the traditional *matière de Bretagne,* which Spenser had chosen in his *Faery Queen,* and in making this confidence he recalled in a Latin poem to Manso, 1639 :

> ' Te pridem magno felix concordia Tasso
> Junxit '.

The 'happy concord' joins Milton too, to Tasso, and, through the rejected Arthur-design, to Spenser, Malory, and the romancers.

His love of music, again, was a Renaissance trait. Milton's blank-verse was a romantic measure, and he continued in his sonnets and odes the verse-forms which Wyatt and Surrey had learnt abroad from romantic masters. His verbal music, too, was romantic. Sir Henry Newbolt, a poet of our day, speaks of Milton's 'natural magic, which takes common words, and suddenly in some way beyond explanation makes of them a strange and memorable picture, a strange and haunting melody, an irradiation, an enchantment'. All these were the ways of Ronsard, not of Malherbe, of the first, not the second, group in the 17th century; and, if part of this evidence is internal, it helps to support our perception of Milton's place in the age of Shakespeare. True, merely as a singer, he was less simple than the authentic Tudor poets[1]. 'Warbling his native wood-notes wild', he said of Shakespeare, but his own notes were more learned and less native to the woods. After all, he was contemporary with ROBERT HERRICK (1591–1674), GEORGE HERBERT (1593–1633) and RICHARD CRASHAW (1612–49), and younger than JOHN DONNE (1573–1631), 'minor' poets, in a useful phrase, of great talents, who, however diverse in expression, are not in the first burst of Elizabethan poetry. But Milton's natural magic with common words, and, indeed, all his dealings with the dictionary, range him with Shakespeare and the Romantics and not with the more 'previous' founders of the future French Academy.

Reforming the Reformation. We must pass quickly over his works. Those who read them need no exposition; those who do not no exposition will convince. In 1644, Milton published *Areopagitica, A Speech for the Liberty of Unlicensed Printing*, and, incidentally, for other liberties as well. In 1644, the French Academy was in being, Herrick was singing to his mistresses, Edmund Waller and Sir John Denham—we shall come back to them—were attending Queen Henrietta Maria in Paris, and Charles I was defeated at Marston Moor. 'Now once again', declared Milton, his singing-robes laid aside, and his energies stretched to the eventful year,

[1] 'In Elizabethan times the art of song-writing was carried to perfection.' A. H. Bullen, in the Preface to his *Lyrics from the Song-books of the Elizabethan Age*.

'Now once again, by all concurrence of signs, . . . God is decreeing to begin some new and great period in His Church, even to the reforming of the Reformation itself. What does He then but reveal Himself to His servants, and, as His manner is, first to His Englishmen?'

And then followed the famous passage enshrined in every anthology of prose, about the 'noble and puissant nation', like 'an eagle mewing her mighty youth, and kindling her undazzled eyes at the full midday beam'. It has the true accent of the Renaissance, alike in its national consciousness and its individual pride. The sea-view of Thomas More, the *virtù* of Machiavelli, and, earlier still, the *antico valore* of Petrarch's Italian heart are in it.

And one point particularly calls for comment, this 'reforming of the Reformation itself', for it supplies the measure and content of Milton's contribution to European letters. There was a moment in the growth of the mind of Europe when Renaissance and Reformation were at one, when both were seeking by one effort to extend by concentration the powers and resources of the human intellect. We might call it the moment of Erasmus, one of the veriest Europeans who ever lived, in the sense in which Dr. Beard wrote: 'The Reformation that has been is Luther's monument: perhaps the Reformation that is to be will trace itself back to Erasmus'.[1] It was to this Reformation that is to be that Milton, a true son of the Renaissance, dedicated himself during the Civil War, invoking not only the Muse of Helicon, restored by the rediscovery of Greece, but also the Heavenly Muse, 'above th' Aonian mount' and 'above th' Olympian hill', who was 'to tell of deeds above heroic'.[2] The iterated 'above' is revealing. He might set his 'deeds above heroic' to the scale of merely heroic deeds. There are descriptive passages in *Paradise Lost* where we can measure the loss to romantic epos of 'the tedious pomp that waits on princes' (V, 354) and of the splendid raiment which Eve did not wear (V, 383), and which Tasso and Spenser would have expanded in many

---

[1] *The Reformation*, 1883; new edition, by Dr. Ernest Barker, London, 1927, p. 73.
[2] See *Paradise Lost*, i, 15; vii, 3; and *Paradise Regained*, l, 14–15.

M

stanzas. But Milton was more than content to do without them. In a long exordium to Book IX of his epic (verses 13–47) he deliberately claims that his theme is ' not less but more heroic ' than that of the wrath of Achilles or the ' rage of Turnus for Lavinia disespoused '. He was ' not sedulous ', he said,

> ' to indite
> Wars, hitherto the only argument
> Heroic deemed '.

His ' deeds above heroic ' could likewise be made epic-worthy —or even epic-worthier.

Milton's Loneliness. We stop here. The *Paradise* poems, the sacred drama of *Samson Agonistes*, the masque of *Comus*, the lament for *Lycidas*, the lyrical odes to Mirth and Melancholy, and the rest of the English and Latin verses survive the Puritan and pamphleteer, the blind father, the formidable husband. Milton, like Dante, a lonely poet, pursued in his own words, ' things unattempted yet in prose or rhyme '. And because the things were unattempted he could reach them only by tentative words. The Miltonic diction, applied more companionably to less rarely attempted things, misses the mark which he attained, and makes a hollow sound. This was the fate of Milton's language when it was used in common air for customary themes. Romantic leaders in a later generation found it uncommunicative and cold ; their half-dead words fell away from the truth, towards which his half-living words had strained. In the history of the growth of the mind of Europe Milton stands outside the critics' categories. He was a romantic poet constrained to classic diction, a Renaissance writer who would reform the Reformation. He stood on a watershed of thought while the streams flowed down and left him solitary, ' with inward eyes illuminated '. But the moment was eternized by his achievement. ' He could not change the character of a people, nor perpetuate his dynasty ',[1] we are aptly told ; but, dying in 1674, he would be content that the Reformation which he enhanced crowned his country in 1611 with the *Authorised Version* of the Bible and in 1678–84 with the two parts of John Bunyan's *Pilgrim's Progress*.

[1] Sir W. Raleigh, *Milton*, London, 1900 ; pp. 264 and 64.

BOOK IV
THE FRENCH RULE AND ITS SEQUEL

FOREWORD TO BOOK IV

THE period covered by this Book is approximately a hundred and fifty years, from the establishment of the French Academy in 1637—in Milton's lifetime, and it might have been in Shakespeare's—to the Fall of the Bastille in 1789. Both events alike were due to the activities of men of letters : the constructive act to the literary group associated with Cardinal Richelieu, and the act of destruction to the nationalists and liberals, who, in England as well as France, had contributed to a reform of the social outlook. More briefly, the period is contained between the death of Milton in 1674 and the death of Voltaire and Rousseau in 1778, roundly a century. But for forty years before Milton died Paris was preparing the age of Reason, and fifteen years after 1778 the worship of Reason was instituted in Paris. From Descartes's *Discours sur la Méthode*, 1637, or even earlier from Malherbe ('enfin Malherbe vint'), who died in 1628, there were direct affiliations with the first phase of the French Revolution. The threads were woven on both sides of the channel, and Edmund Burke was alone in his generation in foreseeing its later phases. 'We are not the converts of Rousseau, we are not the disciples of Voltaire', he warned his countrymen in 1790. But both thinkers had learnt much from England, and Wordsworth and Coleridge in the same year were ready to learn much from France.

A break occurs in our survey at 1700, the year in which Dryden died. He had tempered for English practice the French law which went out from Versailles, while he accepted the law, and handed it on to Pope, who died in 1744 and represents the Augustan age in England. Dryden contrived what Saintsbury has called ' escapes and safety-valves', through which the Romantic spirit found its undeniable expression. Virgil and Homer were not expelled from polite letters. But they became poets of the French Classical school, suffering a new occultation to suit the taste of the modernists, and were translated, the one by Dryden and the other by Pope, into Augustan heroic verse. So, too, Chaucer and Shakespeare were partly edited according to the canons of the new age, and it was due chiefly to Dryden's critical faculty that their partial occultation was not deeper. Shakespeare, again, and, more emphatically, Milton, whose Satan was deemed by Boileau unsuitable as an epic character, owed much to the sanity in criticism of Joseph Addison (1672–1719).

The resurgence of feeling amid reason, through the loop-holes left by Dryden in the neo-Classic screen, marks off the period 1701–78 from the previous fifty or sixty years, and § 1, 'France and England,' in the second part of the present Book will serve to introduce it.

Meanwhile, introducing the first part, we have to note that this 'Querelle des Anciens et des Modernes', which were the French terms for the schools now distinguished as Classical and Romantic, broke out in France towards the end of the 17th century and crossed to England in Sir William Temple's essay on *Ancient and Modern Learning*, 1690, and Swift's *Battle of the Books*, 1697. On paper, it was a dreary controversy; in life and letters, it was settled *ambulando*. For it was what seemed excessive in the zeal of the Pleiad that the zeal of the Academy sought to correct. What Malherbe ultimately brought to French literature as reformed by Ronsard was a scheme of local option rather than of prohibition. Romantic, if an example is wanted, are Shakespeare's daffodils,

> ' That come before the swallow dares, and take
> The winds of March with beauty ' ;

and Classic is Racine's

' Le jour n'est pas plus pur que le fonds de mon coeur '.

The wild pictorialness of the one, decorated with bright images, and the grand parsimony of the other, drawing on the reserves of its own strength (' without o'erflowing full ', as an early practitioner described it), are best characterized by the now familiar epithets. But one writer might exemplify both styles, and they were not always sharply distinguishable. Men could ' talk through the chink of a wall '.

Again, apart from this outworn controversy, which has

tended to make too much of a difference in style, English readers are liable to turn away from French writers in the second half of the 17th century precisely because of their difference from contemporary English writers. The poetry of Shakespeare, the prose of Bunyan, and the cadences of the language of the Authorised Version of 1611, are so intimate a part of our national being, that the French law which these books did not observe makes a difficult appeal to our admiration. The late Lytton Strachey once remarked that Englishmen ' have always detested Racine.' If so, they must fail to appreciate very much that is excellent in English literature as well as in French through the whole of the 18th century. The French law was not destined to be permanent : no rule of taste ever is. A French Revolution was to come, and, whatever its worse consequences, foreseen so clearly by Burke, it was to bring back Romance to European letters. But the rule set by Malherbe and de Balzac, the rule codified by Boileau and exemplified in Racine, was salutary and positive. In its time and place, and particularly in the 17th century and at the Court of Louis Quatorze—

' The classical tendency meant harmony, dignity, and purity' not only in words but in sentiments and construction. It meant indeed something much more classical than the classics. . . . The French classical drama, the greatest literary creation of the second half of the century, is still the typical product of the French mind and one of the living literatures of the world. . . . There never was a literature better suited for export than the drama, the poetry, and the prose of the age of Louis XIV. In the original or in translations, or in imitated or adapted forms, it became the standard literature of Europe '.[1]

A few names may be added for reference in the following pages.

Between 1524 and 1635 occurred the life and work, it will be remembered, of Ronsard, Camoens, Montaigne, Du Bartas, Tasso, Cervantes, Spenser, Marlowe, Bacon, Lope de Vega and Shakespeare.

[1] G. N. Clark, *The Seventeenth Century*, Oxford, 1929 ; pp. 337 f.

Malherbe, critic of the Pleiad and founder of the Classical school, lived from 1555 to 1628.

The Renaissance in Holland is associated chiefly with Hooft, 1581–1648, Grotius, 1583–1645, and Vondel, 1587–1679; Martin Opitz, 1597–1639, represents the same tendencies in Germany.

Recalling next the following events :

> 1618–48, Thirty Years War,
> 1624–42, Cardinal Richelieu's supremacy in France.
> 1625–49, Reign of Charles I in England,
> 1632–54, Reign of Queen Christina in Sweden,
> 1653–58, Cromwell's Protectorate in England,
> 1661–1715, Effective Reign of Louis XIV in France,

we may enumerate a dozen writers in that stirring epoch, in which the law of order, transferred from politics, was imposed on the arts :

> 1596–1650, DESCARTES ; *Discours de la Méthode*, 1637. 'Throughout all Europe the advent of his system caused a revolution in the history of thought '.[1]
>
> 1597–1654, JEAN DE BALZAC ; the Malherbe of French prose style.
>
> 1606–84, CORNEILLE ; *Cid*, 1637. It ' did more than any other single drama to determine for two centuries the character of the theatre all over the Continent of Europe '.[2]
>
> 1608–74, MILTON.
>
> 1613–80, LA ROCHEFOUCAULD.
>
> 1622–73, MOLIÉRE.
>
> 1623–62, PASCAL ; *Lettres Provinciales*, 1656. ' The first masterpiece of Classical taste in our prose literature '.[3]
>
> 1626–96, MME. DE SÉVIGNÉ.
>
> 1631–1700, DRYDEN.
>
> 1632–1704, LOCKE.
>
> 1636–1711, BOILEAU.
>
> 1639–99, RACINE.

[1] *Cambridge Modern History*, Vol. IV, p. 787.
[2] Ticknor, *History of Spanish Literature*, Vol. II, p. 305.
[3] Lanson, *Histoire de la Littérature française*, p. 463.

I. AT HOME

§ 1. MAKING THE RULE.

THERE are two sayings—one contemporary, the other recent—which will help to clarify the distinction between the Pleiad and the Academy as arbiters of literary taste. The respective dates, it will be remembered, are 1549—Du Bellay's *Défense*, and 1637—the incorporation of *l'Académie*.

(1) FRANÇOIS DE MALHERBE, who was born in 1555, a little in advance of the new régime, was seized so thoroughly by its principles that he deemed himself to have invented them. We shall come in a moment to his service to poetics. Here we remark that it was chiefly contained in the commentaries which he wrote on the margins of other poets' works : Philippe Desportes (1546–1616), a disciple of the Pleiad and a favourite model for foreign imitation, was especially selected for this purpose. With scrupulous impartiality he applied his method to his own *juvenilia*, and, when he found a locution which he had since taught himself to disapprove, he would note in the margin : ' Ici je ronsardisais.' So a Ronsardism passed into a solecism very shortly after Ronsard's death.

(2) But time was on the side of the Ronsardisers. J. J. Jusserand, the great French critic, devoted to English studies, who died in 1932, said that Malherbe's ' harmonic ideal was the ticking of a clock ' : invariability, order, expectedness ; no surprise, no free movement, no irregularity. Even the freedom to be a Protestant was abolished in 1685 by the Revocation of the Edict of Nantes, and every road to heaven was prohibited except that authorized by the sermons preached at the Court of Louis XIV by Bishop Bossuet (1627–1704), tutor to the Dauphin, and Bourdaloue (1632–1704), the hardly less eminent divine. Yet, adds Jusserand,[1] ' on ne réfléchit pas, au temps du Roi-Soleil, que le soleil même a un mouvement '.

---

[1] *Ronsard*, Paris, Hachette, 1913 ; pp. 198–99.

That the movement would be accelerated to an eclipse in the Terror of 1793, and that the unchangeable principles of the 18th century would be overturned in a social revolution, which brought literature back to nature and wildness, lay beyond the vision of the anti-Pleiad who marched so securely into the shelter of the French Academy. Thus, these two sayings—' *ici je ronsardisais* ' and ' *le soleil même a un mouvement* '—may serve as touchstones of a critical doctrine which began as a search for Classicism and ended in a Romantic revival.

Malherbe's Legacy. We are concerned here with the beginning, with that instinctive preference for logical order, for ornament arising out of construction and not imported from without, and even for an etiquette of style, which is so strongly implanted in the French genius. ' A wonder edges the familiar face ', says George Meredith somewhere of Earth, or Nature, under the sign of Romance, and it was precisely— or partly, at least—this edging of wonder which Malherbe, expressing the French genius, was resolute to remove. ' Partly ', we qualify it, because neither Ronsard nor his company of wit had fully succeeded in impressing the wonder on men's minds. Shakespeare's daffodils, mentioned above, that ' take the winds of March with beauty ', did stamp that impression; and, when the Romantic revival came at the end of the 18th century, it was largely for Shakespeare's sake that Watts–Dunton, a very competent critic, described it as 'a renascence of wonder '. But the full wonder came after Ronsard, and it did not come, or it did not come largely, on French soil. Had it done so, there might have been no Malherbe, no anti-Pleiad, even perhaps no French Academy. There would have been a French Shakespeare instead. It was the failure of the Pleiad to make a Shakespeare, and the arrest of its development at a Ronsard, which provoked the refusal of the French genius, the native bias of which lay the other way. A romantic wonder had not edged the familiar face. All that happened was that French poesy was said to be defaced by the superficial ' wit ' of Ronsard's ' learned brigade ' and resumed its classical features. The romantic impress was not deep enough to be permanent; and, in the absence of accomplished triumphs in romantic drama and epic, of a *Hamlet*, a *Tempest*, a *Faery Queen*, and a *Paradise Lost* by the innovating Pleiad, the French mind, redirected by Malherbe, and reinforced by social and political causes, turned away from alien seducements to the correct forms and diction which the French Academy was to make its first care. Rejecting Ronsard's experiments in foreign modes and metres, Parisian taste found a more precious beauty in obeying the law of the pendulum than in liberties with cæsura and pause. The response to Ronsard in England, Spain and Holland, and even in the German desert by Opitz, was not repeated in his own country in his time. For his time was anti-individualistic : the time of Napoleon was not yet. It was a time of centralization, of propriety, of academic discipline and commonsense, and of a smoothness,

> ' Though deep, yet clear; though gentle, yet not dull;
> Strong without rage, without o'erflowing, full.'

So Sir John Denham (1615–69), the English poet in Paris, was to write of the Thames in *Cooper's Hill*, and he added the significant aspiration, ' O ! could I flow like thee '.

' *Enjambement.*' This distich of Denham's is famous because it corresponds so exactly to Malherbe's aim in correction of the Pleiad's, and one word in it, by a happy accident, may be used to illustrate a poetic law which Ronsard broke and Malherbe reimposed, and which became a test rule of the neo-Classic school. It is the epithet, ' without o'erflowing '. Overflow was the French verse-maker's worst crime ; every policeman on Parnassus was on the look-out for it. It was *streng verboten* to Parisian poets.

We remember what Boileau, rather ecstatically and in some respects not very accurately, wrote of Malherbe nearly a hundred years after. If it was never fully true, it seemed true to the critic who wrote it, and to the age in which Malherbe's doctrine had become a poets' gospel. ' Enfin Malherbe vint ', we read above,

> ' Enfin Malherbe vint, et le premier en France
> Fit sentir dans les vers une juste cadence :
> D'un mot mit en sa place enseigna le pouvoir,

Et réduisit le Muse aux règles du devoir.
Par ce sage écrivain la Langue reparée
N'offrit plus rien de rude a l'oreille épurée.
Les stances avec grace apprirent à tomber,
Et le vers sur le vers n'osa plus enjamber.'

And then followed the couplet—

'Tout reconnut ses lois, et ce guide fidèle
Aux auteurs de ce temps sert encore de modèle.'

It is a wise child who knows his own father; and if the writers of Boileau's generation chose to honour Malherbe as the first poet in France who drilled their language into the formation in which it was to enter the *Dictionnaire* of the Academy, it is not for us to disturb his laurel. We go back to the sentence before that couplet: 'Le vers sur le vers n'osa plus enjamber'; one verse no longer dared to overflow (leg it over) into the next. This is the point of contact with Denham's aspiration to write poetry like the Thames at Windsor, 'without o'erflowing, full', and this prohibition of *enjambement* became a cardinal principle of the new classical French verse. Not to overrun the sense from verse to verse—not merely to cut off the edge of wonder from the daffodils that took the winds of March with beauty, but also to cut off the verse-end pause between the verb and its object—became an invariable rule; and the observation of the rule against *enjambement* was as strict as the extrusion of romantic sentiment. We shall see it enforced on Corneille, and it persisted in French poetic practice till Victor Hugo, defying it in 1830, made a literary revolution by his defiance. To the types or touchstones mentioned above we may now add the sovereign law *ne plus enjamber*.

Speech and Thought. The verse quoted in a previous paragraph from George Meredith, 'A wonder edges the familiar face' is swiftly followed by his perception,

'Half-strange seems Earth, and sweeter than her flowers.'

To refuse this strangeness of the early Romantic muse, the muse who had to be led back blindfold *aux règles du devoir*, was, of course, a more difficult programme than to purge the dictionary *à l'oreille épurée*. But to some extent the one involved the other. For when no verse overran into the next, less strain was placed on the imagination. If nothing odd or sudden might strike the ear, if the colours painted by words had to harmonize and not clash, if surprise and shock had to be avoided and a clock-like regularity was ideal, then the technical conventions would invite a conventional rendering of phenomena. ' Earth ' would not ' seem half-strange ' when there were no half-strange ways of saying so. Words impose their own conditions, and earth is only sweeter than her flowers to a poet with a taste for edged locutions. Blake in a later age saw ' a heaven in a wild flower ', and to Wordsworth ' the meanest flower that blows ' brought thoughts ' too deep for tears '. But this was not the way of Malherbe or Jean de Balzac, who continued his language-reform, and this was not the correct approach to Nature from the *chambre bleue* of the Hôtel de Rambouillet, where Catherine, transformed to Arthénice, the wife of the reigning marquis, and their fair daughter, Julie de Rambouillet, whom all the exquisites loved, held court in the second quarter of the 17th century and made social conversation a fine art.[1]

What did they talk about all the time, all the long time of reviving peace, and prosperity, and reconstruction, and a growing stability in State and Church ? Of pictures, statues, and landscape-gardening, of tapestry, furniture, and books : particularly of books combined with persons in the heroic romances by HONORÉ D'URFÉ (1568-1625 ; *Astrée*), JEAN OGIER DE GOMBAULD (1576-1666 ; *Endymion*), the SIEUR DE GOMBERVILLE (1600-74 ; *Polexandre*), MADELEINE DE SCUDÉRY (1608-1701 ; *Le Grand Cyrus*), MME DE LA

---

[1] ' From the opening of the Hôtel de Rambouillet (in 1610) dates the organisation of polite society as a conscious force in life and letters, the beginning of the process which was to make literature, poetry and prose, the finest flower of social intercourse, its greatest beauties that elegance and dignity which are the adornment of aristocratic manners. It is only a beginning that we have in these years. In the literature of the period there is still much of the ruder, freer, larger spirit of the 16th century. . . . But before the first sixty years of the century are over, modern French prose has taken shape. In moulding it, the two great influences of Classicism are at work. Balzac represents the one. . . . Descartes stands for the other. . . . Pascal combines the two.' (H. C. J. Grierson, *The First Half of the Seventeenth Century*, Edinburgh, 1906 ; pp. 376-77.)

FAYETTE (1634–93 ; *Princesse de Clèves*), and others, who not only wrote huge novels but also invented a special diction— exquisite or 'precious', as it is described—in which it was appropriate to talk about them. The *Pays de Tendre* of this invention, however artificial in its geography and language, was a sort of idealized Bath and Le Touquet for the refreshment and refinement of the leisured class of Parisian wits, feminine even more than masculine. The present value of the experience was greater than its influence, which was laughed out of fashion by Molière in his *Précieuses Ridicules*, 1659.

Cartesianism. Meanwhile, towards the cleansing of Earth from any half-strangeness that clung to her as Ronsard's deposit, RENÉ DESCARTES (1596–1650) served as the purist in thought. His philosophy (*Discours de la Méthode*) belongs to a separate branch of knowledge and must not detain us here, save to note that he systematized Montaigne's honest doubt and pointed the road to later sceptics and rationalists. More pertinent to literary history is the close connection between his aim at plain reason and the plain writing which he made effective. Authorities agree that Cartesianism is the name of a style as well as of a philosophy, of a mode of language as well as a mode of thought, and that Descartes's method with the problem of how to think implemented the method of Malherbe and Balzac with the problem of how to speak. The *bon sens des honnêtes gens*, the commonsense of straightforward people, was the root-principle of their joint researches, and Descartes was restless in pursuing it. He visited various countries. His central idea, *Cogito, ergo sum* ('I think, therefore I am'), the one certainty amid all the doubts, occurred to him in Germany ; he lay hidden two years in Paris, 1625–27, excogitating his ideas ; he retired to Holland, and returned to France, settling finally in 1649 at the brilliant court of Queen Christina in Stockholm, where he enhanced the lustre which he shared.

There is an acute phrase by Legouis, the French critic, which is worth recalling in this context and which might almost be used as a fourth touchstone. He writes in his *Jeunesse de Wordsworth* of ' the victims of the Cartesian proscription' whom the English poet of the Romantic revival restored to the dignity of speech and thought. Little children,[1] humble folk of the fells and dales, the beggar, the idiot, the ass, trees, flowers, even inanimate objects, which could not say *Cogito, ergo sum*, came back from the darkness of Descartes into the freedom of life and art, with the language appropriate to their states of being; and through the barriers which they broke and the prohibitions which they ignored poured a flood of rejected words, forbidden forms and repressed feelings. Earth could be strange again, there might be a heaven in a wild flower.

We must leave this contrast for the present, but Malherbe's rule, it will be observed, was destined to long repercussions.

Pascal. 'Pascal combines the two', namely Balzac's pursuit of elegance, and Descartes's rationalist requirement of precision. So Professor Grierson told us in a passage quoted in the note on page 177, and for the sake of Pascal's place among the makers of the rule of French Classicism, we lift him a little above his place in chronological order. Balzac and Descartes were his seniors by close upon a generation. But the generations of Romance and Classicism, of Ronsard and anti-Ronsard, were, as has been indicated, not exactly sequent. De Balzac, too, though so closely kin to Malherbe, was born more than forty years after him, and, within certain limits, we may join like to like where we find them.

Not that RENÉ PASCAL, ironic moralist, mathematician and mystic, the brilliant son of a school of Port Royal in the brief epoch of its educational zenith, had much actually in common with the other two. It happened that, as a writer, particularly of the polemical pamphlets known as *Lettres Provinciales* (1656–57), Pascal achieved the double aim of Balzac and Descartes by composing a masterpiece in prose perfect as a model of style and as an appeal to reason. Port Royal—we must say as much as this on a topic not strictly literary—was rehabilitated out of its old religious foundation by Cornelius Jansen (1585–1638), Bishop of Ypres. It shone brightly till

---

[1] It has been observed that Joad in Racine's *Athalie* (1691) is one of very few children in classical French literature : 'le xviie siècle n'a pas connu, n'a pas aimé les enfants. La raison n'a pas assez de place dans leur vie' (Lanson, *op. cit.*, p. 549). Pope's famous verse, 'The proper study of mankind is man' (human nature, not 'external' nature) summarizes the Cartesianism which Wordsworth overwhelmed.

1660, supplying teachers of fine influence to men and women like Racine and Mme. de Sévigné, and making a Greek grammar which was still used at Manchester when De Quincey was at the Grammar School in 1800, and a 'Port Royal Logic' which became a household word. But the Jansenists were in conflict with the Jesuits, and these *Lettres écrites à un Provincial et aux révérends Pères Jésuites sur le sujet de la Morale et de la Politique de ses Pères* (which was the long title of the *Provinciales*) struck a blow at the Society of Jesus from which, according to Saintsbury (and we deliberately cite a literary witness), 'it has never wholly recovered, and it can never wholly recover'.

There we leave the controversial aspect. The Letters were condemned by Parliament and the Pope, and, in their Latin version, were publicly burnt. But their literary value is unsurpassed and has been universally acknowledged. They made a melody of lucid prose and a clear shining after the storms of passion. It was always order which Pascal sought : order in the chaos of the universe, in which one of his treatises formed, according to Sir David Brewster, 'the basis of the modern science of pneumatics'; order in the immense firmament, of which he wrote, 'le silence éternal de ces espaces infinis m'effraie'; order in the conscience of mankind, in which a near experience of death had opened out the 'abyss of Pascal'; and order, therefore, in the composition of French prose, in which his *Lettres* and his posthumous *Pensées* are the very type and model of the classical style.

§ 2. THE RULE AT WORK.

The Classical Century. Great books were written by great Frenchmen in the *grand siècle Louis Quatorze*. We put this at the front of the present Section in order to meet in advance the Romantic-Germanic criticism, which, invaluable as it is, and congenial though it be to Shakespeare's countrymen, failed conspicuously in its appreciation of the genius of France. Take Keats, for example, whose short life (1795–1821)

made so bright a splendour of English poetry, and consider
the verses which he wrote about the Classic-Rationalist school :

> ' Ye were dead
> To things ye knew not of,—were closely wed
> To musty laws lined out with wretched rule
> And compass vile : so that ye taught a school
> Of dolts to smooth, inlay, and clip, and fit,
> Till, like the certain wands of Jacob's wit,
> Their verses tallied. . . . They went about,
> Holding a poor, decrepit standard out,
> Marked with most flimsy mottoes, and in large
> The name of one Boileau ! '

It is the statement of a point of view, but it is not true,
it is not just, and it is not European. The name of Boileau
is written large in Europe, with the names of Corneille,
La Rochefoucauld, Mme. de Sévigné, Molière, La Fontaine,
Racine and others, and he was justified in his view that there
were aspects of the late Renaissance—this is the fact to be
remembered—which, having served their purpose, it was
timely to reform or to reject. ' Law ', ' rule ', ' compass ',
' smooth ', ' tally ', ' standard ', are not in themselves
' musty ', ' wretched', ' doltish ', 'poor ', ' decrepit '. They
are in themselves at all times, and they were particularly at
that time, desirable qualities to cultivate in politics, society
and the arts. And if the cultivation of these qualities (without
the hostile epithets attached to them by Keats) involved the
jettison of certain other qualities, more lawless, less regular
and hardly standardized, and feeling was sacrificed to reason,
there was gain as well as loss in the process. There was, in
the end, more gain than loss, because the clearance of the rank
Romantic undergrowth, the dull Marinisms, the tired
Euphuisms and Gongorisms,[1] with all the elaborate verbiage
of ideas worn thin by repetition, left the ground of Romance
unencumbered when the hour for revival should arrive.
Enfin Rousseau vint : this, too, is a formula of thanksgiving,
and Rousseau was born in 1712, the year after Boileau died.

Maxims, Tables, and *Letters.* Meanwhile, the new law

[1] See page 150 above.

181

N

spread. The light of the Hôtel de Rambouillet was repeated in various *salons* in Paris. The charm of women of society, the wit of *savants* of all classes, the attraction of statesmen and diplomatists, pretty girls, learned ladies, drawing-room love-making, talk of the King and his mistresses, talk of the King and his ministers, talk of the King and his wars, always talk and more talk and yet more talk under the discreet chandeliers—these and other factors were combined to form a setting of cultivated manners, which the memoirs of the age and some visible tokens of its craftsmanship still preserve, though with the essence spilt out.

We make the most of what is left. Inevitably, jealousies developed among the leaders of fashion. A visitor frequenting one hostess might turn his favour to another, and the story of Julie de Lespinasse who for ten years in the middle of the 18th century was a kind of pensioner of Mme du Deffand, and then, when her patroness grew blind, took away some of the chief guests to found a *salon*, is famous in the annals of the time and has been told in *Lady Rose's Daughter* by Mrs. Humphry Ward. Few chapters in literary history, hardly even that of Lorenzo de' Medici's Florence, are more fascinating to read than these records of typically French scenes in surroundings never likely to recur in precisely the same combination : philosophers kissing pink fingers, grammarians gilding the forms of speech, a Court as ante-room to an Academy, ladies' heroes mirroring polite conduct; and over all a sense of growing method, of definition, or definement, if we may use the word, from the laying-out of a garden-path to the formulation of the law of gravitation. The Royal Society and Newton's experiments were coeval with Boileau's early rule. French was at once the language and the law : every civilized State in Europe modelled itself in language and manners, in topics of study and in the method of approach to them, on the patterns of the French, and ' order ', in Pope's triumphant pæan, too near to Revolution to be final, was ' Heaven's first law '.

The Paris *salon*, like the English coffee-house, from which it differed in important characteristics, including particularly the feminine element, developed individual marks. LA

ROCHEFOUCAULD, for example, a nobleman of the highest birth, who was known as the Prince de Marcillac before he succeeded his father as Duke François VI, helped to establish the fame of the *salon* of Mme de Sablé by his series of philosophic epigrams. These were collected in 1665 and again in 1678 to a total number of over five hundred as *Réflexions et Sentences, ou Maximes Morales,* and the maxims, as they are commonly known, are little vessels of Cartesian wisdom cut and polished in academic crystal. JEAN DE LA FONTAINE cultivated the animal-fable, bringing to his popular tales in verse the exact observation and pointed diction of the new classical style. He was called 'the butterfly of Parnassus', partly because he changed his allegiance from one leader of fashion to another, most assiduously to Mme de la Sablière, partly because his life was irregular, and partly because he sipped his honey from various flowers before he settled on his *Fables* in 1668. By brevity of wit and literary skill the *Fables* are of the same vintage as the *Maximes*. La Fontaine illustrated by examples the morality which La Rochefoucauld displayed sententiously. ' Our virtues most often are no more than hidden vices.' ' Self-love is the greatest of all flatterers.' ' The mind is always the dupe of the heart.' 'Virtues lose themselves in interest, as the rivers flow into the sea.' ' How shall another keep our secret if we have not kept it ourselves ? ' So wrote the disillusioned aphorist, selecting out of his experience counsels serviceable to the world in which he lived, and the fabulist, familiar with the same world, brought the animals of Æsop and the Reynard-poets out of their ancient ark again and taught them to dance to the same modern moral tunes. The art of each writer recommended his ethic. In *maxime* and *conte* alike they clothed rational thought in classical diction, and among the makers of the *grand siècle Louis quatorze* La Rochefoucauld and La Fontaine take high places.

Thirdly, in this short list, comes the name of Marie de Rabutin-Chantal, who became the MARQUISE DE SÉVIGNÉ. Left an orphan at seven years old and a widow at twenty-five, this vivacious and temperamental woman belonged by taste and upbringing to the little circle of ' precious ' leaders who frequented the Hôtel de Rambouillet and showed the way to the French Academy. She won renown as a letter-writer, and, though she did not invent that kind of literature, practised before her by Erasmus and Petrarch and before them by their common model, Cicero, she added to it out of the resources of the 17th century an appeal which was at once feminine and French. The letters were addressed to her daughter, Françoise, wife of the Comte de Grignan, who held a governorship in Provence, and they were written with teeming regularity between the date of the daughter's marriage in 1668 and the mother's death in 1696. Mme. de Sévigné had learning and imagination : learning enough to hold her own and a little more in the fashionable society of Paris, where she lived at the Hôtel Carnavalet, and imagination enough to enjoy her retreat to Les Rochers at Vitré, or to Vichy, her favourite spa. Perhaps, too, she used her imagination in order to idealize Françoise, for it must have been an ideal daughter, far superior to the average provincial governor's wife, who would appreciate all the wit and wisdom, all the reflective raillery and grace which were poured into these fifteen hundred letters.

Nor can the shortest list of letter-writers omit the name of Françoise *née* d' Aubigné, MARQUISE DE MAINTENON (1635–1719), who twice made an amazing marriage. Her first husband, more than double her age, was the crippled novelist, Paul Scarron, whose death in 1660 reduced her to the poverty from which he had saved her. In 1669 she was appointed governess to the two sons of Louis XIV and Mme de Montespan, and title and estates became her portion. Her gravity, wisdom, and gifts of service did not vary with her change of fortune, and she brought them as her dowry to King Louis, whose legal consort she became in 1685. In the next year she founded a girls' home at St. Cyr, for which Racine, as we shall see, wrote two sacred plays, and to which she retired after the King's death in 1715. She had a genius for teaching and for correspondence, and her letters rank hardly, if at all, lower than those of Mme de Sévigné.

Et Cetera. We might dwell on the sermons of Bishop BOSSUET (1627–1704) and particularly on his *oraisons funèbres* ; on the famous Dictionary (*Dictionnaire Historique et Critique*)

of PIERRE BAYLE (1647–1706), compiled partly to correct a
slightly older work by Louis Moréri and partly in order to
consolidate the results of contemporary speculation ; on the
pedagogic writings of FÉNELON (1651–1715), including his
popular *Telemaque*, which was used so long as a French
reading-book ; on the scientific writings, hardly less popular,
of the SIEUR DE FONTENELLE (1657–1757), who perforce of
his long life makes a bridge between the learning of two
centuries and crossed it successfully on his *Entretiens sur la
Pluralité des Mondes* ; on the *Caractères* of JEAN DE LA
BRUYÈRE (1645–1696), which extended the ' characters ' of
Theophrastus to those of his own age, and on many another.

It was an eloquent time. Each new recruit to the Academy
had to deliver an inaugural speech, and the funeral oration,
as we have indicated, was as inevitable as death. They lived
in the public eye, these men and women, and subdued or
attuned their griefs and joys to a common public standard,
so that in love-song and elegy, in science and philosophy
in epigram and tale, in conversation and letters, one social
note prevailed and a sense of general order was respected.
It was Edmund Waller, the English poet, a visitor to Paris
in the train of his Queen, who wrote to the Earl of Northumberland on the occasion of his lady's death :

> ' To this great loss a sea of tears is due ;
> But the whole debt not to be paid by you . . .
> You that have sacrificed so great a part
> Of youth and private bliss, ought to impart
> Your sorrow too . . .
> Then with Æmilian courage bear this cross,
> Since public persons only public loss
> Ought to affect . . .
> Yet let no portion of your life be stained
> With passion, but your character maintained
> To the last act.'

He exactly expressed French sentiment. The imparted grief,
the public loss, the restrained passion, the *noblesse oblige*, were
all as Cartesian in principle as the verse was Malherbian in
form ; and that it was composed by an English poet in 1637,

185

the year of Milton's lyrical *Lycidas*, makes its choice in this context more significant. We need not multiply names, if the spirit of the French rule has been made clear.

§ 3. 'Le Théâtre Rempli.'

We come next to its triumph on the stage. A few dates will serve as stepping-stones :

1585–1642	Richelieu	1621–95	La Fontaine
1595–1674	Chapelain	1622–73	Molière
1604–86	Mairet	1636–1711	Boileau
1606–84	Corneille	1639–99	Racine

La Fontaine is recalled in the second group for the sake of his intimate friendship with the three younger writers. His *Psyche* of 1669—a kind of *Trilby* of the 17th century—celebrated in the form of a romance the association of the four, by the names (in the above order) of Polyphile, Gelaste, Ariste and Acante. Amid the jealousies inseparable from genius, especially when confined in a small room, this record of a four-part friendship, extending over many years and surviving King Louis's preference of ' Ariste ' to ' Polyphile ' for a vacant place in the Academy in 1684,[1] is memorable and pleasant.

Richelieu's patronage had founded the Academy a few years before his death. Its first secretary, Valentin Conrart (1603–75), was a member of his circle, and, though Conrart wrote nothing except, as was said, his own name, there moved in the shadow of the powerful Cardinal a little crowd of busy writers, whom he employed or who employed themselves in supporting his literary testament. Corneille, as we shall see, broke away ; some of the shadows are forgotten, but Jean Chapelain and Jean de Mairet flitted among them and helped to popularize the principles which Racine practised with perfect ease and of which Boileau was the most distinguished defender.

[1] Louis XIV kept La Fontaine out of the Academy till he had learnt *d'être sage*, but he was admitted at last.

The 'Unities'.   A leading principle was the dramatic law, neatly formulated by Boileau as follows :

> ' Qu'en un lieu, en un jour, un seul fait accompli
> Tienne jusqu'a la fin le théâtre rempli.'

Thus stated, the law is sound enough. It seemed to Richelieu and the critics that a good play should observe three rules : its scene should be limited geographically to a place readily seizable by the audience ; its duration should not exceed the period covered by its presentation ; and its plot or action should be single, not multiple. After all, there was commonsense in these requirements. As was said by François d'Aubignac, another of Richelieu's shadows, the law was a matter of reason rather than of authority ; Mairet laid down its theory in the preface to his *Silvanaire*, 1631, and Chapelain claimed the honour of converting Richelieu to its worship. Meanwhile, mechanically, it was appropriate. The furniture of the chief theatre in Paris was not suited to shifting times and places, and gorgeous rhetoric got across the footlights more plausibly than sudden stage-directions.

But behind the Unities, thus advocated and sanctioned, lay a bondage of antiquity. Whatever the argument for their observance from stage-carpenters and philosophers of *bon sens*, they came inescapably to French playwrights fully clothed with the authority of Aristotle, who laid down in a passage of his *Poetics* the argument for unity of action on the narrow boards of the unfurnished Attic stage. This argument was expanded by Greek students in Italy into a code for budding dramatists, and the first of many pieces of Renaissance criticism which codified the rules and which exalted Virgil of the Romans as the supreme model for modern poets was the Latin *Ars Poetica* of Marco Girolamo Vida (*c.* 1480–1565). ' Immortal Vida ' Pope called him a little rashly, and Pope's friend, the Virgilian Christopher Pitt, rendered Vida's treatise into English. In this version it passed in due course into Chalmers's collection of *British Poets*—an odd fate for an Italian rhetorician who wrote Latin verse in defence of Greek poetics. Meanwhile, Aristotelians and Horatians had kept the ball rolling in Italy. The unity of time was extracted from that of action by the dramatist and novelist, Giambattista Cinthio (1504–73), and Ludovico Castelvetro (1505–71) added the unity of place. Finally, Piero Vettori (1499–1585) of Florence, who was accounted the leading Hellenist of the 16th century, in a critical edition of the *Poetics*, recognized the three Unities as a present law of the art of drama.[1]

Corneille. Just a century later PIERRE CORNEILLE (1606–84) surrendered to the law. Wrung by Richelieu and his shadows from the reluctant playwright, it was in fact a doctrinal victory. After all, every writer is bound by the law of his material or his model. But the law had sat lightly on writers who felt themselves not merely free but even bountiful in enlarging their own vocabulary both extensively and intensively. When innovation was a function of literature and there were no restrictions on free trade in words, it was a temptation to deal in strange locutions, to encourage immigrants from other tongues, to vary stresses and pauses, and to throw down the barriers of the paragraph. It had sat lightly, too, on writers who, confident in the leisure of their readers, had wound out their dialogues and plots to almost interminable length in fashionable tales of ancient heroes in modern guise. These romantic or quasi-romantic vagaries offended a purist generation. Philologers pruning the language for the *Dictionnaire* of the French Academy were at one with the rationalists of the schools. Their common business was to recall Frenchmen to the art of good writing : away from ingenuities and complications, from twisted sentences and twirled rhythms, back to a simplicity of expression, with each word containing one meaning, each meaning contained in one clause, each play representing one action. It was the doctrine on which they insisted, these reformers of language and thought; and if they became *doctrinaire*, in the baser sense of that epithet, at least their intention was sound. Keeping to our context of the law of drama, the regular play would thus seem the better play. Shakespeare, as we know, proved the contrary. He survived both Thomas Rymer at the end of the 17th and Thomas Bowdler at the beginning of the 19th, and, in France herself, as in less orthodox countries,

[1] See Sir John Sandys, *History of Classical Scholarship*, Vol. II, ch. xi.

he served the cause of the revival of Romance. But the Classical theatre between Corneille's *Cid* in 1637 and Hugo's *Hernani* in 1830 effected its necessary purge and achieved triumphs in its own kind.

Corneille founded that theatre almost in his own despite. After spending a few years in Paris in and out of the Hôtel de Rambouillet and in and out of the favour of Cardinal Richelieu, within whose shadow he felt ill at ease, he produced his first comedy, *Mélite*, at Rouen in 1629. He continued to write for the stage till 1652, when the failure of one of his plays discouraged him for some time. He occupied his leisure with translation work, including a French version of the *Imitatio Christi* by Thomas à Kempis,[1] and returned to dramatic composition between 1659 and 1674 with a series of plays on Œdipus, Attila, Otho and other heroes. It was in this last period that he found a rival in possession of the theatre. PHILIPPE QUINAULT (1635–88) was a kind of herald of Racine, and marked the transition of French tragedy from the incomplete classicism of Corneille to its satisfaction by the genius of the coming master. That transition softened the outline of Corneille's grander and more rugged style by a tenderness which Corneille himself diagnosed as ' a commerce of sighs and flames '. If we may compare Corneille with Marlowe (they had, indeed, much in common), and if we remember that, while Shakespeare and Milton followed Marlowe, Racine and Boileau followed Corneille, we shall apprehend more clearly the nature of the outside pressure which derived a classical theatre from a romantic-minded playwright. That outside pressure included some incidental personal factors : Richelieu's resentment at Corneille's independence, its exploitation by Chapelain and the rest, Corneille's comparative poverty, his jealousy of Quinault, and so forth. But more than all these—behind them, above them, and all round them in the *salons* of Paris—was a growing sense of the psychology of society, of storms of passion moderated by reason, of time and place and circumstances imposing their natural restraints and elevating the conditions of the theatre into a law of social propriety.

[1] See page 48 above.

The essential Cornelian note was struck in his middle period, between 1635 and 1644. This included the tragic plays *Medea*, *Cid*, *Horace*, *Cinna*, *Polyeucte*, *The Death of Pompey*, *Rodogune*, and, among his greater comedies, the *Menteur* of 1642. With the production of the *Cid* in 1636–37 his claim to primacy had to be reckoned with. It was the time of the foundation of the Academy and of the publication of the *Méthode* of Descartes. Did the claimant to leadership on the stage conform with the views of those leaders ? This question could not be put by. It was a matter of doctrine, as we have said, and, in dictating the answer, the Unities were made the test of conformity. Chapelain had proved them to be founded on the same basis of reason as the Cartesian universe, and, discovering that the *Cid* fell short of the full unity of place, he devised a contractual formula which Richelieu at last approved and which the Academy presented to the harassed dramatist. Corneille accepted it at the pen's point : he became an Academician in due course, and his next play was dedicated to the Cardinal.

Such, briefly, was the quarrel of the *Cid*. At longer range we note that the play was founded on and partly translated from the *Mocedades* ('youthful adventures') *del Cid* of Guillen de Castro y Bellvis (1569–1631), a Spanish dramatist in the Lope[1] school, which had been produced at Madrid in 1618. There the hero of the old Spanish chronicle had been raised to the height of power and passion on which Corneille, like Marlowe, chose to keep his tragic characters ; and the conflict between will and fate, which was at once the strength and weakness of Corneille's genius, with something of the rhetoric accompanying it, was likewise added by Castro to the simpler tale of chivalric adventure which he had derived from national legend. Noting, too, that Corneille's *Menteur* was founded on the 'Suspect Truth' (*Verdad sospechosa*) of the Spaniard, Juan Ruiz de Alarcon (1580–1639), we observe how big was the debt which the French theatre that conquered Europe in the 17th century owed to the brilliant lead of playwrights across the Pyrenees.

It is finally on this plane, and not in the academic atmosphere

[1] See page 146 above.

in which the fetters of the Unities were forged, that Corneille holds his secure place in European literature. In the eight or ten great plays of his middle period, he went chiefly to Spain for his models and to Seneca for his dramatic method. He cared more for the great winds of power which blow on the heights of experience than for the ' natural ' relations which may make a tragedy of human life. The Cornelian hero or heroine, involved in a fateful ordeal, spoke like a philosopher in action. The grandeur of abstract thought was so well matched with the horror of suffering that speech acquired granite lines, and the invincible ego, met by implacable destiny, was overwhelmed but not defeated. ' Dans un si grand revers que vous reste-t-il ? ' Medea was asked, when she had been stript of every possession except fury. The key-note was the *si grand*, and, like thunder crashing across the stage and terrifying the audience with its immensity, came her supreme self-assertion : ' Moi, dis-je, et c'est assez ! ' This cry of an ' unconquerable soul ', the Cornelian *Moi*, as it is called, was sustained throughout his masterpieces, and it was not till inspiration failed, and popular taste was converted to the sentimental appeal of Quinault, that Corneille's eloquence left the audience cold and his grandeur became almost intolerably inhuman. The last great son of the Senecan tradition, Corneille typified its passing in his own record.

Racine. We turn at once to JEAN RACINE (1639–99), who grew up when the Academy was in being, and who moved freely within the confines set by Boileau to art.

To these we shall come. Here we may observe two factors of the Racinian stage and one effect. The factors are Jansenism and Hellenism, the effect is feminism. Taking the last first, at least in a summary way, we may note that Corneille's chief tragedies, as enumerated above, deal with the Cid, Horace, Cinna, Pompey and other heroes, while Racine's chief tragedies bear heroines' names : Andromache, Berenice, Iphigenia, Phædra. There are exceptions on both sides but the observation generally is correct : to play the title-rôle in *Phèdre* has been as much an actor's ambition as to play Hamlet or the Cid. The star-part is feminine, and ' the empire of women in literature ', an eminent French critic has declared, ' dates from

Racine '.[1] Their heroic names did not disbar their women's hearts.

Bishop Jansen's schools have been mentioned above. Racine, orphaned at an early age, was sent first to school at Beauvais, where his independence was expressed in a choice of solitude and a certain aloofness which clung to him throughout his life. But at sixteen he entered Port Royal and found a congenial atmosphere. Pierre Nicole, one of its most eminent teachers, helped to develop the tastes and character of the seclusive and beauty-loving youth, and it is recorded that the gardens and the trees brought him delicate refreshment. To Port Royal he returned when, after 1677, Court cabals and a wounded self-esteem combined with his increasing pietism to prompt his retirement from the theatre. In 1689 and 1691 he wrote *Esther* and *Athalie* for Mme de Maintenon's pupils at St. Cyr, surely a fairy-tale episode in the lives of a playwright and a queen. For he had found the 'grace' of the Port Royalists, whose history he wrote and within the precincts of whose cloisters he was buried in 1699.

Racine's Hellenism is partly to be discovered in the titles of his plays, the *Thébaïde*, produced by Molière in 1604; the *Grand Alexandre*, 1665; *Andromache*, 1667, which has been called his *Romeo and Juliet*, and which achieved a like triumph to the *Cid's*; *Mithridate*, *Iphigénie* and *Phèdre*, which closed the series in 1677. *Britannicus*, *Bérénice* and *Bajazet* belong to the same group, and Racine's election to the Academy occurred in 1673. But the Hellenism was more than a choice of topics. He put Greek plays on the French stage in the sense that he relied on character-study for his contact with his audience. Their eyes and ears were so fully occupied with the action on the stage that their attention was undistracted by any interest beyond it or behind it. Thus, he observed the Unities like Sophocles, not like Mairet, leaving them to observe themselves. Take the tragedy of *Phèdre*, for example : the plot is luminously simple. Phædra loved Hippolytus, her stepson, and Theseus, her husband, came home from his rumoured grave. Racine sought no relief from these conditions of jealousy and crime. He brought no ghosts on the stage, no

[1] Lanson, *Histoire de la Littérature française*, page 546.

witches, no rustic grave-diggers. His theme was the hearts of men and women, and by the mobility and variations of this theme he satisfied the abstract rights and the practical requirements of the dramatic art. 'Le comble des horreurs,' declared Phædra, was contained in one word : ' J'aime ! ' (not *Moi*, the person, but *aimer*, what she felt), and in his display of insulated emotions Racine effected works of art as pure as the long history of the stage has to show. Better than Seneca's devices or the improvisations of Romance, they suited the Court of Louis XIV and the taste of his literary arbiter, Boileau. Men and women—or women and men— were talking about themselves all day long, summarizing their motives into maxims, illustrating their acts by fables, analysing their opinions in letters, novelizing their letters into books. Outside themselves was ' external ' nature, where reason did not rule. So the realm of reason was selected as the sufficient horizon for the *bon sens des honnêtes gens*, and ' " whoso does not feel the beauty and force of this unity, of this order, has not yet seen broad daylight, but only the shadows in the cave of Plato." There speaks the whole or the best of French Classicism ; and there is its eternal message to the art of literature.'[1] It is perfect within its limits and in its kind.

Molière. Lastly, in this account of *le théâtre rempli*, we reach the writer who filled it most successfully and whose comedies still appeal to the eternal spirit of humankind. Take the commonest empiric test, applicable to Molière as to Shakespeare : he is full of well-worn quotations. His caps always fit, because he fashioned them for Everyman, the first and last of all *dramatis personæ*. 'Nous avons changé tout cela ' ; ' Tu l'as voulu, Georges Dandin ' ; Jourdain talking prose without knowing it : we need not multiply instances of his expression of the comedy of life. ' If Life is likened to the comedy of Molière,' says George Meredith, ' there is no scandal in the comparison ' ; and in the same *Essay on Comedy* he writes :

' Politically it is accounted a misfortune for France that her nobles thronged to the Court of Louis Quatorze. It was a

[1] Oliver Elton, *The Augustan Ages*, Edinburgh, 1899 ; pp. 153-4. The quotation within the quotation is from Fénélon.

boon to the comic poet. He had that lively quicksilver world of the animalcule passions, the huge pretensions, the placid absurdities, under his eyes in full activity ; vociferous quacks and snapping dupes, hypocrites, posturers, extravagants, pedants, rose-pink ladies and mad grammarians, sonneteering marquises, high-flying mistresses, plain-minded maids, inter-threading as in a loom, noisy as at a fair.'

In a short history of European literature this should be enough about Molière. Biography is aware that his real name was JEAN BAPTISTE POQUELIN (1622–73) ; that he was an upholsterer's son ; that, like Shakespeare, he was a strolling player, mixed up with a family called Béjart, a young member of which he married in 1662, not without some scandal still not resolved ; that he enjoyed the favour of Louis XIV, who installed him as manager of the Royal Theatre, though, as a professional actor, he could neither become a member of the Academy nor sit at the King's table ; and that he wrote a large number of plays, including ballets and masques, among which the best known titles are *Les Précieuses Ridicules*, 1659, *Sganarelle*, 1660, *L'École des Maris*, 1661, *L'École des Femmes*, 1662, *Tartuffe*, 1664, *Don Juan*, 1665, *Le Misanthrope*, 1666, *Le Médecin malgré lui*, 1666, *Georges Dandin*, 1668, *L'Avare*, 1668, *Le Bourgeois Gentilhomme*, 1670, *Les Femmes Savantes*, 1672, and *Le Malade Imaginaire*, 1673. We are aware, too, that, despite royal protection, Boileau's approval, and many loyal friends, Molière, as he called himself after 1644, was pursued by obloquy of various kinds apart from the damaging Béjart gossip. Some of them said he could not write, because his characters spoke the language of their class : we remember how Sir Philip Sidney ' dare not allow ' Spenser to frame his style ' to an old rustic language, since neither Theocritus in Greek, Virgil in Latin, nor Sanazar in Italian, did affect it '.[1] Others loaded him with the vices of his personages, deeming him indecent, impious, incestuous ; they even sought to refuse him Christian burial, though they could not stir one leaf of his bay. To all this his works are the reply ; his sole object was to please, and to keep *le théâtre rempli*.

[1] See page 120 above.

Omitting these foolish things, not worthy of one of his own comedies, the historian may illustrate Molière's greatness by a comparison with what came after. His chief plays were written, we observe, between 1659 and 1673. In 1726, Swift wrote *Gulliver's Travels,* and there is a passage in that book which shows how the comic spirit of Molière had hardened into bitter satire during the intervening fifty years. In the country of the Houyhnhnms, says Captain Lemuel Gulliver,

' was neither Physician to destroy my body, nor Lawyer to ruin my Fortune ; . . . no encouragers to Vice , by Seducement or Examples ; no Pride, Vanity, or Affectation ; no Fops, Bullies, Drunkards ; . . . no ranting, lewd, expensive Wives ; no stupid proud Pedants ; . . . no Scoundrels, raised from the Dust for the sake of their Vices, or Nobility thrown into it on account of their Virtues ; no Lords, Fiddlers, Judges, or Dancing Masters.'

No Court of Louis Quatorze, in a word. Man was stript by Swift, flake by flake, of the artificial coverings of civilization, which Molière had held up to laughter. All the company of his comedies was expropriated, all their conduct was beneath the contempt of the honest beasts in their stables. ' He seemed therefore confident,' relates Gulliver, ' that, instead of Reason ' —governing the Cartesian universe—' we were only possessed of some quality fitted to increase our natural vices.'

We shall come in due course to the acrid Dean. Here we anticipate our narrative in order to set in relief how brilliantly and how leniently withal Molière arrested the passing spectacle and used it for everlasting delight. Ranting wives were sent to an ' École des Femmes.' False physicians met a ' Malade Imaginaire '. ' Femmes Savantes ' and ' Précieuses Ridicules ' rebuked pedantry and affectation. Tartuffe and Don Juan discouraged vice ; and so on through the rest of the gay and splendid comedy which Meredith likened to life. For truly it is an infinitely greater thing to let men and women speak for themselves, in their humours and habits as they are, and yet not to fail to measure their final value, than, by blackening the shadows, to put out the lights of contemplation. ' Gelaste ', as La Fontaine called him, the Greek name for the laughing man, took what he wanted where he found it, from Plaûtus, Terence, the playwrights of Spain, or the plays of lesser Frenchmen before him, who are known only by his levy on them, but he made unique dramas out of common themes within the bounds of the French classical theatre. Hypocrisy, infidelity, misanthropy, avarice, pedantry, pretence : everyone condemns them when he sees them, whether sincerely or conventionally. But not everyone recognizes them clearly in the society in which he moves and by which he lives ; fewer still have the courage to impale them and call them by their proper names ; and rarest of all is the genius of a Shakespeare, a Dickens, or a Molière, to dissipate their evil in laughter. Finally, in joining the names of the inventors of Falstaff, Pecksniff and Tartuffe, it is, perhaps, not irrelevant to remark in how short a span their life-work was done : Shakespeare was fifty-two, Dickens fifty-eight, and Molière fifty-one when he died.[1]

Intersection II.

Between our account of the French rule at home and the reaction to it in other countries, brief mention is due to the critics and philosophers who directed the mind of the 17th century, and to the diarists who reflected it. In a longer history of literature they would be included in the main narrative. A short history must practise economy, and readers may be referred accordingly to the histories of philosophy by specialist writers such as F. D. Maurice and Robert Adamson, and to the *History of Criticism* by George Saintsbury (3 Vols. : Edinburgh, 1900).

[1] We add here a brief comparative estimate from the pen of the late Catulle Mendès, a Romanticist of Victor Hugo's school :

' Le poète Pierre Corneille fut plus grand que Racine, bien que Racine ait eu de charme et d'intimité poignante ; fut plus grand que Molière, bien que Molière en ses œuvres vastes et généreuses ait parlé une langue si extraordinairement adéquate au vouloir de sa pensée ; mais Corneille, lyrique et épique, écrivit pour le théâtre, tandis que Racine, tragique, et Molière, comique, furent le théâtre même ; et il n'y eut, ou XVIIᵉ siècle, ni ode ni épopée '.

Corneille, that is, was the greatest poet of the three, but was compelled to write for the stage in an epoch empty of lyric and epic poetry. Racine and Molière were born playwrights.

Even so, some crossings occur. Political philosophy, for example, is inseparable from the history of literature as made by Dante and his successors, and, formerly, by his Roman master, Virgil. The literature of Utopia is philosophic, derived from Plato and Lucian, and we have noted in the present Book how the Cartesian doctrine of the Knowable (or the Worth-knowing) fitted in with the search of the French intellect for compact and seizable shapes of being, Milton wrote, we may recall, in 1644, of a ' concurrence of signs ' pointing to big changes in thought. With those signs the quick reader will associate the foundation of the French Academy in 1637, the English visit of Comenius, the Czech educational reformer, in 1641-42, and the first stirrings among the leaves which led not long after to the incorporation of the Royal Society in 1662, ' bringing all things as near the Mathematical plainness as they can ',[1] and to the genius, dominantly mathematical, of PIERRE GASSENDI (born 1592), PASCAL (born 1623), SPINOZA and LOCKE (born 1632), NEWTON (born 1642) and LEIBNIZ (born 1646) : the last four a towering quartette. The influence of mathematical speculation on moral and metaphysical philosophy is reflected in the writings of NICOLAS MALEBRANCHE (born 1638), who investigated *la Recherche de la Vérité*, of PIERRE BAYLE (born 1647), the lexicographer of knowledge, and, in the next generation, of the third EARL OF SHAFTESBURY (born 1671), GEORGE BERKELEY, Bishop of Cloyne (born 1685), and ALEXANDER POPE (born 1688), whose name brings us back to literary history.

Mr. G. N. Clark's admirable monograph on *The Seventeenth Century* (Oxford, 1929) contains a chapter on its philosophy, and, if we may condense that short survey, we would point out that medieval thought and the conclusions of its School-men were necessarily superannuated by the movements proceeding from the Renaissance. Certain values in Scholas-ticism have proved permanent, but it relied too securely on an ' authority external to philosophy ', and ' there was always a point where reasoning must stop and submit to dogma '.

---

[1] From the *History* (1667) *of the Royal Society* by Bishop Thomas Sprat, an original F.R.S.

O

Literary history confirms this statement: Rabelais, the physician, for example, had to circumvent that danger-point by taking recourse to rhapsody or rodomontade; Spinoza, the gentlest of pious men, who supplied his frugal needs by making lenses, was attacked as an atheist by Christians and Jews alike; and the fate of Galileo, who died in 1642, the year of Newton's birth, shows again how the natural sciences, shyly emerging into self-expression, were repulsed by 'prevailing opinions about ultimate problems.'

'Nous avons changé tout cela.' Forward minds in the 17th century might have quoted these words from their leading humorist, as they took advantage of the conditions of their own times:

'The Humanists had derided the Scholastic studies; the Protestants had flouted the authority of the Church; the new rationalists like Montaigne had turned aside from the hope of certainties and declared themselves for scepticism, suspense of judgement, doubt.[1] Above all, there was the new activity in mathematics. A fresh start in philosophy had to be made, and it was made to such purpose that from this time the history of philosophy can be understood with very little knowledge of what went before.'

Then Descartes came, who 'hoped to unlock all the secrets of nature by keys like that of mathematics', and, after Descartes, John Locke, for whom, as was said in *The Times Literary Supplement* on the tercentenary of his birth in August, 1932, 'mathematics was something more "sure" than physics', and who, in Voltaire's eager eulogy, 'discovered the human reason to man, just as an excellent anatomist explains the springs of the body.'

It would be interesting to comment on these epithets. Voltaire—we shall come to him in due course—died in 1778,

[1] Darwinism in the 19th century led to a suspense of judgment similar to that which marked Cartesianism in the 17th. So, Tennyson in *In Memoriam*:

'There lives more faith in honest doubt,
Believe me, than in half the creeds,'

and George Meredith in *Modern Love*:

'Ah! What a dusty answer gets the soul,
When hot for certainties in this our life.'

eleven years before the French Revolution, for which in his
life and work he had struck doughty blows. His multifarious
writings, his intercourse with great men, his retirement from
them to a seat of superior greatness, made him at once a
present leader and a prophet; and Paris, it has been said, had
to be Voltairean before it could be revolutionary.[1] Assuming
now these conclusions, which will be substantiated in their
proper place, we would recall here from Book II another
' excellent anatomist ', Machiavelli. He anatomized his ruler,
it will be remembered, explaining the springs of his body
politic, and showing how the levers should be pulled so as to
produce a semblance of might. Infinite dole was imputed to
Il Principe : the massacre of the Huguenots, for example,
on St. Bartholomew's Day, 1572, and other grave consequences of the doctrine that absolute might is absolute right.
Part of the evil is written-off to-day : Machiavelli's analysis
of absolutism did as much to unmake it as to make it. But
Acton's warning is still valid ; the illustrious Florentine
philosopher exposed forces not yet extinct : ' religion,
progressive enlightenment, the perpetual vigilance of public
opinion, have not reduced his empire, or disputed the justice
of his conception of mankind.' As with Machiavelli, so with
Locke. Both were scholars busy with statecraft ; both lived
in distracting times, the one in Florence with the fallen
Medici, the other in England of the Commonwealth and
Revolution; and to Locke as to Machiavelli have been
ascribed positive results of his teaching which the teacher
himself could never have foreseen. Thus, recalling from the
eve of the French Revolution Voltaire's testimony to Locke
as the discoverer of ' the human reason to man ', we observe
that during twenty days in 1793 more than two thousand
churches in Paris were converted into 'Temples of Reason';
and there are those who would associate with the same
discovery by Locke, Spinoza and their peers in the 17th
century, the temples of Marx in Moscow to-day. Truly might
General Smuts say, in his Presidential Address at the British
Association in 1931 : ' One of the gravest tasks before the

---

[1] We quote Mendès again : ' Que la Lumière soit ! et Voltaire fut, Cette
lumière-là, c'est la Raison . . . et naquit le monde moderne.'

human race will be to link up science with ethical values';
and Sir Alfred Ewing, from the same chair in the following
year: 'In the slow evolution of morals man is still unfit for
the tremendous responsibility' entailed by the progress of
discovery.

We pass these controversial aspects. By his *Essay concerning Toleration*, 1667, his *Essay concerning Human Understanding*, 1690, his Treatise *On Education*, 1693, and other
writings, John Locke, of Wrington, in Somerset, who was
educated at Westminster and Christ Church, Oxford, and who
retired in 1691 from travel and practice as a physician to a
quiet home at Oates, in Essex, immensely enhanced modern
style in English prose and takes high rank as a maker of the
modern mind:

'The headlines of Locke's bequest to the 18th century
are indicated by the words Individualism, Reason, Utility,
Toleration, Property: all of which words might be summed
up in the first of them. No wonder that the century witnessed
in England the rise of a gospel of self-interest which made
the wealth of a nation consist in setting the individual free;
and in France that titanic evolution of the pent-up forces of
the individual which made the French Revolution so epoch-
making.'

So wrote a former Master of Balliol[1], and, conjoining
Locke with Machiavelli before him and with Spinoza, his
exact contemporary, we see what passions intrude upon the
literary evaluation of philosophy—even when it starts from
the sure foothold of mathematics.

A paragraph is due to Nicolas Boileau (1636–1711),
known, too, by the surname of Despréaux, whose influence
on the writers of the *grand siècle* has been mentioned up and
down the foregoing pages. Criticism is less vital than
philosophy, and numberless treatises in verse and prose
bearing a variant of the title of *Ars Poetica* and tracing their
way back to Roman Horace in the 1st century B.C. have little
more than historical value. The name of Vida occurred in
the last Section: Horace furnished his armoury; Boileau

---

[1] A. L. Smith, in *Cambridge Modern History*, Vol. VI, p. 815.

polished his shafts; Pope crowned him with immortality; Pitt and Chalmers made him a British poet. He is the shadow of a dead name to-day. So Keats, railing at Boileau, may be comforted. The poet died at twenty-five, the critic at seventy-five years of age. In a third of the time the former won more than a hundred times the renown. Still, Boileau dominated the French scene and laid down the law of applied Classicism. He interpreted for the writers' craft the prevailing tendencies of the age towards purism, directness, simplicity. A better Latinist than Hellenist, and a better Parisian than either, he lifted from Italian critics certain canons of taste which were founded on Aristotle and Horace. He severely deprecated curiosity about the world outside the Greek ambit. The ' ancients ' had reflected in their writings all that was proper to see in ' nature '. The rest was supernatural, external, requiring an *enjambement* of the mind unsuited to reasonable men. ' Rien n'est beau que le vrai ', he wrote, and the pagan Classics had invested truth with the utmost attainable forms of beauty; nature unmethodized, nature in the rough, need not be explored over again; it was a time to take stock, as the mathematicians were aware, and to set in order the littered slopes of Parnassus.

No one can deny the value of Boileau's services to his Court and his times, and, beyond them, to other literatures. But he was better at censure than at praise, which is no recommendation for a critic, and ' the good that he did,' Saintsbury tells us,[1] ' is terribly chequered by the consideration that, in sharpening certain edges of the French mind, he blunted and distorted others in a fashion which, after two hundred years, has not been fully remedied '. Leaving for the moment the fuller meaning of the further remark that ' Boileau did not, like Dryden, leave escapes and safety-valves to the spirit that was too mighty for the narrower channels of poetic style ', we may conclude with the historian's final estimate :

' A great man of letters, perhaps ; a craftsmanlike " finisher of the law ", and no ill pedagogue, in literature certainly : but a great critic ? Scarcely, I think.'

[1] *Op. cit.*, Vol. II, page 300.

Lastly, in this Intersection, which forms a kind of annexe to the house of pure letters, we would refer to the diarists and memoirists. France and England were alike very fortunate in writers of this class, and four names call particularly for mention :

GILES MÉNAGE, 1613–92. | SAMUEL PEPYS, 1632–1703.
JOHN EVELYN, 1620–1706. | DUC DE SAINT-SIMON,
                                                 1675–1755.

Ménage, a Latinist, an *Académicien*, a frequenter of the Hôtel de Rambouillet and a member of the ' Precious ' set in Paris, wrote frankly for publication. His *Menagiana* in four volumes possess valuable anecdotal interest, and he is said to have been the model for Vadius, in Molière's *Femmes Savantes*, Act III, Scene v, who, after a laughable encounter of rival wits, declares :

' Je te défie en vers, prose, grec et latin '.

Evelyn was one of the group with Queen Henrietta Maria in Paris. He was a founder of, and a secretary to, the Royal Society, and a noted collector and *virtuoso*. He kept his diary till within three weeks of his death, and it was published in 1818.

Larger in scope and more fascinating in manner is the ten years' intimate record of daily doings and happenings kept between 1659–69 by Mr. Pepys of the Admiralty. Like George Meredith, he was a tailor's son ; he was educated at St. Paul's School, like John Milton, and took his degree at Cambridge, where, in the library of Magdalene College, he deposited the MS. of his *Diary*, which was written in a code of his own invention. Parts of it were deciphered in 1825, and an enlarged edition was issued in 1875–79 by Mynors Bright, then President of the College. The whole series, except for a few passages wholly unfit for publication, appeared in 1893 under the editorship of H. B. Wheatley. A little book by a Frenchman, M. Lucas-Dubreton (translated by H. J. Stenning ; Philpot, 1925), throws some unflattering lights on Pepys, the man, and, indeed, though indulgent to his foibles, he does not flatter himself. But his *Diary* is a unique document, of perennial human interest, and of wide historical and social importance.

Likewise hidden from the public for more than a century were the *Mémoires* (21 vols., *ed. pr.*, 1829–30) of Louis de Rouvroy, duc de Saint-Simon, a descendant of Charlemagne and very self-consciously a ' peer of France ' (*pair de France*). A certain Marquis de Dangeau (1638–1720) had written Court annals of his time, which Saint-Simon read and annotated in a spirit of lofty disgust at the lacquey's mind of the pensioner of Louis XIV. For the duke had no use for a king who opened his palace to all the talents. A feudal aristocrat by breeding and taste, he regarded Louis XIII as ' the King of gentlemen ', and his disdain of modern times was almost equal to that of the Honourable Mrs. Skewton, who, it may be remembered, in *Dombey and Son*, worshipped

' Those darling bygone times, with their delicious fortresses, and their dear old dungeons, and their delightful places of torture, and their romantic vengeances, and their picturesque assaults and sieges, and everything that makes life truly charming ! '

With her Saint-Simon would have said, ' How dreadfully we have degenerated ! ', and he marked his sense of propriety by scrupulously referring to Voltaire, then at the height of his renown, as ' the son of a notary whom my father and I have employed '. But he wrote splendid, almost romantic prose, and his notes to Dangeau were expanded by him into a graphic account of the *grand siècle* as he saw it from above—even above the *grand monarque* in his glory. Some of the more important characters he drew two or three times over, thus immensely enhancing our knowledge of them, and he was particularly successful in deploying crowds across the stage. Thus, he re-opened Versailles in the 19th century.

II. AND BEYOND

§ 1. FRANCE AND ENGLAND.

To and fro, to and fro went the shuttle, weaving the threads of French taste into the fabric of English literature. The translators were busy all the time; the group of Englishmen in Paris with Queen Henrietta Maria during the period of the Civil War—John Evelyn, Abraham Cowley, Edmund Waller, Sir William D'Avenant, Sir John Denham—brought home their harvest about 1650; and, conversely, Charles de Saint-Évremond, letter-writer, critic, Parnassian, whose ninety years (1613–1703) covered the century, made his home in England from 1661–65 and again from 1670 till his death, when he was buried in Westminster Abbey. JOHN DRYDEN too, covered most of the century (1631–1700), and, though he left 'escapes and safety-valves' for the free British hate of fetters, he was so deeply submissive to French influence that he recognised Waller and Denham as models and reformers of English speech, and built much in criticism and drama on Chapelain, Boileau and Corneille.   A potent force in the English theatre of the Restoration was Molière, and 'even where the debt may not be specifically ascertainable', we are told (and passage after passage can be itemized), 'the tone of the play, the method of its conduct, and the conception of its personages declare the dominant influence of France.'[1]

England Unconquered. We can see this influence in the making. We see it in what Dryden *said* of Waller, that he 'first made writing easily an art', and we see it in what Waller *wrote* on the occasion of the death of the Lady Northumberland in the verses quoted on page 185 above. There we remarked on the contrast between his elegiac muse and that of Milton (*Lycidas*) in the same year (1637). Milton did not write prose according to the pattern of the Royal Society ('as near the Mathematical plainness as might be'), nor verse according to the specification which Waller and Denham had brought back

[1] *The Cambridge History of English Literature*, Vol. VIII, p. 134.

from France (' Strong without rage, without o'erflowing full ').
The style of his *Areopagitica* and *Paradise Lost* and of Bunyan's
Pilgrim's Progress was never that of Dr. John Wallis (1616–
1703), the mathematician, or of Sir William Petty (1623–87),
the political economist; nor did Denham's *Cooper's Hill* finally
supersede the *Authorised Version* of 1611 as the standard of
English diction. For awhile, like the Blue and the White
Niles, the two styles flowed through English meadows in
parallel streams ; then the Classical predominated ; presently
the Romantic will re-emerge.

For the debt, England's debt to France, the French influence
on Waller, Denham and company, will be amply repaid.
Alexander Pope, in a poetic *Epistle* to King George II,
declared in 1733 :

> ' We conquer'd France, but felt our captive's charms ;
>   Her arts victorious triumph'd o'er our arms.'

But Dryden, sixty or seventy years earlier, who, after all, had
lived through the invasion of French arts, was by no means
so certain of their victory.

> ' I am of opinion,' he said in one place, ' that neither our
> faults nor their (the French) virtues are considerable enough
> to place them above us.'

And at another time he wrote :

> ' For my part I desire to be tried by the laws of my own
> country ; for it seems unjust to me that the French should
> prescribe here till they have conquered.'

And yet again he objected to the corruption of

> ' our English idiom by mixing it too much with French : that
> is a sophistication of language, not an improvement of it ;
> a turning of English into French, rather than a refinement of
> English by French.'

These temperate utterances reassure us us that the French
rule will not dominate England in the sense of putting out
the lights of Chaucer, Shakespeare and Milton. Pope might
write in the same passage :

> ' Late, very late, correctness grew our care,'

205

as if ' correctness ', like Boileau's ' Malherbe ', was the advent
to which all the nation aspired. He might exalt for our
imitation and delectation

> ' Exact Racine and Corneille's noble fire,'

and, while allowing a ' tragic spirit ' to Shakespeare, he might
regret that

> ' fluent Shakespeare scarce effaced a line.'

But Dryden had anticipated these criticisms. In the very
century and epoch of French Classicism, he had plumped for
moderation in its use, and for a frank enjoyment of ' God's
plenty ' in the older literature of England. ' Many beauties of
the stage,' he declared, had been banished by too much rigour
about the Unities, and

' what is more easy,' he asked, ' than to write a regular French
play, or more difficult than to write an irregular English one,
like those of Fletcher or of Shakespeare ? '

The French purge recommended by Dryden did not involve
a Racinian immersion.

The Hundred Years' Alliance. Historically, therefore, and
particularly in a short history, it is probably truer, as it is
certainly more convenient, to treat France and England as one
country in respect to their literary activity between the middle
of the 17th and 18th centuries. Exact segments into centuries
are not obtainable. It would be pleasant to select the dates :

> 1674, Death of Milton.
>
> 1778, Death of Rousseau and Voltaire,

and to say that, between them, this *entente littéraire* subsisted.
But men die without respect to historians, and the most that
we can aver is that, roughly, there were about a hundred
years, between the execution of Charles I. in 1649 and the
execution of Louis XVI in 1793, during which there was
formed a solid block of Franco-British or Anglo-French
literary achievement. We mention those regal events because
the Civil War in England gave our exiles in Paris their
opportunity of acquiring French taste (it was ' When the
tired nation breathed from civil war ', according to Pope,

that 'correctness grew our care'), and because the French Revolution led through Trafalgar and Waterloo to a revulsion from French example. The *entente littéraire* broke in pieces during the Napoleonic Wars, and Nelson's legacy of hate infected even the pure muse of Tennyson till late in the 19th century[1].

Let us get this clear at the outset. We are reminded on competent authority that

'No great stir had been created at the first appearance of Revolutionary France on the European stage. Observers on this side of the Channel had looked the new actor up and down and concluded that he was not unlike themselves—almost an Englishman, a very old-fashioned Englishman, about a century behind the times'

(an Englishman, that is to say, of the Revolution of 1688, when the literary *entente* was in full force). But

'presently those seemly garments of the orthodox cut fell off, and a new and utterly un-English figure was disclosed, gaunt, ferocious, in rags and a red cap, with bared teeth and a dripping knife.'[2]

Or, in the contemporary evidence of Wordsworth:

'The goaded land waxed mad . . .
Frenchmen had changed a war of self-defence
For one of conquest, losing sight of all
Which they had struggled for;'

losing sight of all which had caused the young poet to exclaim concerning the hopes held out in 1789:

'Bliss was it in that dawn to be alive,
But to be young was very Heaven!'

---

[1] This statement must be accepted without detailed proof. Speaking to Daly in 1891 about the song, 'There is no land like England,' in *The Foresters*, Tennyson said: 'I wrote that song when I was nineteen. It has a beastly chorus against the French, and I must alter that if you will have it.' Stopford Brooke, in his *Tennyson* (London, 1894) writes: 'Tennyson became, with a conscious reversion to the type of the Englishmen of Nelson's time, the national opponent, even the mocker of France and the French character.' George Meredith's noble *Odes in Contribution to the Song of French History*, inscribed to John Morley, were eloquent but unpopular on the other side.

[2] *Wilberforce*: *A Narrative*, by R. Coupland, Oxford, 1923; p. 150.

In other words, the hundred years' alliance, which began about the middle of the 17th century, with Saint-Evremond as a kind of liaison-officer, and the terms of which Dryden modified to suit English theory and practice, might have been continued beyond the end of the 18th if the course of the Revolution in France had not diverted the aims of its precursors. Good men of the class of William Wilberforce,[1] including George Crabbe (1754–1832), a most respectable poet, and Dr. Richard Price (1723–91), a Nonconformist divine, had actually been celebrating the centenary of 1688—one revolution on the eve of another—when Burke's *Reflections on the Revolution in France* fell like a bolt from the blue. His disclosure of that 'un-English figure' interrupted the progress of Reform and determined, among other precious things, the prevailing literary co-operation. It is true that Dr. Johnson had joined in equal reprobation both Rousseau and Voltaire, but it is not less true that for a century before their death in 1778 French and English writers and thinkers had pursued like aims in a common style. They gave and took in varying proportions. Neither can justly claim a victory over the other. But severally or jointly at different times their influence was supreme in Europe, and the Augustan age in England in the 18th century was the heir of the *grand siècle Louis Quatorze*, which closed with the King's death in 1715, following that of Boileau in 1711, of Racine in 1699, of Bossuet in 1704, and, let us add, of John Dryden in 1700, John Locke in 1704, and of Baruch (Benedict) Spinoza, the Dutch Jew, their contemporary, who was only fifty-five when he died in 1677.

Dryden. The greatness of Dryden, then, resides alike in resistance and attainment. He was convinced that what Waller and Denham had learned in the *salons* and *Académie* of Paris was rich with good counsel for English letters. But he was not less convinced that imitation should be checked

---

[1] There is an interesting reference to Wilberforce's campaign against the slave-trade in Wordsworth, *Prelude*, Book X. The poet was not much depressed by its failure, since he believed that, 'if France prospered' (in her revolutionary propaganda),

'This most rotten branch of human shame
Would fall together with the parent tree.'

by knowledge-values acquired on our native soil, ' the genius of our countrymen in general,' as he wrote in one of his famous prefaces, ' being rather to improve an invention than to invent themselves.' So his own originality ' was essentially originality of treatment ' [1]; by his saving power he ' determined the bent of a great literature at a great crisis ',[2] and he will not be refused to-day the high praise bestowed on him by Dr. Johnson :

' To him we owe the improvement, perhaps the completion of our metre, the refinement of our language, and much of the correctness of our sentiments. By him we were taught *sapere et fari*, to think naturally and express forcibly. He showed us the true bounds of a translator's liberty. What was said of Rome, adorned by Augustus, may be applied by an easy metaphor to English poetry embellished by Dryden— he found it brick, and he left it marble.'

Johnson's reference to Augustus is prophetic. Dryden ushered in the Augustan Age, and, welcoming the restoration of Charles II in his poem *Astræa Redux*, he evoked expressly the

> ' Happy age ! Oh, times like those alone
> By fate reserved for great Augustus' throne !
> When the joint growth of arms and arts foreshow
> The world a monarch, and that monarch you.'

True, he had sung the obsequies of Cromwell as tunefully as he greeted the Stuart's return. He succumbed to, though he repented, the temptation of writing loose comedies for fashionable audiences, relaxing the comic muse of Molière to the taste of the Restoration stage, soon to be filled with the plays, which do not call here for further notice, of Sir George Etherege, William Wycherley, William Congreve, Sir John Vanbrugh, George Farquhar, Thomas Otway, the tragic dramatist, and others.[3] But he was feeling his way all the time. Placed where he was and when he was, between two countries,

---

[1] Sir A. W. Ward, *Cambridge History of English Literature*, Vol. VII, p. 57.
[2] Prof. Churton Collins, *Essays and Studies*, London, 1895, p. 1.
[3] The *floruit* of these playwrights is between 1660 and 1720. The most recent authority is Bonamy Dobrée, *Restoration Comedy*, Oxford, 1924, and *Restoration Tragedy*, Oxford, 1929.

two forms of government, two æsthetic theories, he explained his position with transparent honesty in his *Apology for Heroic Poetry* (1677):

'I will not run into their fault of impressing my opinions on other men, any more than I would my writings on their taste; I have only laid down, and that superficially enough, my present thoughts, and shall be glad to be taught better by those who pretend to reform our poetry.'

It was a time of suspended judgment, and so, in quite another sphere, Dryden's *Religio Laici*, 1682, confessed his faith as a Protestant layman, in equipoise between Rome and the Deists, while his *The Hind and the Panther*, 1687, defended his conversion to the Church of Rome. So, too, his political satires, *Absalom and Achitophel*, 1681, *The Medal* and *Mac-Flecknoe*, 1682, prove no contention to-day. Like the *Hudibras* of Samuel Butler (1612–80), they are void of present interest, rolling empty vessels of controversy on a full tide of verbal music. But they leave undiminished his greatness as playwright, critic, and poet. He rendered the *Æneid* of Virgil into admirable heroic verse; he first familiarized English prose with the flexile, lucid and dexterous manner which was to make the reputation of Addison and his successors, and he handed on the national measure of the heroic couplet perfected alike in its ' correctness ', as containing the sense in the sound, and perfect, too, in its mastery of the art of polite diction. He wrote several distinguished odes: *Alexander's Feast, or The Power of Music* and *A Song for St. Cecilia's Day* among them[1]; and he wrote *Annus Mirabilis* (1666) in which he used a quatrain instead of a couplet. But apart from these few metrical experiments in which he still maintained dignity and precision he found the couplet adequate to the needs of the poet's craft. He wrote of Waller, that he

' first showed us how to conclude the sense, most commonly

---

[1] The odes are full of well-known phrases. We select:
  'None but the brave deserves the fair.'
  'And thrice he routed all his foes, and thrice he slew the slain.'
  'Like another Helen, fired another Troy.'

in distichs, which, in the verse of those before him, runs on for so many lines together, that the reader is out of breath to overtake it.'

They did not care to be out of breath in Dryden's time. They lived in a sober age, which was sparing of its breath as of other properties. The Bill of Rights was passed in 1689, the Bank of England was established in 1694, and the nation which organized its defences and tied the strings of its purse, which studied astronomy and geology[1] instead of sailing on strange seas to new lands, and which concurred with the laureate's dictum :

> ' All will at length in this opinion rest—
> A sober prince's government is best,'

was content to stay its muse on the heroic couplet. Dryden had no use, as he wrote, for ' fanatic bays ' ; he even con-jectured that the creation of only one sun proved that

> ' Heaven, though all-sufficient, shows a thrift
> In his economy, and bounds his gift.'

Independently, then, of French example, which brought so much that was valuable to English life and letters, including such French locutions as ' chagrin ' and ' adroit ' and in one place an unnaturalized ' fraicheur ', Prof. Courthope correctly advises us that ' out of the English political spirit was developed in English poetry the classical form.' Dryden, ' glorious John ' as he is known, was no Francophil patron of a Gallo-Classic hero in taste. He was English in all his being, as English as Tennyson, though a better European, and gossip preserves a pleasant picture of him seated in Will's coffee-house at the corner of Russell Street and Bow Street, in the cosiest ingle-nook of the room, as the acknowledged chief and referee of all who frequented that resort. But it was his good fortune to live in an age when ' the stamp of a Louis ',

---

[1] The names occur of Seth Ward (1617–89), Robert Boyle (1627–91), John Flamsteed (1646–1719), Edmund Halley (1656–1742), Sir Hans Sloane (1660–1753) and John Woodward (1665–1728). Among other scientists are John Wallis and Sir W. Petty (above), Sir Josiah Child (1630–99), Sir Christopher Wren (1632–1723) and Newton himself (1642–1727).

as he himself wrote, ' is not much inferior to the medal of
an Augustus Cæsar,' and loyally, conscientiously, and very
brilliantly he sought to transfer that impress to the literature
of his own country, desiderating similar conditions. He was
jealous of Spain and France :

> ' Heaven, that seem'd regardless of our fate,
> For France and Spain did miracles create,'[1]

Their novelists, dramatists, letter-writers and critics had
risen to Academic rank, recalling the triumphs of the Ancients,
and he was jealous for England's equal honour, for her equal
place in the comity of Europe :

> ' And now Time's whiter series is begun,
> Which in soft centuries shall smoothly run . . .
> Our nation with united interest blest,
> Not now content to poise, shall sway the rest.'

To this sway, which was to be divided, we now come.

Note on the Heroic Couplet.

There are, briefly, three phases in the history of this national
metre. Chaucer, who introduced it into England in his
Legend of Good Women and later in his *Canterbury Tales*, took
it ultimately from the French lyrist, Guillaume de Machault,
who died in 1377 ; he seized its epical value, and manipulated
it in paragraphs for narrative purposes before blank verse
rivalled it and replaced it. Dryden and Pope in the 17th and
18th centuries used it more rigidly in self-contained couplets,
and provided a compensating excellence of heightened
epigrammatic force. Keats (in *Endymion*) broke this mould,
which had become monotonous in Crabbe and other poets,
and disguised the rhymes and the pauses so successfully that
the measure was hardly distinguishable from blank verse.
Tennyson, a disciple of Keats, abandoned the couplet
altogether, and produced in blank verse the lost effect of rhyme
by his rare skill in repeating the sounds of vowels, consonants,
and syllables.

[1] *Astræa Redux*, 13–14 and (below) 292 ff.

§ 2. DRYDEN TO ROUSSEAU.

We come to a period of many names, but with one or two threads running through them. In order to show the profusion we set down first some of the names.

Writers and Books. Dryden died in 1700, Voltaire and Rousseau in 1778, and there flourished in that span of a man's lifetime :

In *England*—Swift, Pope, Richardson, Fielding, James Thomson, Chatterton, Johnson, Sterne, Gray, Sir Horace Walpole, Adam Smith, Goldsmith, Burke, Bishop Percy, James Macpherson, Edward Gibbon. Addison, Steele and Defoe lived till 1719, 1729 and 1731, respectively, and Wordsworth, Scott, Coleridge were born in 1770, 1771 and 1772.

In *France*—Lesage, Prévost, Marivaux, Voltaire, Buffon, Rousseau, Diderot, Turgot, Beaumarchais, Saint-Pierre, with Germaine Necker (the future Mme. de Staël), Chateaubriand and others growing up.

In *Germany*, restored from the devastation of the Thirty Years' War (1618–48)—Winckelmann, Lessing, Bürger, Klopstock, Wieland, Gottsched, with Goethe and Schiller beginning work, and with the ' Sturm und Drang ', or youthful ' Geniezeit ' (the epoch of genius, 1767–87), already in eruption.

In *Denmark*—Ludwig Holberg (1684–1754), and in *Italy*— Carlo Goldoni (1707–93), each of whom has been called the Molière of his respective country.

It was a splendid time into which the Augustan age debouched, and the Emperor Augustus, surveying the scenes of his uncle's Northern campaigns, might well be proud of the use to which his name is put.

Next, in the terms of the books they wrote. A complete nominal roll would be tiresome, but we may enumerate the following, in addition to the complete works of Rousseau and Voltaire :

1709, the first issue of *The Tatler*.
1711, the first issue of *The Spectator*.
1715, Lesage's *Gil Blas*, vols. 1 and 2.

P

1719, Defoe's *Robinson Crusoe*.

1726, Swift's *Gulliver's Travels*.

1726–30, Thomson's *Seasons*.

1731, Prévost's *Manon Lescaut*.

1733, Pope's *Essay on Man*.

1735, Marivaux' *Paysan Parvenu*.

1740–41, Richardson's *Pamela*.

1748, Klopstock's *Messias*.

1749, Fielding's *Tom Jones*.

1751, Gray's *Elegy*.

1755, Winckelmann's *Greek Painting and Statuary*. Johnson's *Dictionary*.

1759, Johnson's *Rasselas* and Voltaire's *Candide*. ('Par nobile fratrum.')

1766, Lessing's *Laokoon*. Goldsmith's *Vicar of Wakefield*. Smith's *Wealth of Nations*.

1768, Sterne's *Sentimental Journey*.

1774, Goethe's *Young Werther*.

1776, *Wirrwarr, oder Sturm und Drang*, a passion-play by F. M. von Klinger (1752–1831), which gave its name to the period.

The Commonwealth of Europe. Still not unravelling this confusion of best-sellers and epoch-making books, we may consider their interaction, which is really the interplay of the feelings which evoked them and which they invoked. The choice, again, is very large, and we select our illustrations almost at random.

Pierre de 'Marivaux (1688–1763), for example. In 1722 he imitated Addison by founding a French *Spectator*. A few years later, his sentimental novels, *Vie de Marianne* and *Paysan Parvenu*, gave a lead to Samuel Richardson in *Pamela*, to Fielding in *Joseph Andrews*, and less directly to Ludwig Tieck in *William Lovell* (1795). Tieck (1773–1853), a fine product of the vintage of the 'seventies, we shall meet again as the colleague of A. W. Schlegel in the classic German translation of Shakespeare's plays.

The *Spectator* under various titles recurs up and down

these years. J. J. Bodmer and J. J. Breitinger (Johann Jakob both : they used to sign their joint articles ' J.J.J.J.') started one at Zurich in 1721. J. C. Gottsched (1700–66), a lonely and rather pathetic figure who defended the cause of neo-Classicism, kept one going at Leipzig from 1725–27. But there were defections from his standard, and three Leipzig rebels were associated in founding a similar paper with contrary views : Adolf Schlegel (1721–93), the father of greater sons, Arnold Ebert, translator of Young's *Night Thoughts*, and Christian Gellert, who wrote fiction *à la* Richardson.

So, too, with *Robinson Crusoe*. That Crusoe feeling of manliness in solitude spread with extraordinary rapidity through the tents of Israel in those days, and poured healing on the artificialities of bewigged and powdered social life. There was a regular factory of ' Robinsonaden ' in Germany, where King Frederick II of Prussia, surnamed the Great (1712–86), was training his subjects to self-consciousness. The first German version of Defoe's romance was ready as early as 1720. An *Insel Felsenburg* by J. G. Schnabel, in which the conception was expanded, appeared in four volumes in 1731–43, and was re-issued in six by Tieck. J. H. Campe's juvenile *Robinson Crusoe*, 1779, passed through a hundred and twenty editions before the end of the century, and the *Swiss Family Robinson* by J. R. Wyss (1746–1820) has almost rivalled its prototype in popularity. Moreover, the Crusoe motive found expression out of his surroundings. Manon Lescaut's cavalier preferred adventure and love to worldly gear ; Candide visited strange gardens before returning to cultivate his own, and other characters in the fiction of other countries were impelled by like desires.

Robinson Crusoe was a common man. In this aspect he differed significantly from the heroes of the Racinian stage, of Milton's epic, and of Elizabethan drama. The author of *The Art of English Poesy*—we have quoted him before[1]—remarked towards the end of the 16th century that ' the actions of mean and base personages ' (he instanced ' a craftsman, shepherd or sailor ') ' tend in very few cases to any great good example ', and the

[1] See page 113 above.

playwrights and novelists followed suit. But they thought otherwise at the beginning of the 18th. Thus, George Lillo (1693–1739) and Edward Moore (1712–57), two not very notable writers, experimented in a kind of domestic drama, which keyed down the heroic to the plebeian level. The theme of Lillo's *George Barnwell* 1731, was the ruin of a London apprentice, and his *Fatal Curiosity*, 1736, declared expressly: 'From lower life we draw our scene's distress.' Low life, life below stairs, was the fashionable *milieu* at this time. Richardson's letters of instruction to 'handsome girls who were obliged to go out to service, how to avoid the snares that might be laid against their virtue,' were the well-known origin of *Pamela*, and Pamela's virtue dulled the glitter of the gallants of the Restoration stage. The common man came into his own again, restoring Chaucer to Fielding and Dickens. From Lillo and Moore there proceeded the domestic drama of France and Germany: the *comédie larmoyante* or *tragédie bourgeoise* of the one, the *Schicksalsdrama* or *bürgerliches Trauerspiel* of the other. Writers as eminent in other fields of literature as Denis Diderot (1713–84) and Gotthold Lessing (1729–81) contributed plays in this kind. Lessing translated two of Diderot's into German. Diderot wrote Richardsonian novels and an *Éloge de Richardson* on his death in 1761.

The Threads: (1) *Shakespeare*. In the foregoing paragraphs we have sought to display the profusion of books in the first three-quarters of the 18th century and their interlacing in England, France and Germany. We shall seek now some binding threads.

The first thread running through them is Shakespeare. By the law which went out from Versailles at the end of the 17th century Shakespeare was a barbarian playwright who overflowed the pauses of his verse and the sacred unities of time, place and action. His ghosts, witches and crowds and his sudden licences in stage-directions could not be reconciled with the poetics of Boileau, law-giver to Parnassus. So there followed a partial slump in Shakespeare, exploited at home, as we saw, by Thomas Rymer (1641–1713). But it did not prove of long duration. The 'escapes and safety-valves' left by Dryden in the stretched fabric of French criticism let in

Shakespeare to the theatre again, and, though Dryden himself
saw fit to revise some of his plays *à la mode*, and Pope ventured
to deplore that ' fluent Shakespeare scarce effaced a line ',
the darkness was soon lifted. Much of the new light came
from Germany. True, Professor Gottsched of Leipzig, who
was born in the year of Dryden's death, sustained the
melancholy thesis that Shakespeare was not *hoffähig*—not
presentable at the Court of Versailles from which the dramatic
law proceeded. But he fought a losing cause. The younger
dons deserted his drooping banner, and, one after another,
with increasing power, sallied forth as convinced Shakespeareans. This was the time of the rise of the Schlegel family,
which was to give the valiant brothers, August Wilhelm
(1767–1845) and Friedrich (1772–1829), to the Romantic
revival, and Elias Schlegel (1718–49) now anticipated his
greater nephews with a valuable plea for Shakespeare study.
Christoph Wieland (1733–1813), author of *Oberon*, a fairy-
romance much admired by Goethe, translated eleven of Shakespeare's plays into prose and the *Midsummer Night's Dream*
into the metres of the original. J. G. Herder (1744–1803),
Hellenist and Romanticist, helped to rouse the 19th century
to appreciation, and a big step forward was made when
Friedrich Schröder, a leading actor-manager, put *Hamlet* on
the boards of the Hamburg theatre, with ghost and disunities
complete. We need not multiply evidences. Out of every
German romantic workshop, every school of national
sentiment, fresh and vital criticism of Shakespeare was the
staple credential which was produced. By every sign it was
apparent, that, since Shakespeare had been ruled out by
Boileau, he must be brought back by a critic of equal
weight, and Lessing, playwright and antiquary, wrote
accordingly the *Hamburgische Dramaturgie* in 1767–68. This
master-work in two volumes, which restored sanity to the
Aristotelians, was preceded in 1759 by his brilliant
contribution to the study of Shakespeare in a journal of the
Spectator type called ' Letters relating to Modern Literature.'
   Light came from Germany, as we remarked, and,
appropriately, the period of its emanation is known as the
Aufklärung, or Enlightenment. It dates from about 1740,

and it is justly associated with the reign of Frederick the Great, who ascended the throne in that year. Goethe said of that monarch, whose life was written by Carlyle : ' The first true and higher self-consciousness came into German poetry through Frederick the Great and the Seven Years' War.' Schiller, who planned a *Frederician*, declared of the German muse that she went ' unprotected and without honour' (*schutzlos, ungeehrt*) from Frederick's presence. Both statements are defensible, for the King's most significant act as a patron of letters was to invite Voltaire to Potsdam. He tried to Europeanize Prussia by wrapping his capital in plaster of Paris. In those days, 1750–55, it was a practical idea. A century earlier, in 1649, Queen Christina of Sweden had invited Descartes to Stockholm, and these domestications of genius in foreign surroundings were a sign of its federal force. ' Whatever the explanation may be,' writes M. Faguet, the eminent *Académicien*, in the *Cambridge Modern History* (Vol. V, page 71), ' for nearly a hundred years (after 1700) France occupied a position towards every other European nation analogous to that of a nurse.' So, under Voltaire's influence, summoned by Frederick the Great, Germany was nursed back to literary self-expression ; and, if her native writers went unhonoured in the cradle, their maturity was richer in consequence. Meanwhile, whether stimulated by Voltaire or another, a chief factor of the enlightenment was Shakespeare ; and, when Germany's re-entry into letters was crowned by a score of noble names, the Romanticists, headed by Goethe, in his recital of the apprenticeship of Wilhelm Meister, handed Shakespeare back to his own countrymen—Coleridge, Lamb, and the rest—enhanced, adorned, and adored.

Indirectly, at any rate, we may ascribe it partly to Voltaire. His immense, transcendent genius, spread in Europe throughout this period, had been battened on Shakespeare in England, where he was a visitor in 1726. A couple of Cæsar tragedies, *Brutus*, 1730, and *Mort de César*, 1731, proved his discipleship to the greater dramatist and his departure from the canons of Boileau. There was an unchartered ghost in his *Sémiramis*, 1748, Othello has been traced in his *Zaïre*, 1733, and Macbeth in his *Mahomet*, 1742. True, his enthusiasm waned ; his countrymen's too eager worship of Shakespeare made him jealous of his own fame. In later life he was even anti-Shakespeare, but his conversion did not stop the translators—Pierre Letourneur (1736–88), J. F. Ducis (1733–1816) and R. J. Turgot (1727–81) particularly—nor could it tarnish the laurel of so brilliant an actor as Talma (1763–1826) in leading Shakespearean parts. Thus, in France, as in Germany and as, much later, in Russia, Shakespeare was a chief factor of the new enlargement which spelt liberty and romance. In drawing the threads together, this is certainly the first.

(2) *The Outlet for Feeling.* The second is harder to extricate. We cannot associate with a single writer the thread running through our period which may be designated by the name of feeling. It was distributed, and yet it can be collected.

Consider briefly what is implied by the vogue of James Thomson (1700–48) and Edward Young (1683–1765), descriptive poets, and of George Lillo and Edward Moore, dramatists. The former pair are very little read to-day, the latter not at all. Even Samuel Richardson (1689–1761) belongs to the class of novelists whom ' no gentleman's library should be without' rather than to the class which every schoolboy reads. Yet how widespread were their readers in France and Germany in their own lifetime, and not merely widespread but enthusiastic. They were broadcast, even in those slower days of the stagecoach and the sailing-ship. Thomson wrote, with a certain David Mallet, who died in 1765, a play, or masque called *Alfred*, 1740, in Act III, Scene v, of which occurs the famous jingle, ' Rule Britannia '. But, though this song survives his name, his contemporary fame was not derived from it, nor yet chiefly from his plays, *Sophonisba* and others, nor from his *Castle of Indolence* in Spenser's metre. It rested most securely on his four books of *The Seasons* in blank verse, with their echoes from Milton and Virgil and their future echoes in Coleridge and Shelley, and with their obvious obedience to the laws of poetic diction as observed by Pope. Neither Thomson's *Seasons* nor Young's *Complaint, or Night Thoughts on Life, Death, and Immortality*, published in nine parts, 1742–45, strike us as front-line books to-day. They are probably a little more popular than Lillo's and

Moore's plays, a little less than Richardson's novels, but all
five writers alike are inferior, say, to Shakespeare and Milton,
whom Addison was following Dryden in restoring to public
esteem.

Now, look at the response on the Continent. With Lillo
and Moore we have dealt above. Pierre Letourneur, whose
version of Shakespeare, 1776, was subscribed, among others,
by the Empress Catherine of Russia,[1] thought it worth while
to add to his labours by translating Young's *Night Thoughts*,
which are justly credited again with a strong influence on
Rousseau and, through him, on the French Revolution. Yet
how mediocre a poet Young was, and how uninspiring a
teacher. George Eliot, in her essay on ' Worldliness and Other-
Worldliness ' assures us that

' Young has no conception of religion as anything else
than egoism turned heavenward, and he does not merely
imply this, he insists on it. . . . His ethics correspond to his
religion. . . . Virtue, with Young, must always squint. . . .
To his mind, the heavens are " for ever *scolding* as they shine " ;
and the great function of the stars is to be a " lecture to
mankind ". . . . It is this pedagogic tendency, this sermonis-
ing attitude of Young's mind, which produces the wearisome
monotony of Young's poems.'

It was not a bright example to France and Germany, where
Young found his translator in J. A. Ebert (1723–95) and
imitators in many of the Leipzig poets.

Turn next to Thomson's *Seasons*. These were translated
into German by Berthold Brockes (1680–1747), whose
' Earthly Pleasure in God ' (9 volumes, 1721–48) was composed

[1] We cannot pause at the cosmopolitan Courts, which derived from King
Louis XIV of France, Queen Christina of Sweden, and earlier rulers, a tradition
of patronage in art and letters. King Frederick II (the Great) of Prussia is
mentioned in these pages ; the Empress Catherine of Russia was a Princess of
Anhalt when she married the Grand-Duke Peter, Heir Apparent, in 1744. She
became sole autocrat in 1762, and was in constant correspondence with Voltaire,
Diderot, and others. In 1770 King Louis XVI of France was married, at the
age of sixteen, to Marie Antoinette, the Habsburg Archduchess. Baron F. M.
de Grimm (1723–1807), a Frenchman of German origin, acted as a kind of
Court newsman in this age. He wrote Paris letters on literature, etc., in the
form of an intimate journal, first published in 1812, to the Duchess of Saxe-
Coburg, the Empress of Russia, the Kings of Prussia and Poland, and other
rulers.

in the same vein. Thomson was studied and imitated again by A. von Haller (1708–77), E. C. von Kleist (1715–59), and others, including Johann Peter Uz (1720–96), who was known as the German Horace—all earnest and eager writers, forming themselves into a group or school united in patronizing God's handiwork with a sort of tearful joy.

For there were always tears in their eyes. Even the admirable Richardson, a printer by trade, who began novel-writing at fifty years of age, made domestic sentiment a channel for easy weeping—' sob-stuff ', they call it to-day. When Clarissa, his second heroine, died—out of contrast to his earlier Pamela's happy ending—it is said that England's wail of lament spread across the Continent of Europe. It rose to a flood in Germany, where feeling had been discouraged and repressed during the barren years of fighting and reconstruction; and the sorrows of unrequited love, of muted effort, bereavement and early death, were associated with the conventional phenomena of rain, waterfall and autumn tints, until at last direct observers of nature swept the whole bag of tricks into the limbo of ' poetic diction '.

The reaction was stronger than the facts warranted. When Matthew Arnold wrote of the sequel to ' the literature of genius stretching from Marlowe to Milton ' as ' our provincial and second-rate literature of the eighteenth century ', he was using exaggerated terms, nor was that century, as he declared, merely an ' age of prose and reason '. He was thinking particularly of the special language which a poet assumed with his singing-robes, and which had been so emphatically condemned by Wordsworth (1770–1850), whom Arnold was writing back into honour. But he forgot that there were protestants before him. One example tells more than a volume of criticism, and as early as 1744, in the very year of Pope's death, we find Joseph Warton (1722–1800), a son and brother of Professors of Poetry at Oxford, anticipating the Romantic Movement which Rousseau was to teach to Wordsworth. In *The Enthusiast* : *or The Lover of Nature* Warton wrote :—

> ' O taste corrupt ! that luxury and pomp,
> In specious terms of polish'd manners veil'd,

> Should proudly banish Nature's simple charms !
> All-beauteous Nature ! by thy boundless wealth
> Oppress'd, O where shall I begin thy praise,
> Where turn the ecstatick eye, how ease my breast
> That pants with wild astonishment and love !
> Dark forests, and the opening lawn, refresh'd
> With ever-gushing brooks, hill, meadow, dale,
> The balmy bean-field, the gay-clover'd close,
> So sweetly interchang'd, the lowing ox,
> The playful lamb, the distant waterfall
> Now faintly heard, now swelling with the breeze,
> The sound of pastoral reed from hazel-bower,
> The choral birds, the neighing steed, that snuffs
> His dappled mate, stung with intense desire,
> The ripen'd orchard when the ruddy orbs
> Betwixt the green leaves blush, the azure skies,
> The cheerful sun that thro' earth's vitals pours
> Delight and health and heat ; all, all conspire
> To raise, to sooth, to harmonize the mind,
> To lift on wings of praise, to the great sire
> Of being and of beauty, at whose nod
> Creation started from the gloomy vault . . .
> What are the lays of artful Addison,
> Coldly correct, to Shakspear's warblings wild ? '

This is typical of much poetry of the period, not in England only but in all countries, and it directly contravenes Pope's contemporary aim at correctness, as a canon superior to the profusion of Shakespeare's pen. We may smile at Warton's taste in epithets : *balmy* field, *lowing* ox, *playful* lamb, *choral* birds, *azure* skies, etc., but we should really reserve our smiles for Arnold's choice of epithets for Warton's century, since surely neither ' prose ' nor ' reason ' caused him to pant with astonishment and love. The vices of the diction are obvious, but the virtue of its sentiment was genuine, and in Young and Thomson and their contemporaries there was much pure music, much honest feeling and true characterization, as they tapped their way back to ' Nature's simple charms '. French and German opinion was not misled in employing them as patterns for imitation, and those patterns, though they contained some frigidities of diction, conveyed to a discerning eye warm colours and genuine sentiment. Dr. Nichol Smith correctly writes, in his introduction to the *Oxford Book of Eighteenth Century Verse* :

'If we are disposed to search in this volume for the explanation of such catchwords as " the poetry of the Town," "the tyranny of Pope," "the domination of the heroic couplet," we are likely to be disappointed.'

It was ' a period of definite achievement ,' and its initiative is not to be washed out in the flood-tide of Romance revived.

Its immediate value for foreigners, its *preceptive* value, if we may call it so, lay in its minor note of direct moral instruction. When Richardson set his hand to the edification of serving-girls, when Gray meditated in a churchyard ' the simple annals of the poor,' when Thomson saw ' social labour lift its guarded head,' and Lillo drew his action from ' lower life,' these writers made a direct appeal to the conscience of Europe, preparing, as we are aware, for social and moral revolution. That their appeal was couched in language which found a ready way to men's hearts, that human feeling and natural phenomena were fused or forced into harmonious relationship—

> ' All, all conspire
> To raise, to sooth, to harmonize the mind,'

this was an implement of its success, and it is arguable that the success was quickened by the fact that many of the writers were not in the first rank. The mood was communicated more readily to the middle classes. Burke perceived this imminent danger in the new thought, and there is a sense in which the note of the 18th century was sublimated after the ordeal of the French Revolution.

The Forgers. Fused or forced, we said just now, and, amid all this transfusion of feeling and translation of books, there was bound to be some forcing of sentiment. The conspiracy between Nature and man would sometimes have to be assisted.

JAMES MACPHERSON (1736–96) and THOMAS CHATTERTON (1752–70 ; he committed suicide in that year) both forced the sentiment at which they aimed. Macpherson, a Scottish antiquary, who became M.P. for Camelford and was buried in Westminster Abbey, saw that an ' Ossian ' was missing from the epic cycle of national origins, and as brilliantly as boldly he set to work to supply it. After publishing a volume of *Fragments of Ancient Poetry in the Highlands*, 1760, he produced in 1762–63 *Fingal* in six Books and *Temora* in eight, each being subtitled ' an ancient epic poem translated from the Gaelic language.' The advertisement to *Fingal* stated that there was ' a design on foot to print the Originals as soon as the translator shall have time to transcribe them for the press.' It was known that the Ossianic cycle of the old and lost Irish prose sagas revolved round the heroes Finn MacCumhall and Ossian, his son, and, in Scotizing the Gaelic Finn into a Caledonian Fingal, Macpherson satisfied Highland pride by providing romantic Scotsmen with their *Iliad*. His ' Ossian ' proved a resounding success. Turgot translated it into French and Melchiore Cesaroti into Italian. The Italian version accompanied Napoleon all the way from Egypt to St. Helena, and may have helped to make European history. Certainly, it helped to make Goethe's poetry and to create a new literature in far-off Russia. Joined with the genuine *Reliques of Ancient English Poetry* by Bishop (THOMAS) PERCY (1729–1811), it gave a most powerful impetus to the revival of medieval studies in folklore and ballad and is one of the pillars on which the Romantic Movement was established.

It was an unkind fate which compelled Macpherson to produce the goods. But the scholars demanded the ' originals ', and late in life, as Professor Ker writes, ' he had to sit down in cold blood and make his ancient Gaelic poetry. He had begun with a piece of literary artifice, a practical joke ; he ended with deliberate forgery, which, the more it succeeded, would leave him the less of what was really his due for the merits of the English Ossian.'[1] A Committee of the Highland Society was appointed to inquire into the matter. The Chairman of that Committee was HENRY MACKENZIE (1745–1831),

[1] *The Cambridge History of English Literature*, Vol. X, p. 230.

whose *Man of Feeling*, 1771, and other novels belonged to the age of reviving sentiment; and Scott, among others, who owed so much to the Percy–Macpherson–Mackenzie type of fiction, exposed the fraud in the *Edinburgh Review* (July, 1815). But its ' merits ' remain. It served the needs of its own time, and, paraphrasing a famous saying by Voltaire, we may add that, since Ossian was not extant, it was necessary to invent him. His immense vogue is the measure of the need.

The second brilliant forger of this time was ' the marvellous boy, the sleepless soul that perished in his pride,' as Wordsworth called Chatterton. He was the son of a Bristol schoolmaster, and learned the beauty of the antique from the architecture, charters and Black Letter Bible of St. Mary Redcliffe Church in that city. He invented a Thomas Rowley of the 15th century, and wrote his poems. He wrote, too, a Rowley's history of painting (*Ryse of Peyncteyne yn Englande written by T. Rowleie*, 1469) which he sent to Sir Horace Walpole, who ignored him. In London, to which he made his way, he found no release from poverty except by the fatal dose of arsenic which he swallowed at eighteen years of age. But Chatterton, too, is among the romantic founders.

By hook or by crook, then, we may say—and these extreme cases illustrate the crooked means—writers between 1700 and 1778 satisfied with increasing zeal the demand for surprise and difference. The worn sameness of experience was proving intolerable. Meredith's perception was stealing over consciousness :

' She wears no more that robe of printed hours ;
Half strange seems Earth, and sweeter than her flowers.'

So earth had to be re-mapped for the survey of the sons of man. Dr. Johnson in 1747 planned a new *Dictionary of the English Language*, and Denis Diderot in 1750 issued the prospectus of his *Encyclopédie, ou Dictionnaire raisonné des Sciences, des Arts, et des Métiers* in 35 volumes. The new spirit would be served, alike in language and in thought.

Pope was dead (1744), and there died with him the narrow doctrine which he expressed so attractively in his brilliant *Essay on Man* :

> ' Know, then, thyself, presume not God to scan,
> The proper study of mankind is Man.'

But mankind would not be refrained from scanning God, and the proper study of Man should now include not merely the polite man among his equals, but the naked man of Defoe, the rustic man of Goldsmith, the lower man of Lillo, and the economic man of Adam Smith. Dead men, too, should be revived in their habits and humours as they had lived. Lessing and Winckelmann brought their hammers, their foot-rules and their balances to the statues and monuments of Greece and Rome. Macpherson and Percy went to folklore and ballad, and taught the muse of history how to make use of their resources. Everywhere were opening casements, extended frontiers and new horizons. As the period 1770–78 draws near to the Revolution which it was preparing, we mark a deeper study of God and man in all their varied manifestations.

Men of Feeling. We cannot enumerate these manifestations. We may take from Henry Mackenzie, however, the Scottish novelist whose name occurred above in connection with the ' Ossian ' forgery, the general epithet of men of feeling, in order to characterize this new class of writers. His own *Man of Feeling*, 1771, forms a link between Richardson and Scott who was born in that year; and Mackenzie was an early champion of his fellow-countryman, the new poet, ROBERT BURNS (1759–96), and an admirer of Lessing and Schiller.

In the same class was LAURENCE STERNE (1713–68), author of the nine volumes, 1760–67, of *The Life and Opinions of Tristram Shandy* and of *A Sentimental Journey through France and Italy by Mr. Yorick*, in two volumes, 1768. There was ' feeling ' on Mackenzie's title-page and ' sentiment ' on Sterne's, and this is, perhaps, as much as is requisite to the present rapid reference to their works. Sterne was the better writer of the two, and Sir Horace Walpole in a letter of April 4th, 1760, bears witness that, ' at present, nothing is talked about, nothing admired, but what I cannot help calling a very insipid and tedious performance : it is a kind of novel, called *The Life and Opinions of Tristram Shandy* '. This mixed testimony of a contemporary is worth quoting, because it illustrates the two opinions between which men halted in the 18th century. Even Byron, at the century's end, could describe Sterne as a sentimentalist who preferred ' whining over a dead ass to relieving a living mother.' The same thing, we shall see, might have been said of Rousseau, and we should note that Wordsworth's ass in *Peter Bell* entered literature through Sterne's gate. Goethe, too, was a Sterne man, and said in one place that ' Yorick-Sterne was the finest spirit that ever existed : who reads him feels himself at once free and fine.' We may put the matter in another way. There is a passage in *Tristram Shandy* where ' Uncle Toby ', after ' infinite attempts ,' manages to catch a blue-bottle fly and release it through an open window. ' Go, poor devil,' he says, ' get thee gone ; why should I hurt thee ? This world surely is big enough to hold both thee and me.' It is sentimental : perhaps, too much so ; but it contrasted remarkably in 1760 with Pope's easier way with insects a few years earlier :

> ' The bliss of Man (could pride that blessing find)
> Is not to act or think beyond mankind ; . . .
> Why has not Man a microscopic eye ?
> For this plain reason, Man is not a fly.'

The curiosity estopped by Pope was re-admitted by the men of feeling.

We might pursue these re-admittances through many channels. ANTOINE FRANÇOIS PREVOST (1697–1763), for example, commonly known as l'Abbé Prévost, lived in Holland and England from 1727–33 and picked up the threads of the pattern which Goethe described as ' free and fine ' (*schön*). We have mentioned his translations from Richardson, his imitation of the *Spectator*, and so on ; and more special mention is due to his *Histoire du Chevalier des Grieux et de Manon Lescaut*, 1731, which is one of the great love-stories of modern literature. Oliver Goldsmith's *Vicar of Wakefield*, 1766, is another of the formative novels.

On a former page, writing of Robinson Crusoe, we remarked that he was a common man, and that common men were now coming into their own again. We shall see in the next

Section how much of this 'return to nature' was due to the
influence of Rousseau. Here, in conclusion to our present
survey, and avoiding a mere catalogue of names, we turn to
the supreme type of the common man in America. His
inalienable right to freedom and happiness was the basis of
the Declaration of Independence in 1776, which fulfilled all
the tentative aims and philosophic hints formulated in the
Old World. 'America's dream and ideal', says the modern
historian,[1] ' rest on the Jeffersonian faith in the common man ; '
and, even if the American idea contemplated by Thomas
Jefferson ' has been a dream,' we read on, ' it has also been
one of the great realities in American life. It is all that has
distinguished America from a mere quantitative comparison
in wealth or art or letters or power with the nations of old
Europe. It *is* Americanism, and its shrine has been in the heart
of common men.'

We pause here. French, German and English writers
between 1700 and 1778 modified the French rule of exactness
which Pope had acquired from Boileau, and they did not live
to see the baleful policy against which Burke warned his
fellow-countrymen. Perhaps their sentiment was too lachry-
mose, their ' sob-stuff' too overpowering, their lives too
much in contrast with their professions, their conscience
slower than their genius. But their achievement was immense.
They emancipated the common man. They made his feelings,
wishes and powers the measure of truth and the theme of
literature. ' The provision which we have here made is no
other than Human Nature,' wrote Henry Fielding in Chapter I
of *Tom Jones*, 1749, and Tom and Jones are common men's
names. By this provision the Old World was reformed and
the New World was founded, and if all the political hopes of
1789 and 1776 have not come to complete fruition, this is not
the fault of the visionaries who went before the politicians.
So we come at the last to Rousseau.

[1] *The Epic of America*, by James Truslow Adams, London, 1932 ; pp. 134,
174.

§ 3. ROUSSEAU.

Jean-Jacques Rousseau, whose life and work lie wholly within the limits of this Book, was born in 1712 and died in 1778. He belongs to the company of the immortals—Shakespeare, Dickens, Molière are among them—who fulfilled life without longevity.

His Achievement. He altered the face of Europe, and helped to found the constitution of America. He altered the face of Europe not merely, though clearly, in a political sense : he altered it, too, like a beauty-doctor, bringing out lovely lines and curves hitherto not plain to observation. He was a natural landscape-gardener, disclosing in nature unadorned, and not twisted by the hand of man, sources of refreshment and healing, a cool lap and a tranquil breast. Mountain-scenery particularly appealed to him, and if, as will presently appear, he was comparable to Petrarch as a herald of a new way of life, he may be compared with Petrarch, too, in his recourse to the hills for help. ' Rousseau, Sir, is a very bad man,' said that very good man, Samuel Johnson (1709–84) to the greatest of all biographers, James Boswell (1740–95). Boswell was recently home from France, where he had met many of the leading writers, and perhaps he did not fully concur with this opinion. But Johnson was right in his place and time. In Burke's England, Rousseau was a bad man, and no one knew it better than Burke. ' We are not the converts of Rousseau ', he declared, as we have seen, to his fellow-countrymen in 1790. But times change, and England is not Europe. Burke's anti-Revolution tract was also a tract anti-Rousseau, in so far as Rousseau was an author of the ideas expressed in the Revolution, and those ideas in that intensity would have been bad for English practice. Yet nothing that Rousseau desired, where his desires can be formulated, has been denied to Englishmen : the Reform Act of 1832, the Abolition Act of 1834, and so on. Bad and good are relative terms, when applied to political projects, and the scholars and statesmen of our day do not repeat Dr. Johnson's strictures.

Professor C. E. Vaughan, for example, in the *Cambridge*

Modern History, Vol. VI, reminds us that Immanuel Kant (1724–1804), the illustrious German who finished what Luther began,

'compared the moral revolution wrought by Rousseau in his "discovery of the deep-hidden nature of man" to the intellectual revolution inaugurated by the discoveries of Newton . . . . Nothing', he adds, 'could illustrate more clearly the significance of the ideas first proclaimed by Rousseau than the supreme value attached to them by a thinker so cautious and so profound.'

And in his Cambridge edition of *The Political Writings of Rousseau*, he says, in words which we have borrowed above:

'Rousseau gave men faith in their power to redress the wrongs of ages. And he held forth an ideal of civic life which has changed the face of Europe.'

Lord Cromer, the Empire-builder, wrote:

'Rousseau made the world think. He introduced new ideas, which were often wrong, but almost always fruitful';

and Lord Morley, Liberal statesman and author of the *Life of Gladstone*, declared that Rousseau

'first in our modern time sounded a new trumpet-note for one more of the great battles of humanity.'

'The ideas first proclaimed by Rousseau'; 'new ideas'; 'first in our time': these testimonies to Rousseau as an innovator come aptly from the distinguished countrymen of Johnson and Burke, to whom his ideas were anathema. We may put it that 'The Club' of 1763, of which Burke and Johnson were original members, would have welcomed Morley and Cromer, despite their admiration for Rousseau.

It is on Rousseau as thought-provoker and pathfinder, as the Socrates of the 18th century, that the secure judgment of the world has been pronounced; and Schiller, surely no 'bad man', who lived through the French Revolution to the year of the Battle of Trafalgar, found the comparison with Socrates inadequate.

'Socrates ging unter durch Sophisten,'

he wrote : Socrates was destroyed by Sophists ;

    ' Rousseau leidet, Rousseau fällt durch Christen,

Rousseau suffered, Rousseau fell by Christians,

    ' Rousseau, der aus Christen Menschen wirbt,'

Rousseau, who turned Christians into men.

We are estimating Rousseau's achievement, not the reaction to his ideas in his lifetime, nor the follies of that life itself. Again and again it has happened, in the history of the making of the mind of Europe, reformed in the 16th century and later formed again in the 18th, that its ideal makers must be differentiated from the realists who apply their teachings and pervert them to uses not designed. The mind eloquent in Kant and Goethe, in Wordsworth, Shelley and many more, owed much of its noble sense of social honour to the difficult and morbid genius which taught revolutionaries in Paris to address one another as *citoyens*. We wrote by anticipation on page 21, that, ' the Revolution of the 18th century was the sequel to the Reformation of the 16th.' Petrarch died in 1374, Rousseau in 1778 ; the Reformation followed the one, and the Revolution the other ; Rousseau and Kant were wanted to complete what Petrarch and Luther had begun, and even to undo a part of what had been ill-done in four centuries of imperfect experimentation.

His Life.   Does mankind merit vessels of flawless crystal ?

    ' I feared, loved, hated, suffered, did and died,
        And, if the spark with which Heaven lit my spirit
        Had been with purer nutriment supplied,
        Corruption would not now thus much inherit
        Of what was once Rousseau . . .
        If I have been extinguished, yet there rise
        A thousand beacons from the spark I bore.'

So Shelley of Rousseau in 1822, and, while the beacons were multiplied in the 19th century, we must notice the vessel with its flaws.

Jean-Jacques's mother died when he was born, and his father, a watchmaker at Geneva, was a ne'er-do-well who deserted him at ten years old. Six years later, he began the shiftless life, or the life of many shifts and changes, which he led till death released him, miserable, poor, and obscure. He was sometimes a footman, sometimes a music-copier or a teacher of music, often in debt, always quarrelsome, jealous, and suspicious even of those who befriended him. He was taken up—the ugly word is not out of place—by rich women older than himself, Mme de Warens at Annecy, Mme d'Epinay at Montmorency, and was recommended by his talents from time to time to Diderot in Paris, King Frederick the Great at Neufchâtel, then under the suzerainty of Prussia, and the Scottish historian, David Hume (1711–76), in England, which Rousseau visited in 1765. For many years after 1743 he had a lodging in Paris in the squalid rue des Cordiers. The house is known to-day as the Hôtel J. J. Rousseau, and biographers recognize it particularly as the place where the superannuated footman formed his liaison with the kitchen-maid Thérèse, whom he married by a ceremony of his own invention in 1768, and who left him two years afterwards for a stable-lad. The low business is unredeemed by any ideal. Rousseau is properly reputed the ' father of Romanticism ' in Europe, but no spark of romance illumined his human relations as husband and father. The five offspring were deposited, successively, like litters of kittens, in a Foundling Hospital. Thérèse, whatever her feelings, might not keep one baby in the basket. We must leave this mystery to God, whom, potentially, Rousseau rescued from the deists. The restorer of faith, the worshipper of nature, the defender of the poor, the champion of the oppressed, the prophet of in-dividualism, the reformer of education, the well-spring of Byronism, the fountain-head of feeling, refused the elementary rights of motherhood to the woman whom he chose as mate. Baptist crossed with Caliban, is the best epithet we can formulate for a character which defies analysis. His own posthumous *Confessions*, as immodest, or a-moral, as they are truthful, expose what cannot be explained, and the imaginary voices which haunted him and tormented his lonely, dying years, attest the greatness of his imagination.

His Writings. Quite briefly, the list of these is (1) contri-butions on music to Diderot's *Encyclopédie*; (2) an essay written for a prize offered in 1749 by the Dijon Academy on the topic, ' Has the Progress of the Sciences and Arts tended to Corrupt or to Purify Manners ? ' ; (3) a further discourse, published at Amsterdam, 1755, ' On the Origins and Foundation of Inequality '. By this time Rousseau was accounted *philosophe*, and a public was ready for (4), 1761, *La Nouvelle Héloise, ou Lettres de deux Amants*, in which the problem of a return to nature was discussed from the point of view of sex-love and family-life. Richardson imposed the form of letters, Richardson and Prévost jointly inspired the tone of tender sentiment which took female Paris by storm, and the old story of Abelard gave the lovers their names. What was new, and direct from Rousseau's brain, was the doctrine of individual right defeated by social wrong, and the place of the family as the nucleus of society. Its sequel was (5) 1762, *Émile, ou de l'Éducation*, of which (6) the *Profession de Foi du Vicaire Savoyard* forms a part. In the same year and likewise at Amsterdam appeared (7) *Du Contrat Social*, which, like the rest of his writings, applied to bookish philosophy the test of common human conditions of the heart as well as of the head.

No one takes it all literally to-day. Rousseau said himself, that ' those who boast that they understand the whole of it are cleverer than I am,' and a scheme of conduct which has to be taken in parts will reveal paradoxes and contradiction. Nothing is easier than to be cleverer than Rousseau, or, more exactly, than to be clever at his expense. Nietzsche, for instance, said that Rousseau returned to nature *in impuris naturalibus*, and crueller *mots* have been coined by smaller men. The central doctrine of his thought, that society is to nature as evil is to good, is capable of disproof along half a dozen lines of history. But the light shines in darkness. Rousseau is greater than his writings as he was greater than his life. He made our life natural ; he made nature ' une inspiratrice et une confidente ; il l'a suscitée autour de nous, non comme un domaine ou un décor, mais comme une conscience frémissante, tour à tour docile ou souveraine.'[1] It is by this method with nature, correcting the method of

[1] De Mornet, *Le Romantisme en France au XVIII⁰ Siècle*, Paris, 1912 ; p. 269.

Descartes and the Encyclopedists, that Rousseau's final influence proved supreme. 'Willingly or unwillingly, at first hand or from imperfect echoes, every one who studies education must study Rousseau,' wrote R. H. Quick, the historian of education, at the beginning of the English half-century of busy educational reform which started with the eighteen-seventies; and E. Paulsen, the German historian of philosophy, wrote in the same sense : 'For three hundred years the maxim of the Renaissance, that education is the presupposition of morality, had been accepted. Then Rousseau entered his emphatic protest.' He gave men what Wordsworth called, simplifying both Rousseau and Kant, 'a heart that watches and receives.' This faith, declares Paulsen, 'is the only way of approach to the super-sensible world. Learning of the schools, theology and metaphysics are of no advantage here '.

Rousseau leads us to heights of the spirit, as he unfolds the hills of his beloved Alps. 'Forbode not any severing of our loves,' wrote Wordsworth of those hills, and the love was ultimately knit in Geneva and Königsberg by Jean-Jacques Rousseau, the French watchmaker's son, and Immanuel Kant, the son of a German saddler. 'It was in Rousseau ', says Morley, 'that polite Europe '—note the epithet ' polite ', so appropriate to the broken symbols of the 18th century—'first hearkened '—and observe the temporal ' first '—' to strange voices and faint reverberations, out of the vague and cavernous shadow in which the common people move.' Common people moving out of the shadow ; these form the vast company of Rousseau, and though they moved in places to ill deeds, for which, maugre Burke, it is vain to blame Rousseau, they moved in long procession towards the light. Out of the shadow of the factories into the light of the fields :

' God made the country, and man made the town,'

wrote William Cowper (1731–1800). Out of the shadow of the old pedagogy into the light of the new, heralded by J. H. Pestalozzi (1746–1827), the Swiss educational reformer. Out of the shadow of inhibition and repression into the light of full sensibility :

'Der Gefangene hatte das Licht vergessen, aber der Traum der Freiheit fuhr über ihn wie ein Blitz in die Nacht;'

'the prisoner had forgotten the light,' wrote Schiller in his *Räuber*, 1781, 'but the dawn of freedom broke upon him like a flash into the night.' The 18th century was the prisoner of bounds and limits; Rousseau unsealed the forgotten light, and taught the common man his dream of liberty.

It was said in the *Gentleman's Magazine* in April, 1755, by a reviewer of Dr. Johnson's *Dictionary*, that therein he had 'beat forty French, and will beat forty more.' The reference, of course, was to the forty Immortals of the French Academy, whose *Dictionnaire* Johnson had rivalled single-handed. So he was ready and more to combine with Burke and kindred patriots in saving England from the French evil, which was routed at last at Waterloo. The historian concedes these facts: they are written in letters of red and gold. But the mind of Europe has sought other modes of more tranquil expression than those which we commemorate in martial colours.

Take, for instance, the year 1759, well within the period under notice and very close to the year of Johnson's *Dictionary*. It was the year, or near it, of Minden and Quiberon Bay, of Clive in India and Wolfe at Quebec.

> 'Hearts of Oak are our ships,
> Hearts of Oak are our Men,
> We always are ready,
> Steady! Boys, steady!
> We'll fight and we'll conquer again and again!'

So sang David Garrick in 1759, 'to add something more to this wonderful year.' Garrick was Johnson's friend and pupil; they had come together in London as young men. But was Johnson so certain of the 'wonder', so resolute to fight again? Or was he alert to forces directing men to victories of peace no less renowned than of war? His *Rasselas* and Voltaire's *Candide* were both published in 1759, in the midst of 'the great decisive duel between England and France for the possession of the New World',[1] and France and England

[1] Sir John Seeley, *The Expansion of England*, London, 1883, p. 28.

met in those books, above the duel for the New World in a generous effort to found a new spirit in the Old. Forces were at work in 1759, correcting wrongs of society and industry, and ameliorating the relations of mankind ; Sir Leslie Stephen aptly joins those two tales—the Frenchman's and the Englishman's, written while their countries were at war—as

'among the most powerful expressions of the melancholy produced in strong intellects by the sadness and sorrows of the world.'[1]

There is more imagination in this perception and in the conjunction of Johnson with Voltaire than in the denunciation of the latter by the former and the echo of his sentiment by Edmund Burke.

1759 was a wonderful year. Hearts of oak are still tough in English breasts, and 'We'll fight and we'll conquer again and again '. But it was a more wonderful year and full of other wonders than Garrick indicated to Seeley. A higher patriotism guides us to loftier heights. We had fought not in vain for 'the choice of life ' renounced by Rasselas, and the right way out of his 'happy valley ', for the removal of causes of social wrong, and for a hope more secure than that which Dr. Pangloss recommended to Candide. The duel for the possession of the New World was less significant than the reforms of the old. In that fight Rousseau was leader, and his torch-bearers in England, France and Germany are at one now in acclaiming his initiative.

§ 4. The End of an Age.

Postscript to Rousseau. We have reached 1778, when Rousseau and Voltaire died, and, so reaching, we see how artificial are pauses in history. Every *terminus ad quem* slides into a *terminus a quo* ; ' the vessel splits, the thought survives ' ; a thousand beacons may have been ignited at an extinguished spark.

[1] *Samuel Johnson* (English Men of Letters), p. 50.

So, Rousseau did not die in 1778. Two years before, the Declaration of Independence had been formulated by Thomas Jefferson in his spirit; twelve years after, Burke was proclaiming that good Englishmen were not his disciples. The Bastille fell in 1789, and out of the nurseries of the seventeen-seventies came a long procession of great writers, eager and hopeful to build upon its ruins.

We seem to be repeating former things. 'The dreamer awakes', we read above,[1] in the epoch when Boccaccio escaped from Dante in a galley rigged by Petrarch, 'the dreamer awakes, and tastes the air, and sees the colour of life, and feels the delight of moving his limbs. . . . He has come out of the prison-house of the theological system '— *Ecrasez l'infâme*, Voltaire had cried out upon it, —'and is abroad again in the homely disorder of our familiar world '. Now, a new escape is being planned. Liberty in France and America is winging its way out of the system of 18th-century philosophy. Prison-houses are being pulled down, and the common man, rejoicing like a bridegroom, finds it bliss in that dawn to be alive.

The economists corroborate the poets. We suggested just now the contrast between the victories of war and of peace, and illustrated it by comparing Garrick's poem in 1759 with the contemporary tales of Voltaire and Johnson. In this context we may quote from a survey of London life in the 18th century[2] the historian's evidence, that

'The new spirit which (rightly or wrongly) regarded the miseries of man as due not to original sin or an inscrutable Providence, but to bad laws and a bad environment, was beginning to be concerned not only to relieve distress but to deal with its causes. As most of our social and industrial evils have a longer history than is often supposed, so has the process of improvement and reform. The advance in health, cleanliness, order, sobriety and education, which has obviously been going on in London since 1850, can be traced since at least the middle of the 18th century '.

[1] See page 25. The quotation is repeated from Sir W. Raleigh, *Some Authors* Oxford, 1923; p. 3.
[2] By Mrs. Eric George. London, 1925; p. 20.

At the time of the Black Death in Europe they ascribed the
miseries of law and environment to original sin, and they
were still ascribing them to an inscrutable Providence when
John Wesley (1703–91) and his brother Charles were routing
the Deists. But men were strong to escape. Dr. Johnson,
though he had already written *Rasselas*, was not all-wise when
he added in 1770 his famous couplet to Goldsmith's *Deserted
Village* :

> ' How small of all that human hearts endure,
> That part which laws or kings can cause or cure '—

at least not if he penned it in a spirit of *laisser faire*—and
Wordsworth was not all-foolish when, at whatever peril to
the muse, he invoked the blessing of God on universal free
education.[1] For the removal of the causes of social wrong
and the initiation of means of industrial welfare were live
issues at the end of the 18th century. The common man was
moving out of the shadow, and it is perhaps not fanciful to
say that the Reform Act of 1832 and all that it implied in
moral progress might have been ante-dated by half a century
if the Jacobins had not outpaced the Whigs.

Paine and Godwin.   Leaving these larger speculations we
return to our proper sphere of literature. We return to it in
the company of two writers, THOMAS PAINE (1737–1809)
and WILLIAM GODWIN (1756–1836), who, though not important to our topic, assist the transition to the new age.
Paine wrote *Commonsense* in 1776, which argued in favour of
American Independence, *Rights of Man*, 1790–92, in reply to
Burke's *Reflections on the Revolution in France*, and *The Age of
Reason*, 1793. The *Rights of Man* is said to have been sold to
the number of more than a million and a half copies in this
country alone, and naturally Paine was well-known in France,
where he was imprisoned, and in America, where he died.
Godwin wrote some novels of note, and, principally, *Political
Justice*, 1793, which had immense influence on English
radicalism. Between them they count for much in the formation of the new social consciousness.

Mme de Staël and the German Romantics.   Of great in-

[1] See *The Excursion*, Book IX, at the passage beginning : ' O for the coming
of that glorious time.'

fluence, too, was GERMAINE DE STAËL (1766–1817), who, it
ls remarkable to recall, was contemporary with JANE AUSTEN
(1775–1817). The former died in Paris on 14th July and the
latter in Winchester on the 18th of the same month, and it
is a fascinating if a vain amusement to try to imagine what a
journalist of to-day would have made of that double event
in July, 1817. The quiet spinster, whose orbit was confined
to Georgian drawing-rooms in the western counties, and
whose delicate and exquisite art evoked an intense human
interest out of the ordinary round of walking, talking, driving,
dancing, dining and visiting : and the passionate amorist,
famous in every country and sometimes forbidden in her
own—it would strain the wit of a Landor to indite a conversation between the two. They never met, of course, and
in their lifetime Germaine was a bigger force than Jane.
To-day, *Sense and Sensibility*, *Pride and Prejudice*, *Mansfield
Park* and the rest are better known and better liked than
Delphine and *Corinne*, despite the close filiation of Germaine's
genius with the movements of her times. Her spiritual home
was in Germany. Even her affinity to Rousseau (and ' Corinne '
descended from ' Héloise ') was derived through her discipleship to the German writers whom she taught her countrymen
to appreciate. Her *Allemagne*, 1810, with its immense debt
to August Wilhelm Schlegel (1767–1845), taught herself as
well as her compatriots, and was so thorough a lesson in
German methods as to offend Napoleon, who did not approve
of a French inferiority-complex even in literary achievement.
The book was impounded in Paris and was published in
London in 1813 ; and in the following year the *Quarterly
Review* bore witness that the terms ' Classic' and ' Romantic'
had been made familiar in England by Mme de Staël.

Using the passport of Romanticism, issued in her spiritual
home, where the Schlegel circle of ardent men and women,
mixing their tastes like cocktails, produced the *Athenæum* in
1798 (the year of *Lyrical Ballads* in London), Germaine de
Staël moved from country to country with a nimbus of
unfulfilled desire. The children of Rousseau—of his spirit,
not his body : those were left to the fate of foundlings—
formed an international company. And there were stranger

relationships. Germaine might have called Gibbon father, for the learned historian of *The Decline and Fall of the Roman Empire* was the lover of Suzanne Curchod before she married Jacques Necker, the Genevan minister in Paris; and Germaine, if Mme Necker had had her way, would have become the wife of Chatham's son, William Pitt. But she rebelled from an English destiny, and chose instead the Baron de Staël, Swedish ambassador in Paris, as 'the next best thing to marrying no one'. So wedded, she was more free, in accordance with the standards of her class (for the range of domestic liberty was limited), to take unconsecrated lovers. The most faithful of these was BENJAMIN CONSTANT (1767–1830), translator of Schiller's *Wallenstein* and author of *Adolphe*, 1806; and through sixteen hectic years this consciously romantic couple broke each other's heart in every capital of Europe.

Politician, critic, talker, letter-writer, traveller, novelist, Germaine de Staël is to-day most rememberable as the carrier of Romance and the inventor in fiction of the *femme incomprise*. If we may attempt for one moment to play the part of the journalist in July, 1817, without aspiring to the higher part of Landor, we would say that her difference from Jane Austen lies precisely in that margin of mystery. Jane's *femmes* are thoroughly *comprises*: 'the business of her life', we are told of Mrs. Bennet in *Pride and Prejudice*,' was to get her daughters married; its solace was visiting and news', and there was no room for misunderstanding in this programme. It would not have suited Germaine. As the heroine of her own adventures, always looking at her reflection in the romantic mirror, the common things and simple lines of life were projected on to a screen, which showed them with edges and vibrations, in the patterns of which was discovered a new way to truth. The transmuting magic of romance changed the seen world in all its parts and made it one with the unseen. J. L. TIECK (1773–1853), Schlegel's collaborator in the German version of Shakespeare, sang it in the famous invocation:

> 'Mondbeglänzte Zaubernacht,
> Die den Sinn gefangen hält,

Wundervolle Märchenwelt,
Steig' auf in der alten Pracht,'

which may roughly be Englished :

'Witchery of the moonlit night,
Holding all our senses fast,
Realm of faery, wonder-bright,
Rise in splendour of the past.'

F. L. VON HARDENBERG (1772–1801), known as Novalis, and celebrated as the prophet of Romanticism, epitomized it in a single phrase : 'Die Welt wird Traum, der Traum wird Welt' ('the dream and the world áre one'), and pursued the 'Blue Flower' of mystic longing to the utmost distance of space and time ; and Goethe himself expressed it in the final chorus of *Faust* :

'Das Unzulängliche,
Hier wird's Ereigniss ;
Das Unbeschreibliche,
Hier ist es gethan.'

('Here the uncompleted finds completion, and the unseizable is achieved ').

Mme de Staël was a missioner of transcendental feeling, which 'is at once the solemn sense of Timeless Being—of " That which was, and is, and ever shall be " overshadowing us—and the conviction that Life is good. " Live thy life " is the Categorical Imperative addressed by Nature to each one of her creatures according to its kind'.[1] We have swung from Descartes to Kant.

Sir Walter Scott. More perfect and less tendencious a pursuer was the pure, clean muse of WALTER SCOTT (1771–1832), who likewise followed the blue flower across the hills and revived the colours of olden time. Among the books and essays on Scott which marked the centenary of his death in 1932, none was more illuminating than the article contributed to *The Times* newspaper on September 21st in that year by Prof. Trevelyan, O.M. There we were told that the

[1] *The Myths of Plato,* by J. A. Stewart, London, 1905 ; p. 40.

author of *Waverley* (as he was known in his period of anonymity) 'did more than any professed historian to alter mankind's vision of its past.' His imagination married to his method made the bygone arise in its *alte Pracht*, and by their conjunction the *Unbeschreibliche* was *gethan*. Writing with full responsibility as Regius Professor of Modern History at Cambridge, Dr. Trevelyan pointed out for the first time that

' The difference between Gibbon and Macaulay is a measure of the influence of Scott. Gibbon's work comes as near to perfection as any human achievement. It is able to approach perfection partly because of its limitations. It does not attempt the warm and intimate reality of human affairs in all their perplexed and romantic detail, but deals in a few facts and some very broad generalizations. Gibbon is a wonderfully accurate historian ; he tells the truth, but he does not attempt to tell more than a small portion of the truth. Living as he did before Scott, he conceived of mankind as essentially the same in all ages and countries. This was, indeed, a view characteristic of the eighteenth century with its cosmopolitan outlook, untroubled by national or sectarian prejudice. The " Philosophers " and the early French Revolutionists would have measured all human problems by the same rule. Against that unreal unity of mankind Burke protested. Scott illustrated and popularized Burke's protest. . . . And ever since Sir Walter showed mankind this new and richly variegated pattern of history, not as a mere narrative of events, still less as a mere generalization, but as " a fair field full of *folk*," mankind has craved after Scott's view rather than Gibbon's, as being both more interesting and nearer the fullness of the truth. The professional historians have tried to follow suit, though never with the perfect success that Gibbon achieved in his more limited task.'

And Others. We are fortunate in being able to quote this high authority for a change which, as the context shows, is essential to the transition from the 18th to the 19th century through the self-expression of mankind in society and politics. We might expand our survey to include yet a dozen or more names. There was BERNARDIN DE ST.-PIERRE (1737–1814)

in France, whose *Paul et Virginie*, 1787, was one of the key-
books of the new rule of sentiment; who, as a native critic
remarks, not perhaps without a touch of irony, planted the
trees on French boulevards and introduced pianos into French
lunatic-asylums; and who brought into literary use a new
terminology of nature. St.-Pierre's colour-vocabulary was
based on exact observation, not invention, and, like Dr.
ERASMUS DARWIN (1731–1802) at Lichfield, a correspondent
of Rousseau, he made ' flowers, plants and trees into men and
women '. When Wordsworth declared in 1798, ' 'tis my faith
that every flower enjoys the air it breathes,' he was speaking
in the spirit of Dr. Darwin and St.-Pierre, which Rousseau
had breathed into their nostrils. There was ROBERT BURNS
(1759–96), the short-lived Scottish peasant-poet, who, *teste*
Wordsworth again, ' brought Poetry back to Nature.' It was
a common cargo at this century's end, when to ' return to
nature ' was at once a habit and a profession; and perhaps
we may particularize more precisely the vivid Scotsman's
eager delight in proving the resources of his native language
and in treating animals and flowers not only as men and
women, like Erasmus Darwin, but as little friends familiarized
by diminutive names. Burns, with his mousies and daisies,
' lived nearer to the brown earth,' it has been well said,[1]
' upturned for sowing and crowded with life, than any other of
our poets,' and it was from the crowded life of the common
soil that the true music of nature was evoked. An inspired
faun they have called him, and, though he and William Cowper
(1731–1800) and Scott himself in his ballads belong to the
school of poetry which Pope represented in its zenith, and
which died down in the twilight notes of William Shenstone
(1714–63) and the rest, Burns, too, is a herald of the dawn.

There was GOTTFRIED AUGUST BÜRGER (1747–94) at
Göttingen, who was hardly longer-lived than Burns, and
whose ballad *Lenore*, 1774, made a beam in the morning sky
of the Romantic movement. William Taylor (1765–1836), a
busy Germanophil, translated it for the *Monthly Magazine*,
where, at Lamb's instance, it was read by Coleridge before he
wrote his *Ancient Mariner*. Scott made his own version of it

[1] By Prof. Elton.

in *William and Helen*, 1796, and plunged into German literature in its wake, so that Bürger's debt to Bishop Percy and the *Reliques* was amply requited out of the common storehouse of romance. Then, too, or rather later, there was ESAIAS TEGNÉR (1782–1846), Sweden's national poet, whose *Frithjof's Saga* has been translated eighteen times both in Germany and England, and who owed much and repaid more to the movement which Macpherson served by his *Ossian*. Above all, there was FRANÇOIS RENÉ DE CHATEAUBRIAND (1768–1848), whose *Génie du Christianisme*, 1802, with its two romantic tales, *René* and *Atala*, is a book of first-class significance. It invented the literary use of the Bible, its value as a model of style, which Swinburne appreciated so well, and it practised a more imaginative kind of criticism than had been used by modern writers before him. From Byron to Joseph Conrad later writers are deeply in Chateaubriand's debt.

The Age of Voltaire. Here, then, we leave the 18th century. Its chief representative in France was VOLTAIRE (1694–1778), whose progress across the age leaves the impression of a trail of advancing light. His works are so many, his influence was so wide, his personality was so powerful, alike in his brilliant youth and his patriarchal eld, that no brief record can be just to his immense genius and authority. Poet, philosopher, critic, historian, Voltaire adorned literature at half a dozen points. He was fearless in fighting wrong—and wrongs; evil in the abstract and evil in specific cases. He pleaded, *écrasez l'infâme*, ' crush the foul thing,' of credulity, or religion, but he likewise said, *si Dieu n'existait pas, il faudrait l'inventer*, and, in his advocacy of the oppressed, he displayed Christian virtues, if he did not profess Christian dogma. He is less readable in the 20th century than in the 18th, less a man of letters than an impregnable rock, a force in the background of modern principles :

' When the right sense of historical proportion is more fully developed in men's minds, the name of Voltaire will stand out like the names of the great decisive movements in the European advance, like the Revival of Learning, or the Reformation.'

Thus John Morley opened his book on Voltaire in 1872, and it is an exordium to history rather than to literature.

'The existence, character and career of this extraordinary person,' he went on, 'constituted in themselves a new and prodigious era.'

We think, not of Voltaire's tales and plays, but of his influence on the epic of America and the drama of Revolution in France. For 'the peculiarities of his individual genius'—a big claim for one man—'changed the mind and spiritual conformation of France, and in a less degree of the whole of the West' (including the West across the ocean), 'with as far-spreading and invincible an effect as if the work had been wholly done, as it was actually aided, by the sweep of deep-lying collective forces. A new type of belief, and of its shadow, disbelief, was stamped by the impression of his character and work into the intelligence and feeling of his own and following times.'

So, Voltaire's works are resumed in his work; Voltairism is more than Voltaire. He learned much in England and taught much in Prussia. He went before Rousseau and instructed him. By his mark on thought it became free thought.

'We are not the converts of Rousseau nor the disciples of Voltaire', wrote the English statesman within a dozen years of their death. The brief interval and the high authority show that they had already passed into history—passed even into legend, we may say. They counted for far more than men of letters, and their influence was vaster than their books. In this sense their work belongs to an ampler survey than is contained in a history of literature. But they belong to the smaller survey, too, and the men of letters who came after them, and to whom we turn now in the next Book, do not deny their discipline and faith.

R

BOOK V
REVOLUTIONARY EUROPE

FOREWORD TO BOOK V

BY coincidences helpful to historians, Cervantes and Shakespeare died in 1616, Rousseau and Voltaire in 1778, Scott and Goethe in 1832. With the first pair the Renaissance closed, with the second the 18th century, and with the third we may associate the close of the Revolutionary half-century which it inaugurated.

When Scott and Goethe died, Byron and Shelley were dead, Wordsworth, though living, was nearly silent, Keats was dead, Tennyson had published his first volume, and the Reform Act, postponed for thirty years since Burke led the Whigs into anti-Jacobinism, now at last became law. 1830 was a crucial year in French literature. Russia's Pushkin died in 1837, and Italy's Leopardi by another coincidence in the same year, which happened to be that of the accession of Queen Victoria whose name is given to her age in England.

The present Book deals mainly with that half-century, from the seventeen-seventies to the eighteen-thirties, and with the men who administered Rousseau's legacy, redeeming it from misprisal and abuse and substituting Morley's view for Burke's. The hundred years which have since elapsed, and which are very near to living memory, are more briefly characterised in an Epilogue. Special emphasis is laid on 1859, when Darwin's *Origin of Species* levelled walls as obstructive as any which had fallen in Paris seventy years before ; and then this short history of European literature is left to the judgment of its readers.

I. REVOLUTIONARY EUROPE

§ 1. GOETHE.

IN the series of 'Periods of European History' edited
by Mr. Arthur Hassall,[1] the volume called *Revolutionary
Europe* comprises the years 1789–1815. This break at the
Battle of Waterloo is politically defensible; the defeat and
capture of Napoleon left the stage free for new action. But
a literary history of Europe may not less defensibly extend
the terminus of revolution. Shelley died in 1822 and Byron
in 1824, and to neither poet did Wellington's victory bring a
change of inspiration. Dowden's *French Revolution and English
Literature*[2] does not stop at 1815, and what is true of literature
in England is true of it in other countries. A more appropriate
terminus of revolution, as a contemporary source of literary
inspiration—contemporary, as distinct from the sources of
Tolstoy's *War and Peace* and *The Dynasts* of Thomas Hardy—
is found in 1832, when Scott and Goethe died, and Carlyle
was writing his history of the Revolution, and England went
back across the storm-area to the abandoned causes of reform.[3]
In this view, the epoch of Revolution covers, roughly, the
lifetime of Scott, or the years from Rousseau's death to
Goethe's, or from the Fall of the Bastille to the Reform Act—
a symbol of destruction to a symbol of construction. They all
end in 1832.

A Complete Seer. 'Bliss was it in that dawn to be alive':
we have quoted Wordsworth's apostrophe more than once,
and recall again the next verse: 'But to be young was very
heaven.' But was it all bliss and heaven on a long view?
Wordsworth was nineteen when the Bastille fell, Scott was

---

[1] 8 vols., London, 1895–1910.   [2] London, 1897.
[3] 'The effects of the Revolution in England had been to inspire the majority
with an unreasoning dread of change. But for this feeling Parliament might
have been reformed, Nonconformists freed from their disabilities, and the
Slave Trade abolished, before the end of the (18th) century'.—Dr. G. P. Gooch,
in *The Cambridge Modern History*, Vol. VIII, p. 762.

eighteen, Coleridge seventeen, Southey fifteen. Scott's contacts came later : he lived apart ; the three Englishmen were
in close communion. Coleridge and Southey had married
sisters, and with a third brother-in-law, Robert Lovell, they
all played at a young men's dream of a pantisocracy (a
free and equal State) on the banks of the Susquehanna.
Wordsworth and Coleridge fraternized, and collaborated in
Lyrical Ballads, 1798. Wordsworth succeeded Southey as Poet
Laureate in 1843. Surviving into Victorian England, did they
forget the radiance of the dawn ?

JOHANN WOLFGANG GOETHE, too, was alive in that dawn.
But, more fortunately, perhaps, he was not young. Born at
Frankfort-on-the-Main in 1749, he was forty when the
Bastille fell : just the right age for ripe judgment, and long
past the rapture of the teens. He had made his Italian journey,
the *Italienische Reise* of 1786–88, and all his rapture was reserved
for that experience. 'From the day I entered Rome,' he
declared—October 28th, 1786—'I count a second birthday,
a rebirth,' and this was a maturer dedication than that of the
English lad in France in 1790. For Goethe's journey to Italy
(let us settle this at once) was partly an escape and partly a
fulfilment. It was a flight from the Grand Ducal Court at
Weimar, where the conditions of life, though of his own
choice and very much to his liking, were cramping and
restrictive,[1] and it was the realization of a longing for the
springs of Helicon undefiled.

This Hellenic note, which is heard throughout his writings,
is nearer to that of Keats than of Wordsworth. Keats's
yearning for the sunshine of the South—

> ' O for a beaker full of the warm South,
>   Full of the true, the blushful Hippocrene,
>   With beaded bubbles winking at the brim,
>   And purple-stained mouth ;
>   That I might drink, and leave the world unseen,
>   And with thee fade away into the forest dim '—

recalls the appeal of Goethe :

---

[1] His *Torquato Tasso* play (see page 118 above) reflected in part Goethe's
personal experience as Court-poet to Duke Karl August at Weimar.

' Kennst du das Land wo die Citronen blühn,
Im dunkeln Laub die Gold-Orangen glühn,
Ein sanfter Wind vom blauen Himmel weht,
Die Myrte still und hoch der Lorbeer steht,
Kennst du es wohl ? . . .
　　　Dahin ! 　Dahin
Geht unser Weg ! O Vater, lass uns ziehn ! '

The light shone from the skies of Italy on the lemon-groves
and golden orange-orchards, with the soft breezes, the stilly
myrtle, and the growing bay. There, by God's grace, his
road pointed, there his yearning would be sated. There he
would quaff his cup at the eternal and ever-renewed founts of
beauty and joy in Rome, not in Paris amid the fallen stones
of a broken prison-house, which Wordsworth picked up so
ecstatically[1]. We are not questioning the sincerity nor even
depreciating the currency of the revolutionary enthusiasm of
our own young poets of the seventeen-nineties, whether
dreaming in Bristol of the Susquehanna or walking in France
by the Loire ; indeed, we yield to none in reverence for
Wordsworth. But we suggest that Goethe's better fortune in
surveying the French Revolution with a grown man's eyes
made him a more complete seer, gave him less or nothing to
retract, as was Wordsworth's doom before his death, and
enabled him to concentrate with larger vision on the truth
behind the appearances of human fate. This contrast between
Goethe's Italian journey and Wordsworth's French journey
a year or two afterwards, if it has ever been noted before, has
not yet been seized in its full significance. Both lived through
the Revolutionary era ; Goethe, after his return to Weimar,
even took part in the campaign against France. But the
German poet who died in 1832 in his eighty-third year was
more fortunate in his generation than the English poet who
died at eighty in 1850, and he became a more complete
European. He had neither hoped nor feared too much, and
he kept his sense of heaven till the end. Where we quote it
does not matter, but no account of Goethe can omit it, and
it seems appropriate here to reproduce the loveliest song in

[1] See *The Prelude*, Book IX, vv. 66 ff.

his *corpus* of lyric verse, by which Goethe exactly expressed his faith :

> ' Ueber allen Gipfeln
> Ist Ruh '.
> In allen Wipfeln
> Spürest du
> Kaum einen Hauch.
> Die Vögelein schweigen im Walde.
> Warte nur, balde
> Ruhest du auch.'

Peace on the Heights. His compatriots never attained this restfulness—at least with the exception of IMMANUEL KANT (1724–1804) and possibly of G. W. F. HEGEL (1770–1831), Kant's successor in mental philosophy. Kant is equated with Luther as a deliverer of the German spirit, and, through Germany, of the spirit of mankind. Once, in 1794, his researches into natural and revealed religion brought down on him the threat of a ' cabinet order ' from the reactionary Prussian Court, an incident which points the analogy between the Kantian and the Lutheran liberation. His three *Critiques*, of ' Pure Reason ', ' Practical Reason ' and ' Judgment ' (*Urteilskraft*), his *Metaphysic of Morals* and his *Logic* constitute a philosophical system which revolutionized thought and made clear thinking and honest faith reconcilable terms in an age which was presuming their divorce. Hegel, too, in his country and time, and by transference in other countries and at other times, invented a resting-place for work-weary seekers and a breathing-space for uneasy speculation.

We must not stay with the philosophers. They implement poetry, but do not make it. But our reference to these German philosophers on the bridge between the 18th and 19th centuries helps to illustrate Goethe's supreme gift as a thinker without party in an age of action. He stood, like Dante, above the factions, even though, like Dante again, he belonged to a country and took his part. ' A ship without a pilot in great tempest ' Dante called the Italy of his day, and Goethe, too, found the ship of State labouring in the storms of revolution and war. He sought a higher peace than of arms and treaties.

254

Pacem summa tenent, there is peace on the heights, he had read in Lucan's *Pharsalia*, and at Ilmenau, in September, 1783, he inscribed on a wall of a hut the verses quoted just now. His peace (*Ruhe*) was to be spread over vaster hills than Rousseau had unfolded for refreshment. It included Kant's moral reconcilement and Hegel's transcendental unity. For Goethe, too, sought to unify knowledge. He was more than an amateur in several branches of science, particularly in optics and osteology, with their application to colour and physics, and his idea of *Ruhe* surpassed definition and defied articulate analysis. He would have claimed to be an exact thinker only in the sense that he thought about thinking and it was in this sense that he attained a summit of peace beyond the reach of his contemporaries.

From Lessing (1729–81) onwards we might enumerate a long list of German critics and teachers who enhanced the dignity of man and added to his moral stature. J. G. HERDER (1744–1803), J. G. FICHTE (1762–1814), J. P. RICHTER, Carlyle's ' giant Jean Paul ', (1763–1825), F. E. D. SCHLEIER-MACHER (1768–1834), F. L. VON HARDENBERG, ' Novalis ' (1772–1801), F. W. VON SCHELLING (1775–1854)—a bigger canvas than we can stretch would include these figures and others in the picture of Germany among the nations. By their help she withstood the blows of fate. ' Deutschland found Prussia,' wrote Carlyle, ' a solid and living State, round which the Teutonic people should consolidate itself.'[1] Fichte roused her from abasement to self-consciousness. Scharnhorst or-ganized her fighting forces, Baron von Stein directed her counsels, Wilhelm von Humboldt was her Minister of Education. E. M. ARNDT (1769–1860) sang her into freedom. THEODOR KÖRNER (1756–1813) crowned his patriotic verse, like Philip Sidney and Rupert Brooke, by a soldier's death. And other nations hurried to her for healing ; Carlyle himself and Coleridge in England, Mme. de Staël in France and so forth.

Reaction. The end was not as the beginning. That solid and living State, created by Fichte, Humboldt and the rest,

[1] *History of Frederick the Great*, XX, 13.

hardly survived its makers, hardly survived the Battle of
Leipzig, October 16–19, 1813, in which Napoleon was
defeated and his triumph at Jena was avenged. The implacable
militarism of the Hohenzollern destroyed the nation which
it had hammered into shape. It was better to have died on
the battlefield with Scharnhorst and Körner than to live
with Arndt and Stein. The facts speak for themselves. Arndt
was dismissed from his chair of history. Stein was driven out
of public office. Free speech was ranked as high treason.
Seven professors at Göttingen were forced into retirement;
three others were expatriated. One of these was JAKOB GRIMM
(1785–1863), who, with his brother WILHELM (1786–1859),
was joint-author of the tales (*Kinder—und Haus—Marchen*,
1812–15), which are as valuable in folklore as they are popular
in nurseries. For not even fairies were exempt from the
Prussian rule of blood and iron, which was imposed with
successive strokes in 1864, 1866, 1870 and 1914. The national
spirit, so powerfully aroused, perished by excess of power, and
'those moral effects of the War of Liberation, from which
so much had at first been hoped, now seemed to have been
lost utterly and for ever,'[1]

Herein lay the tragedy of HEINRICH HEINE (1797–1856).
He could find no foothold in a State in which no exercise of
patriotism was accepted unless it conformed with the opinions
of authority. The *Kultur*, which had driven out the fairies
attendant on the gentle, learned brothers Grimm, drove Heine
into voluntary exile, and when he strung his lyre in a strange
land his songs were bitter as well as sweet. He expressed many
moods in those songs, as, indeed, he was subject to many
passions; but in one set of verses out of the ample lyric
volume of his poetry, he spoke as sincerely as his fellow-Jews
in Babylon. We translate it literally :

> 'Once I possessed a lovely Fatherland.
> The oaken-tree
> Grew there so tall, the violets peeped soft.
> It was a dream.
> It kissed me German-wise and German spake

[1] Bryce, *Holy Roman Empire*, XXIII.

(You'll not believe
How fine it sounded), saying " I love thee " !
It was a dream.' ·

The Higher Teutonism. Goethe's Teutonism was of stouter
stuff. By these losses, narrownesses and errors his larger vision
may be measured. True, he was Goethe, the inconstant lover,
who loved and sang and rode away, not once but many times
in his long life. He was Goethe, the municipal dictator, who
was content to superintend the theatre at Weimar, and to
wait on the whims of its Grand Duke. He was Goethe,
playing with bones and stones while Napoleon was trampling
Europe ; Goethe, who rarely visited his loving mother and
put up with his daughter-in-law's domestic chaos. He was all
this and more—or was it less ?—to men and women incapable
of hero-worship or of its first condition of heroic insight.
But he turned from common standards with a grave smile.
' Was uns alle bändigt—das Gemeine ' could not detain him.
His body was of the earth and expressed its native urgencies,
but a serene and an unbound spirit looked out from his
wonderful eyes which fascinated all beholders. We think of
that spirit escaping from the flesh, and of the immortal music
evoked by fleeting love. We think of Goethe meeting
Napoleon, and recognized by him as a brother,' Voilà un
homme ! ' cried the conqueror to the poet. We think of him
in camp and field, when he followed Duke Karl August to
the French war, meditating peace in the clash of arms and
eternal things amid temporal illusions. On that eminence
minor differences disappeared. Patriotism was not enough for
the star-gazer. Imperial France, he wrote, is repeating the
crime of Lutheran Germany, and is driving fair deportment
(*ruhige Bildung*) underground. What would he have said of
Bismarckian Germany ? He was not rapt by pæans to liberty.
Apostles of freedom are all alike, he averred ; each seeks in
the last resort his own dominion. He was not impressed by
portents of democracy. Let the little take warning by the
great, he announced ; when the great are overthrown, the
many become the oppressors of the many. This was not the
temper of a martial leader, hardly even of a loyal German,

they might have said. But the kings and the conquerors departed ; the poet remains. When the German Empire had followed the French, and 1919 had undone 1871, Germany spent several months of 1932 in organizing successive celebrations of the centenary of Goethe as the supreme genius of her race. They might not reach his height, but they could aspire to it, and might draw their difficult breath in its rare air of renouncement, of *Entsagung*. For Goethe, too, like the eager revolutionaries, kept an open door to heaven. *Wer nie sein Brod mit Thränen ass*, he wrote, ' who never ate his bread with tears, who never sat weeping on his bed through nights of trouble ', *Der kennt euch nicht, ihr himmlischen Mächte*, ' He knows you not, ye heavenly Powers ! ' Bliss was it in that dawn to be awake, and we should part with reluctance from the legend that Goethe's last utterance was ' More light ! ' *Mehr Licht*.

His Writings. The tale of his writings is long and is complicated by overrunning and harkings-back. Their final significance in Europe—their comparative influence in Germany and abroad—is more important than their titles and order. Thus, the novel, or ethical life, of *Wilhelm Meister* in his *Lehrjahre* (Apprentice-years) and *Wanderjahre* was begun about 1778 and was completed in 1829. There was more than one version of his *Torquato Tasso* and several books of his *Italienische Reise*. He had a period of devotion to scientific writings on plants, colours, etc. His *Westöstlicher Divan*, translated by Edward Dowden, was a work of old age, 1814–19. His most youthful work of note was the play *Götz von Berlichingen*, 1773, the type of a ' noble German ' of the 16th century. Scott translated it in 1798, and ' we in England cannot forget that it may have been the acorn from which sprang the spreading oak of our *Waverley Novels* '.[1] Even wider was the spread of his next book, the novel called *Die Leiden des jungen Werthers* (' The sorrows, or sufferings, of young Werther '), 1774, after which Goethe was known for many years as ' the author of *Werther* '. It enjoyed a kind of Byronic fame, filling every young heart with dissatisfied Wertherism, and to Goethe's biographers it possesses (as,

[1] J. G. Robertson, *The Life and Work of Goethe*, London ,1932 ; p. 50.

indeed, do most of his works) a further subjective interest, derived from one of his love-affairs—this time with Lotte Buff; it was affected, too, by the suicide of his intimate friend, K.-W. von Jerusalem. A subjective work *de longue haleine* was his *Dichtung und Wahrheit* ('Fiction and Fact') of 1810–14, 1821 and 1830–31. He wrote plays: *Iphigenie*, 1786, *Egmont*, 1787, *Hermann und Dorothea*, 1796; a Reynard-epic, *Reinecke Fuchs*, 1793; 'Roman Elegies' and 'Venetian Epigrams'; an epilogue to Schiller's *Glocke* and a prologue to Carlyle's *Life of Schiller*, in generous and wholehearted commemoration of his close friendship and part-collaboration from 1794 to 1805 with the great national dramatist, J. C. F. von Schiller (1759–1805); ballads and other lyric verse, and much else in various kinds, while his letters, diaries and conversations (*Gespräche*), chiefly with his last secretary, J. P. Eckermann, extend to another library of books.

Above all, and through sixty years, 1772–1831, he wrote *Faust*, Parts I and II. He was sensible of time on his side in this ample leisurely composition of an epic-drama which ranks with the works of Lucretius, Dante and Milton. His transformation of the old German folk-tale of power-lust into a symbolic poem of spirit-hunger, universalizing in an epoch of unrest, hardly paralleled in the history of man, his own exalted sense of attainable tranquillity, is familiar to critics and students, and must not detain us here either by its majesty or by its loose ends. ' At the time when he first came in contact with the story,' we are told, ' Faust-dramas were being announced by authors from all corners in Germany '.[1] But all the corners of Germany were too narrow for Goethe's genius. The Greek in him Hellenized the Faust of German folklore. Its rude fun and crude morality were humanized on earth and purged in heaven, as if Kant had edified Shakespeare's Shylock. Deliverance was vouchsafed to the questing soul:

> ' Wer immer streben sich bemüht,
>   Den können wir erlösen '.

To him that giveth-up much is given.

---

[1] *Men, Myths and Movements in German Literature*, by W. Rose, London, 1931; p. 81.

We cannot summarize this world-drama in a paragraph. To many the interest of Part I is contained in its unsurpassed acting values: the cellar, Gretchen, Mephistopheles. To others the final chorus of Part II is the utmost expression of human wisdom:

> ' Alles Vergängliche
> Ist nur ein Gleichniss;
> Das Unzulängliche,
> Hier wird's Ereigniss;
> Das Unbeschreibliche,
> Hier ist es gethan;
> Das Ewig-Weibliche
> Zieht uns hinan '.

Meanwhile all will subscribe to Sir Frederick Pollock's estimate :[1]

' The whole of our education and experience bids us to renounce and resign : *dass wir entsagen müssen*. The problem of man's life is to reconcile himself to this. One ready way is the superficial way of the many, to proclaim that all things are vanity. But the path of wisdom, sought only by a few, is to cut short the pains of resignation in detail by resignation once for all ; to rest one's mind on what is eternal, necessary, and uniform, and possesses ideas which remain undisturbed by the contemplation of a transitory world. This was the secret,' he adds, ' of Spinoza for Goethe.'

And this is the revelation, we add further, of Goethe's *Faust* for mankind.

§ 2. ENGLAND AND FRANCE.

Anti-Burke. It will be recalled that Dr. Richard Price (1723–91), an eminent Nonconformist divine, had been celebrating the centenary of the bloodless and glorious Revolution of 1688 when Edmund Burke was moved to condemn the contemporary movement in France. It was not

---

[1] *Spinoza : His Life and Philosophy*, 2nd edn., London, 1899 ; p. 370.

a time for nice distinctions between revolutions. It was a time for prison-breaking and cutting-off heads, for threatening kings and asserting popular principles, and it ill became a minister of religion, in the opinion of the Minister of State, to treat a name of shame as a name of glory.

Still, there were those who differed from Burke. Dr. Price died in 1791, a year after the publication of the *Reflections on the Revolution in France*. But the French Revolution was still in being; the American colonists were working out their independence; Tom Paine, meditating *The Rights of Man*, became a French *citoyen* in 1792; SAMUEL TAYLOR COLERIDGE (1772–1834) was talking at Cambridge, high-falutin' talk, as it might be called to-day, and there were other indications that Burke's strictures did not convince some younger men.

Two items particularly we would select out of the speeches and writings of the time for the sake of certain later affiliations. In April, 1785, Dr. R. Watson, Bishop of Llandaff, had preached an Anniversary Sermon to the Stewards of the Westminster Dispensary. He printed his discourse in 1793 and added thereto an Appendix ' on the French Revolution and the British Constitution.' It was published at twopence, and the Loughborough Association recommended it ' for the support of the Constitution to the serious attention of the Public.' WILLIAM WORDSWORTH (1770–1850), a youthful member of the public and a future collaborator in *Lyrical Ballads* (1798) with S. T. Coleridge, sat down at once to the composition of *A Letter to the Bishop of Llandaff on the Extraordinary Avowal of his Political Principles, contained in the Appendix to his late Sermon.* He signed himself, ' A Republican ', a signature which matters the less since his retort went unpublished till 1876. Nor is his argument material to-day, save to note that he compared the Right Reverend defender of the British Constitution to a ' drunken man reeling towards his home ' with ' business on both sides of the road '. Wordsworth lived to change his views on kings, bishops, and Mr. Burke. He lived to succeed Southey as Poet Laureate, and to appoint his nephew, the Bishop of Lincoln, as his literary executor. He changed his views on more intimate things than any concerning Church or State. In the flush of his dawn of bliss in France he had fallen in love at Orleans with Annette Vallon, who bore him a daughter, Caroline, later the wife of a certain J.–B. Baudouin. But he let Annette and Caroline go. Willingly, even deliberately, he obliterated them, and the closely guarded secret of their existence was not disclosed till 1916.[1] We are not criticising Wordsworth for inconsistency. In times of revolution consistency is not a virtue. Our point is that Burke's view of the French Revolution was not shared by the authors of *Lyrical Ballads*.

The second item likewise had repercussions. We have already mentioned William Godwin (1756–1836), whose *Enquiry Concerning Political Justice*, 1793, became the leading text-book of English Radicalism. In 1797 he married Mary Wollstonecraft, a woman of tragic experience, who died in the year of her marriage at the birth of her daughter, Mary. Mrs. Godwin, like Wordsworth, was anti-Burke, and she did not hide her name or her opinions. She was an admirer of Dr. Price, and her zeal for the poor and the oppressed was not appeased by the squirearchy's promise of their relief by compensation in the next world. So she wrote boldly and rather brilliantly a present *Vindication of the Rights of Man*, as he was expressing himself in France. This was in 1791. Many years afterwards a boy rising twenty sent a spontaneous letter to William Godwin, saying among other things that he was thinking of composing an inquiry into ' the failure of the French Revolution to benefit mankind.' The boy's name was PERCY BYSSHE SHELLEY (1792–1822), and his naïf letter must have touched the older man's heart, despite his second marriage to Mrs. Clairmont in 1801. His daughter Mary became Shelley's second wife[2] in 1816 and survived the poet till 1851, and his stepdaughter, Clara Clairmont, became the unmarried mother of Byron's daughter Allegra. So the generous spirit of Mary Wollstonecraft, a pioneer of the feminist movement by her *Vindication of the Rights of Women*,

[1] By the investigation of Professor G. McLean Harper, *William Wordsworth : His Life, Work and Influence* (3rd edn., 2 vols. in 1, London, 1929). The evidence was confirmed and expanded by Professor E. Legouis, *William Wordsworth and Annette Vallon* (London, 1922).

[2] We omit the ' chatter about Harriet ' Westbrook, Shelley's first wife, whom he married in 1811, whom he deserted for Mary, and who drowned herself in the Serpentine in Hyde Park on November 10, 1816.

1792, met the generous spirit of her son-in-law, who was five years old when she died. Burke's warning to the disciples of Rousseau fell on deaf ears among the poets.

Wordsworth. It is tempting to linger in the English scene with the great writers, who, from almost every shire, Cumberland, Devon, Sussex, Warwick, brought, like the Canterbury pilgrims, their meed of story and song. That many of them died in the South, Keats in Rome, Landor in Florence, Byron in Greece, Shelley by drowning off Leghorn, is another sign of the *Kennst du das Land* which drove Goethe to his Italian journey, and which caused Schiller, his finest critic, to write to him in the course of their eleven years' intimacy : ' Had you been born a Greek, or even an Italian, your way would have been infinitely shortened '.

Meanwhile, the greatest of these English writers found his Greece and Italy within. William Wordsworth, the Cumbrian, and a country-dweller all his life, made but one journey abroad—one formative journey, that is to say—when he went to France between 1790 and 1792. His famous dawn of bliss was at Calais, on July 13, 1790, the eve of the Feast of Federation, where he saw, or believed he saw,

> " In a mean city, and among a few,
>   How bright a face is worn when joy of one
>   Is joy of tens of millions."
>   (*Prelude*, VI, 347-349).

He articulated his belief in Book IX of the same poem, verses 519-32, stating that he shared the conviction of his French mentor, the Republican General, Michel Beaupuy,

> ' That a benignant spirit was abroad
>   Which might not be withstood, that poverty
>   Abject as this would in a little time
>   Be found no more, that we should see the earth
>   Unthwarted in her wish to recompense
>   The meek, the lowly, patient child of toil,
>   All institutes for ever blotted out
>   That legalised exclusion, empty pomp
>   Abolished, sensual state and cruel power,

Whether by edict of the one or few ;
And finally, as sum and crown of all,
Should see the people having a strong hand
In framing their own laws ; whence better days
To all mankind '.

Whatever his political inconsistencies, whatever his personal disloyalties, he never varied in this belief. Though he would not publish *The Prelude*[1] in his lifetime, preferring to keep it by him for half a century, patching and doctoring its text with a mature man's conscientious endeavour to put an old head on young shoulders, he never compromised his hope for ' better days for all mankind.' *All* mankind is significant. Not Frenchmen only should share in the new order. Not France only was cheated, when

' now, become oppressors in their turn,
Frenchmen had changed a war of self-defence
For one of conquest.'
(Prelude, XI, 206–08).

The original objects of their warfare, in which *(ibid.*, 110–12)

' the meagre, stale, forbidding ways
Of custom, law, and statute, took at once
The attraction of a country in romance,'

were still and always *his* objects. *Their* objects had changed, not his, and Nature, mending her lover's heart, held up *(ibid.*, XIII, 29–32)

' before the mind intoxicate
With present objects, and by the busy dance
Of things that pass away, a temperate show
Of objects that endure.'

The passing things had to be universalized, romanticized. *Alles Vergängliche ist nur ein Gleichniss.* The things that endure

---

[1] *The Prelude, or Growth of a Poet's Mind*, an autobiographical (or autopsychological) poem in 14 Books of blank verse (Childhood, Schooltime, Cambridge, Vacation, Books, London, France, etc.) was written between 1799 and 1805 and was published posthumously in 1850. The text has been collated by Prof. E. de Sélincourt in a definitive edition, and a valuable commentary will be found in *La Jeunesse de Wordsworth* by Prof. Emil Legouis.

had to be interpreted in order to prove the law of permanence
and immanence :

> ' Alas ! What differs more than man from man !
> And whence that difference ? Whence but from him-
>   self ? . . .
> The sleepless ocean murmurs for all ears ; . . .
> The primal duties shine aloft like stars ;
> The charities that soothe, and heal, and bless,
> Are scattered at the feet of Man—like flowers.'

So he wrote in Book IX of his *Excursion*, the ponderous
second part of a spiritual epic, of which the other two parts
were not written ; and in his *Ode to Duty* he prayed :

> ' My hopes no more must change their name . . .
> Flowers laugh before thee on their beds,
> And fragrance in thy footing treads ;
> Thou dost preserve the stars from wrong ;
> And the most ancient heavens, through thee, are fresh
>   and strong '.

It was to a deeper than present joy, whether realizable by
Frenchmen or others, that Wordsworth recalled a generation
which had set its heart on temporal things : to a ' joy in widest
commonalty spread ' ; to ' the deep power of joy ', by which
' we see into the life of things ' ; to the mood in which he
felt

> ' A presence that disturbs me with the joy
> Of elevated thoughts ; a sense sublime
> Of something far more deeply interfused,
> Whose dwelling is the light of setting suns,
> And the round ocean and the living air,
> And the blue sky and in the mind of man ;
> A motion and a spirit, that impels
> All thinking things, all objects of all thought,
> And rolls through all things. Therefore am I still
> A lover of the meadows and the woods '.
>   (*Tintern Abbey*, 1798) ;

and in which he prayed :

> ' And O, ye Fountains, Meadows, Hills and Groves,
> Forbode not any severing of our loves ! . . .
> Thanks to the human heart by which we live
> Thanks to its tenderness, its joys, and fears,
> To me the meanest flower that blows can give
> Thoughts that do often lie too deep for tears '.
> *(Ode on Intimation of Immortality*, 1803–06).

Wordsworthians do not readily stop quoting, and, indeed, Wordsworth's readers have been multiplied in every decade. Particularly in times of stress, whether national or personal, his poetry inspires and consoles. His simple love of the countryside, with the heart of all humanity in its ' grave livers ' ; his poems of feeling and imagination, quickened to transcendental insight ; his sonnets, more rousing in their patriotism than Fichte's *Addresses to the German Nation* ; his lyric songs, ballads and odes ; even the 9 Books of *The Excursion* and the 14 of *The Prelude* are a part of the English heritage and have affected the mind of Europe. For more and more, as the Terror receded, Wordsworth won the disciples refused by Burke to Rousseau, to whose nature-lore and child-lore the English poet is so immensely indebted. Poets and professors of poetry have laid their offerings on his shrine : Coleridge, Matthew Arnold, Frederic Myers, Stopford Brooke, Edward Dowden, Walter Raleigh ; and if one clue among many to his secret may be hazarded in conclusion, we would suggest that readers look for the occurrence of the words ' deep ' and ' joy ' in his poetry. Their frequency is remarkable, since the morning when he stood a-tiptoe in Calais and came home to warn us in stately phrase :

> ' We must be free or die, who speak the tongue
> That Shakespeare spake ; the faith and morals hold
> Which Milton held.'

Shelley. The glory of Shelley was love—free, open, beautifying love, radiant in vision, musical in expression, illuminating everything that he wrote. It was fused with political enthusiasm into a love of public liberty, expressing

> ' the eternal law,
> By which those live to whom this world of life
> Is as a garden ravaged ' ;

and to a repair of that ravaged garden (*Epipsychidion*, 185–87) his heart and his head were devoted. WILLIAM BLAKE (1757–1827) was moved by mystic longing for a like ideal, and he is the only poet-artist who could have designed illustrations to Shelley's poems. So Mary Shelley wrote of her dead husband :

' To defecate life of its misery and its evil was the ruling passion of his soul. . . . He looked on political freedom as the direct agent to effect the happiness of mankind ; and thus any new-sprung hope of liberty inspired a joy and an exultation more intense and wild than he could have felt for any personal advantage.'

Remembering to-day how young he was, how full was the flood of his poetry, and how many hopes of political liberty sprang to new birth in his brief lifetime, we shall be less surprised at his occasional incoherence, at the occasional dizziness of that soaring spirit. For his love, he sang, was no other than

> ' The desire of the moth for the star,
> Of the night for the morrow,
> The devotion to something afar
> From the sphere of our sorrow,'

and it might not always see the near things of the day.

Shelley's readers will discover for themselves the magic of his language, in which the meaning melts into the sound and the words are mixed with the music which they make. Not all that he wrote maintains its vogue. But his *Adonais* (the elegy on Keats), his *Ode to the West Wind*, his *Sensitive Plant*, some choruses in his dramas, his *Hymn to Intellectual Beauty*, such a sonnet as *Ozymandias*, and many lilting lyric poems, are among the everlasting possessions. Reading Shelley aloud, we hear with our feelings as well as with our ears :

> ' From rainbow clouds there flow not
>   Drops so bright to see
>   As from thy presence showers a rain of melody.'

So Shelley of the skylark, and so Shelley's readers of the poet.

Byron. George Gordon, LORD BYRON (1788–1824) was a libertarian, like Shelley, and followed a ' new-sprung hope of liberty ' to a hero's death in Greece. He was heroic, almost legendary, in his lifetime. Always his eyes were fixed on more tangible and positive objects than those visualized by Shelley in his abstract dream of justice. He drew back from our fog-bound island the veil which hid the warming sun, faring South in this sense like Chaucer when English literature was young. But Byron enlivened our drab ways and added calories to our system by shock-tactics rather than by scholars'-trove. His amorous adventures, his interesting melancholy, his sudden glimpses of blue sky from Continental Sundays 'out of Church, his irresponsible glee in releasing English villas from conventionality, his quips, his daring rhymes, his rebellious genius—these contributed to the legend of *le Byronisme* and *der Byronismus*, which spread across France and Germany, extended to Spain and other countries, and presently flooded contagious Russia with Byronic heroes complete to the flowing collar.

Perhaps the highest compliment that was ever paid him was his representation as Euphorion, the offspring of Helen and Faust, in Part II of Goethe's epic-drama :

> ' Scharfer Blick die Welt zu schauen '

(keen eyes to see the world),

> ' Mitsinn jedem Herzensdrang '

(sympathy with every heart's desire),

> ' Liebesgluth der besten Frauen '

(love of the loveliest women),

> ' Und ein eigenster Gesang '

(and a wholly individual song),—

this is justly accounted his final epitaph, and it was laid by Goethe on Byron's tomb. Time has undone much of his popularity both at home and abroad. We think less of his work than of its influence, and even that is passing away. But his insurgent brilliance, like that of Napoleon himself, left its mark on the social map of Europe. He crowded into a short life love, travel, adventure, friendship, pride, in a profusion hardly to be measured. Not long after the middle of the 19th century Matthew Arnold ventured to predict that Byron's fame would not be dim in 1900, and his genius is so vital as to justify the prediction that in the year 2,000 his Titanic note, as it has been called, will still resound round the little homes of lesser men, arousing them out of self-complacency.

One word more must be added to make the English scene clear. There was a Revolution in France which, moving Burke and his supporters to grave fears, moved Wordsworth, Coleridge and Southey to bright hopes. Twenty years or so younger than these three poets, Byron and Shelley grew up in the epoch of war and reconstruction. It was a different time, and they were of different origin. They were more objectively zealous in aspiration, and they lived less sheltered lives. Wordsworth never ventured far from the protection of his adoring sister Dorothy. She went with him on his wedding-trip in October, 1802, and she companioned him in the August of that year on his unique visit to his French daughter Caroline. The younger poets did not hide their light. It burnt fiercely and consumed them earlier. Byron had no protector, and Shelley exacerbated his father. It is not fanciful to suggest, looking back through the poetry which they made, to the time and circumstances in which they made it, that they were what is now called class-conscious. Byron was sixth in descent from the Baron created by Charles I in 1643, and Shelley, the heir to a Baronetcy, 'was born in the purple of the English squirearchy'.[1] Thus, they were aristocrats in an age when aristocracy had learnt a harsh lesson. They felt the oppression of the poor, the burden of privilege and prerogative, as a

[1] *Shelley*. By J. A. Symonds; 'English Men of Letters'; London, 1907; p. 4.

crime of their own class against the common people moving out of the shadow. THOMAS CARLYLE (1795–1881), the son of a Scottish mason, was subject to no such inhibition. He could write his *History of the French Revolution* with the same sense of Necessity and Faith as had moved Martin Luther, the ' Hero as Priest' of his splendid lectures on hero-worship ; he could write his monumental *History of Frederick the Great* with whole-hearted admiration for a type of the Great Men who had imposed sweet order upon turmoil and sansculottism. Byron and Shelley had no such contact with the commonalty, and the occasional shrillness of their partizanship, its expression in atheism, a-moralism and so forth, may partly be ascribed to this cause. It was generous, because they were poets, but it was not always fully sane, and it is Byron's exhibitionism, in the current use of that term, which contributed to his wide and sudden fame.

§ 3. THE GREEK SUCCESSION.

Broken Forms. The mould of literature cast in the Renaissance was broken in the Revolution. We might say that it was cast by Italian humanists and broken by French humanitarians. ' We are not the converts of Rousseau, we are not the disciples of Voltaire ' : Burke's refusal is quoted once more in order to emphasize the fact that it was directed at men of letters. Rarely has a statesman of Burke's eminence built his policy on a rejection of foreign literature, and rarely have young English poets—we are thinking particularly of Wordsworth, but Coleridge, Southey and others were concerned— made their début by an excursion into foreign policy. Yet Wordsworth's theory of the poet's craft, expounded in his essays and prefaces into a system of poetics, and requiring, though he did not always use it, a diction drawn from common life, was in some degree the counterpart of the politics which he had learnt from Rousseau and seen in operation in France. In opposing Burke's attitude towards the Revolution, he was opposing the poetic tradition of the 18th century, represented principally by Pope. So he asked for a new vocabulary, a direct approach to natural phenomena and less regular measures of verse : in one word, for romantic freedom instead of classical law.

The movement was frankly a revolt, and the volume by Professor C. E. Vaughan which deals with it in Saintsbury's 'Periods of European Literature' is properly called *The Romantic Revolt*. But it was not consummated in Europe. The demands formulated in the Old World were most fully satisfied in the New, where Walt Whitman (1819–92), the leading poet of America, declared, like Jacob at Luz, that to him every common thing was sacred :

' Lads ahold of fire-engines and hook-and-ladder ropes no less to me than the Gods of the antique wars.'

Modernity was as romantic as antiquity and the commonplace was miraculous :

' To me every hour of the light and dark is a miracle,
    Every inch of space is a miracle . . .
    Every spear of grass,—the frames, limbs, organs
        of men and women, and all that concern them,
    All these to me are unspeakable miracles.'

Not even the authors of *Lyrical Ballads*, 1798, adducing the principle that ' it is the honourable characteristic of Poetry that its materials are to be found in every subject which can interest the human mind,' ventured so far in experimentation as Walt Whitman. Still, in the Old World, as more freely in the New, wild oats were sown on Parnassus, and the familiar gibes of armchair critics—Jeffrey's ' This will never do,' and the rest of them—prove that the guardians of tradition were sensitive of the harvest.

The old mould was being broken. Byron, though he was to die in Greece, wrote at the opening of his *Childe Harold's Pilgrimage* that he dared not call the Greek muse from her sacred hill. Shelley, for all his Greek studies and deep immersion in Hellenic lore, exclaimed in the final chorus of his *Hellas* that ' Another Athens shall arise.' He would ' write no more the tale of Troy ' nor mix his dawn-joy ' with Laian rage ; ' and Wordsworth, except in *Laodamia*, had no use for the gods of Greece. Why, he asked, should the joys of Paradise be sought afar in the realm of myth, when they might be gathered as 'a simple produce of the common day,' and expressed in language of the same extraction ? The revolt of the young poets in England, though never so extreme as it was to become in the Republican writings of Walt Whitman, and though estopped in Wordsworth by changed circumstances and in Byron and Shelley by early death, was very clearly formulated.

Repaired Hellenism. But Greece reasserted her spell. Mitford's *History*[1] was superseded by Grote's, ' Close thy Byron, open thy Goethe,' wrote Carlyle in *Sartor Resartus*, a few years after Byron's death, and the counsel is worth pondering for a moment. We would associate it at once with the German studies to which Carlyle was so much addicted, not merely in his monumental history of Frederick the Great, but in his smaller life of Schiller, his translation of *Wilhelm Meister*, his reverence for Luther, his close reading of Johann Paul Richter, ' the giant Jean Paul, who has power to escape out of hearsays,' and his constant apprenticeship to the philosophers, Winckelmann, Lessing and Herder, who had drawn out a healing Hellenism from the taboos of pseudo-classic orthodoxy. Walter Pater (1839–1904) speaks with discernment of the note of revolt against the 18th century, which we detect in Goethe, who

' illustrates,' he said, ' a union of the Romantic spirit, in its adventure, its variety, its profound subjectivity of soul, with Hellenism, in its transparency, its rationality, its desire for beauty—that marriage of Faust and Helena, of which the art of the 19th century is the child. . . . Goethe illustrates, too, the predominance in this marriage of the Hellenic element.'

Here, surely, is the clue to Carlyle's counsel, given ten years before Pater was born. Greece, recovered with so much pains from the darkness of the early Middle Ages, Greece, raised to so blind authority by the followers of Boileau in the 18th century, was not to be lost again for the poor trove of the idiot boy, the ass, the simple child, the boy at Kilve, the March

[1] See note 1, page 281 below.

buds, and the rest of the humble witnesses whom Wordsworth had summoned to the bar of truth and Francis Jeffrey (1773–1850), his coeval critic, had always concurrently denounced. Nor was Byron's Greek death a full atonement for his denial of the Greek muse. True, Goethe himself had represented Byron as Euphorion, the offspring of the Faust and Helen marriage, from which reconcilement was to begin. ' Aber es geling dir nicht ', he added : but not even Byron's effort was successful ; and, though Goethe admitted that success was a boon which it were idle to implore (' Wem gelingt es ?— Trübe Frage '), yet he emphasized the predominance of the Hellenic element, and for the sake of that predominance Carlyle chose Goethe above Byron.

Goethe, as we saw, went to Italy when Wordsworth found his dawn of bliss in France. He sought the Renaissance-land of Hellenism. He visited with set purpose the cities of the re-birth of Greece : Rome, where Reuchlin, his country-man, had sat at the feet of Argyropoulos[1], and Florence, where Petrarch had spelt out the *Iliad* on his toilsome road to the living dead. Out of Italy in the golden 15th century the soul of Greece had flown across the Alps, bringing to Reuchlin's native Germany powers and faculties, which, though retarded by many years of religious and social warfare, were to flower at last in the 18th century and to call to the secret Greek in Goethe. ' Dahin ! Dahin, O Vater, lass uns ziehn ! ' he exclaimed out of his Greek soul, and ' had you been a Greek, or even an Italian,' Schiller wrote to him, ' your way would have been infinitely shortened.' Short or long, he took that way, Reuchlin's way reversed across the Alps, drawn irresistibly *dahin* by an urge that would not be denied. And at home in Weimar again, finally touching the Faust-legend with the philosophy learnt in Italy from the Greeks, he supplied the Scottish teacher of a hard gospel with a text for the reconcilement between poetry and the moral law :

' Close thy Byron, open thy Goethe ; love not Pleasure, love God. This is the Everlasting Yea, wherein all contra-diction is solved ; wherein whoso works and walks, it is well with him.'

[1] See page 72 above.

JOHN KEATS (1795–1821). The Greek road brings us direct to Keats, who was born in the same year as Carlyle and who was the third and youngest of the three poets— Byron and Shelley are the other two—whose brief lifetime falls within the span of Goethe, Wordsworth, Coleridge and Scott.

Everyone knows his reaction to Chapman's Homer; how he felt

> ' like some watcher of the skies
> When a new planet swims into his ken:
> Or like stout Cortez when with eagle eyes
> He stared at the Pacific; '

and probably everyone knows of his earlier reaction to Edmund Spenser, our English Homer of Chapman's time by descent through Virgil and Ariosto; how Keats borrowed the *Faery Queen* from a schoolfellow, and ' went through it as a young horse through a spring meadow ramping.' Some words stick in the memory and call to one another across the centuries. Petrarch, reading Cicero in the 14th century, apostrophised him in an ecstasy of enjoyment: ' Yours are the springs from which we water our meadow '. It was the same meadow which Keats found in Spenser. His initiation into Elizabethan poetry was his initiation into Hellenism. Like Petrarch, he took his Greek at secondhand: Petrarch, unable to find a Greek teacher, took it from the Renaissance of Greece in Florence; Keats, the London ostler's son, took it from the Renaissance poets of his own country. By his transmission of the Tudor Hellenists to the 19th century, he was to join the age of Shakespeare to that of Tennyson, and he enabled Byron's generation to open their Goethe in Keats. Take his *Hyperion*, for example. Though a fragment in three unfinished Books of 357, 391 and 136 lines respectively, it is recognized as the *Paradise Lost* of pagan myth. He published it in 1820, but he was not content with it. He had been reading Dante in Cary's translation, and towards the close of 1819 he tried to revise his own poem. This second version *The Fall of Hyperion*, called ' a vision ' in Dante's vein, was written only as far as verse 62 of Canto II, and was not

published till 1856, many years after the poet's death. But it
' justifies the surmise that, had his powers not failed, he might
have given to England a poem more nearly comparable than
any other with Goethe's *Faust* '.[1] We are very close to
Carlyle's aspiration.

Keats moved in the company of big men, though he lived
obscurely and for a few years : Dante, Spenser, Milton,
Goethe, Tennyson, Rossetti. His odes *On a Grecian Urn,
To a Nightingale, To Autumn*, his *Eve of St. Agnes* and *La Belle
Dame sans Merci*, his sonnets, his *Endymion* and *Hyperion*, and
the elegiac *Adonais* which his death evoked from Shelley, make
it fitting to measure his fame by theirs. And a bigger man
than any may be added to them. For he possessed, we are
told on grave authority :

' The highest gift of all in poetry, that which sets poetry
above the other arts ; I mean the power of concentrating all
the far-reaching resources of language on one point, so that
a single and apparently effortless expression rejoices the
æsthetic imagination at the moment when it is most expectant
and excited, and at the same time astonishes the intellect with
a new aspect of truth. This is found only in the greatest poets.
and is rare in them ; and it is no doubt for the possession of
this power that Keats has often been likened to Shakespeare,
and very justly, for Shakespeare is of all poets the greatest
master of it.'

This was written by ROBERT BRIDGES (1845–1930), late Poet
Laureate of England. Three poets are conjoined in the
tribute.

Landor. The road from Keats leads directly to ALFRED
TENNYSON (1809–92), who, though Poet Laureate to Queen
Victoria for forty-two years, won the Chancellor's medal for
English verse at Cambridge in the reign of George IV, and,
through Tennyson, to DANTE GABRIEL ROSSETTI (1828–82)
and the Pre-Raphaelite movement. But there are parallel roads
as well as a direct one, and consideration is next due to

---

[1] *The Cambridge History of English Literature*, Vol. XII, p. 86. The writer is the
late Professor C. H. Herford, the leading Anglo-German scholar of his day.

ALEXANDER PUSHKIN, 1799–1837, in *Russia*,
GIACOMO LEOPARDI, 1798–1837, in *Italy*,
ALFRED DE VIGNY, 1797–1863, and
VICTOR HUGO, 1802–85, in *France*,

to whom we might add, if music were literature,

RICHARD WAGNER, 1813–83, in *Germany*.

Before quitting the English scene, however, for this excursion abroad, and noting, by the way, that CHARLES DARWIN (1809–82) was born in the same year as Tennyson, a brief pause may be made at the *Imaginary Conversations*, 1824, 1828, 1829, of WALTER SAVAGE LANDOR (1775–1864).

Landor belongs, it will be seen, to the ripe vintage of the seventeen-seventies, which produced Scott, Wordsworth (by the cipher), Southey, Coleridge, and other great men. He outlived them all, and surpassed them in the sense that he was singularly unaffected by the changing times in which he lived. It has been observed by the prince of modern critics that, ' though he lived to receive the homage of Swinburne, his schoolboy walks had taken him past the house where still lingered the daughter of Addison.'[1] The observation joins 1672 to 1909, and it is appropriate to the junction of diverse strands which Landor's genius illustrates. Generally, we can distinguish in writers the Classical from the Romantic note. We can say that Wordsworth's *Descriptive Sketches* were almost irredeemably ' eighteenth-century ' and that his *Stepping Westward* and similar lyrics are essentially ' romance.' We cannot separate the elements in Landor. They are blended harmoniously in his prose, the bulkier and more permanent part of a body of writings which contain some poems not easily forgotten. This blend of contrary strains is expressed in the choice of *Conversations* as his vehicle. By bringing men and women together to express their individuality, he applied the dramatist's gift to real personages of history. King James I and Isaac Casaubon ; Louis XVIII and Talleyrand ; William Wallace and King Edward I ; La Fontaine and De La

[1] Prof. G. Saintsbury, in *The Cambridge History of English Literature*, Vol. XII, p. 218.

Rochefoucauld; Galileo, Milton and a Dominican; Chaucer, Boccaccio and Petrarch; Machiavelli and Michael Angelo; Princess Mary and Princess Elizabeth; Henry VIII and Anne Boleyn; even Dante and Beatrice; these are selected at random from the five series of such studies which he perfected in 1853.

The special value of this gift to posterity resides in the devotion to scholarship displayed by Landor in an innovating age. Keats died, Goethe died, Wordsworth lingered after the death of Scott, Shelley and Byron, and all through that departure of the great, Landor persisted in his Hellenic studies and in reviving old learning in a new society. It is noted that he was not an exact scholar, and he himself never aimed at popularity: 'I shall dine late', he foretold, 'but the dining-room will be well lighted, and the guests few and select'. As to the scholarship, Swinburne put it best when he wrote of Landor, whom he admired warmly:

> 'Through the trumpet of a child of Rome
> Rang the pure music of the flutes of Greece.'

The same thing might have been said of Petrarch, who like-wise got to Greece through Rome, and who ranks as a Hellenist though he could not read Greek. The degree of Landor's purity as a Grecian is less to the point than the Attic perfection of his style in prose, as to which we may quote Saintsbury again, that 'more beautiful things — from the famous "Dreams," which sometimes fill pages, to the little phrases, clauses and passages which occur constantly—are not to be found in literature, ancient or modern, English or foreign'. This is a great gift from the epoch when Napoleon was dying in St. Helena, and Byron was aiming at shooting stars, and Wordsworth was turning-in on himself, and England was moving towards the Reform Act. The 'guests few and select' who enjoy Landor's hospitality to-day confirm his high seat in the Greek succession.

Greek Scholarship. We are writing a history of literature, not of scholarship, a field which has been most admirably surveyed by Sir John Sandys in his three-volumed *History of Classical Scholarship*. But since we selected Homer as the

277

T

representative Greek poet whose works were recovered with so much pains out of the darkness of the Middle Ages, we may select him again in the full light of modern knowledge, and add the eminent name of FRIEDRICH AUGUST WOLF (1759–1824) to the list of Homerists mentioned above. He was a student at Göttingen and a teacher at Halle, where Goethe attended some of his lectures, and partly by what he taught Goethe and partly by his own contribution to learning Wolf ranks in European literature as a father of the revival of Greek studies. The Romantic movement is immensely indebted to him. His *Prolegomena to Homer*, 1795, is a landmark in the history of Hellenism, and was contemporary with the translation of the *Odyssey*, 1781, and the *Iliad*, 1793, into German hexameters by his fellow-countryman, J. H. Voss (1751–1826), with the *editio princeps* of the *Scholia* to the MS. Codex Venetus A of the *Iliad* by J.-B. D'AUSSE DE VILLOISON (1750–1805), the French Hellenist, and with the illustrations to Homer drawn by JOHN FLAXMAN (1755–1826), the English artist and sculptor—a brilliant band of workers in the same field.

§ 4. THE RUSSIAN MOMENT.

Very late in the comity of nations Russia entered into her inheritance of the Renaissance. One historian tells us that her ' Middle Ages ' extended to the reign (1689–1725) of Peter the Great. Another dates her literary beginning from the year 1739, when MICHAEL LOMONOSOV, a peasant by birth and a scientist by training, published the first of his Odes. The significance of Lomonosov is real; his Russian grammar in 1755 was authoritative in its scholarship and furthered the extraction of a literary out of an ecclesiastical language; he was instrumental, too, in founding the first Russian University at Moscow.

Tsar Peter's sowing was reaped by the Tsarina Catherine II, who reigned from 1762 to 1796, and who wore the name of the ' Semiramis of the North ' with a better title than Queen Christina of Sweden. Catherine, as noted above, was one of

Baron de Grimm's correspondents, and Voltaire, Diderot and others helped her to europeanize her Court. Her Court rather than her country, for, like King Edward VII on a famous occasion, she was loyal to her own class, and the fate of Louis XVI repressed her zeal for reform. Still, the ideas sprung in France had been transferred to Russia, where they flowered in tale and fable, in elegy and ballad, if not in statute and law. A chief agent was VASILI ZHUKOVSKY (1783–1852). His labour as translator was not only immense but intelligent. He made the *Odyssey* a Russian classic. He is said to have visited Stoke Poges in order to acquire the local colour of the churchyard for his version of Gray's *Elegy*, and, like Scott, he was rapt by Bürger's *Lenore*. Very justly he is reputed to have opened the door of Russian literature on the fields of European poetry.

Pushkin. Through that door came ALEXANDER PUSHKIN, who was born in the same year as Heine (1799) and who died in 1837 as the result of a duel. Like his French contemporary, ALEXANDRE DUMAS (1803–70), author of *Monte Cristo*, *The Three Musketeers*, and other famous novels, Pushkin had a negro grandparent, and to this African strain both writers owed a certain exuberance and exoticism. Like Byron, Pushkin was of noble birth and was not unconscious of the fact. He had his Byronic period, his Voltairean, his Shakespearean, and he learnt his native folklore, with its rich mystical elements, from his nurse, Anna Rodionovna. Thus equipped, taught and disposed, he flamed in the morning sky of Russia ' predestiné, lumineux, et insolent de bonheur '.[1] He has been variously called the Chaucer, the Goethe and the Peter the Great of his national literature, and the Russian novelist, Dostoievsky, when he unveiled a memorial to Pushkin in Moscow in 1881, even used the epithet ' pan-human ' to describe his country-man's genius.

An awareness to impressions shut out from Russia hereto-fore and a brilliant and prolific pen brought Pushkin recognition from the start. It was his good fortune not to be spoiled by it. In 1820 his professional duties as a clerk in the Foreign Office took him away from the capital to the

[1] Vogüé, *Le Roman Russe.*

South, where he reacted at once to the wilder appeal of the scenery in the Caucasus and Crimea. There he wrote the first novel in the Russian language, a verse-romance, *Eugène Oniégin*, the heroine of which, Tatiana, dates another literary departure. She is at the head of the line of charming women who walk through the pages of Russian fiction in the natural variety of their circumstances, lovable, truthful, and companionable. This gallery of female types is as famous as any picture-gallery in Europe, and special attention should be directed to Tatiana's love-letter to Eugène, which is one of the classic pieces of modern literature. *Oniégin* was on the stocks from 1823–31, and the same busy years produced the narrative poems of *The Prisoner of the Caucasus*, *The Gipsies*, and a Mazeppa, changed out of deference to Byron, to *Poltava*, and others. There was also the chronicle-play of *Boris Godunov*, going back to the time of the pretended son of Ivan the Terrible, Demetrius, on whom Schiller had likewise tried his hand, and there were epic-idyls, lyrics, and historical works, which owed their inspiration to Russian lore and their forms to foreign models. Young, ardent, fortunate, intense, seizing an untouched kingdom with an artist's vision and a conqueror's zest, Pushkin is numbered among the happy few, who, like Alexander, founded an empire. Much of his work may be read in French and other languages, but the warning of a native critic must be heeded by those who, like the present writer, are neither Russian nor versed in Russian scholarship :

' It is indeed difficult for the foreigner, perhaps impossible if he is ignorant of the language, to believe in the supreme greatness of Pushkin among Russian writers. Yet it is necessary for him to accept the belief, even if he disagrees with it. Otherwise any idea he may form of Russian literature and Russian civilization will be inadequate and out of proportion to reality.'[1]

After Pushkin. A less devout act of faith is required for the appreciation of Pushkin's successors in Russian literature, whom it is convenient to consider briefly in this place. They were banded at first in a club or côtérie, not unlike the Pleiad in old France or the Cénacle in the Arsenal of Paris which

---

[1] *Modern Russian Literature*, by Prince D. S. Mirsky ; p. 8.

was founded in 1824. All three, the Pleiad, the Cénacle, and the Russian Arzamas, which was partly a kind of Eton ' Pop ' (the Russian Eton being the Tsarkoé-Sélo, established in 1811 for the sons of the aristocracy) and partly a club for select members of the Civil Service, were the hunting-grounds of young men in a hurry. Indeed, there was need for hurry in Russia. Out of the dark came the young men, directed by the spirit of Peter the Great to the founts of foreign culture, and into the dark they went when the empress in Catherine overtook the reformer of arts and manners. Take the experience of ALEXANDER RADISHCHEV (1750–1802), for example. In 1773 the Tsarina paid the costs of his translation of a French treatise on the history of Greece. The author was G.-B. de Mably, a *philosophe* in the swim with Diderot and Rousseau, and his book contained reflections on the philosophic bases of democracy and autocracy[1]. In 1790, Radishchev published *A Journey from St. Petersburg to Moscow*. In form and scope it was akin to Sterne's *Sentimental Journey*; incidentally it described the condition of the Russian peasantry and made proposals for their better welfare. But there was a difference between modern Russia and ancient Greece, another difference between theory and practice, and a third difference, measurable by French happenings, between 1773 and 1790 ; and Radishchev, Catherine's protégé, lost her favour for philosophizing about politics in an epoch of political disorder. Sentenced at first to death, and then, by an exercise of clemency, to exile in Siberia, he was not the last martyr among Russian men of letters.

Immediately in the wake of Pushkin was MICHAEL LERMONTOV (1814–41). They were alike in their record of stormy youth and in their early death in love-duels. They were alike in their period of Byronism and in their drafts of inspiration from the Caucasus, to which Pushkin went as an administrator and Lermontov as an exile. His novel *A Hero of Our Days*, 1839, portrayed the first of the subjective heroes, with hearts bigger than their heads, who saunter through Russian fiction,

---

[1] English readers may like to be reminded that the standard *History of Greece* at this time, in which Hellenic liberties were measured by Tory principles, had been written by WILLIAM MITFORD (1724–1827). Mitford was a Colonel in the South Hants. Militia with Edward Gibbon, at whose instance he undertook this task.

unsatisfied in being and negative in doing. His Pechoyin was Lermontov himself, and he was also the type of Russian youth in that age of dangerous living and daring thought. Lermontov wrote an ode on the death of Pushkin, and narrative verse filled with Southern colour, and yet true to the kindred point of the native simplicity of the Russian homeland.

Lermontov died in 1841. In the next year NICHOLAS GOGOL (1809–52; 1809 was a great vintage-year for literature) published Part I of his *Dead Souls*, a picaresque romance in three 'cantos'—Gogol always described it as a poem—of which the second was destroyed by the author and the third was never written. In 1843 he laid down the lines which, in his opinion, Russian literature must follow. Pushkin's lead had issued in a blind alley. It had been necessary, but it was not final. There was a native Russian spirit, which must escape from the vogue of Circassian maids' amours and the gorgeous colours of Southern blooms. The apprenticeship to Byron was a means, not an end, and

'the melancholy, the disillusion, the ideal heavenly virgins,' he wrote, 'the moon, the hate of our kind, vanished youth, treason, daggers, and poisons—the time for these has been, whether in the beautiful works of Pushkin, or in those of his crowd of imitators. . . . The hour of juvenile enthusiasm has passed : the hour of thought has arrived.'

It was a swift passing of a brief epoch, and it might have been a sure beginning of a new if the hour of realization had fallen in the 16th instead of the 19th century. But the iron hand of the censor was over all, Slavophils and Westernizers alike, those who ' thought ' and those who imitated foreign thinkers. When we recall that Dostoievsky, the most ardent Slavophil of the lot and a novelist in the highest rank of creative genius, was led out to be shot in December, 1849, and was reprieved only at the last minute and sent for ten years to Siberia, we see how vain was Gogol's faith in the new way inaugurated by ' the hour of thought.' It arrived too late for tragic Russia, with her fate of nihilism in philosophy and of bolshevism in politics.

A brooding Hamlet of ' maimed wants and thwarted

thoughts ', to quote a forgotten English poet,[1] is the salient hero of Russian fiction in the last century, and he might echo the poet's plaint that these unrequited longings,

> ' answered by the wind,
> Have dried in me belief and love and fear.'

One by one, in their various incarnations, those Hamlet-heroes of *bourgeois* life bore the burden of their negative creed, and expressed the type of philosophic fatalism, the national, semi-Oriental quality of *ochiania*, which means no-belief, no-love, no-fear. IVAN KRYLOV (1768–1844), the fabulist, the La Fontaine of Russia, is said to have exemplified the type in his own person, and it was repeated in the novels of IVAN GONCHAROV (1812–91), IVAN TURGENEV (1818–83), FEODOR DOSTOIEVSKY (1821–81), LEO TOLSTOY (1828–1910), and others. Particularly the *Oblomov*, 1858, of Goncharov, has given its name to the quality, and every hero of Russian fiction is said to have a portion of Oblomov in his composition. Perhaps we may put it in another way, and say that Oblomovism, or the philosophy of a tired idealist in a dressing-gown on a sofa, is inherent in the Russian temperament. Robert Browning writes somewhere of his contempt for ' the unlit lamp and the ungirt loin,' and George Meredith tells us of Earth's summons to active life :

> ' Accept, she says ; it is not hard
> In woods ; but she in towns
> Repeats, accept.'

The destiny of the Russian gentleman led him from the woods to the towns, and passiveness in circumstances requiring action was Oblomov's answer to destiny, or hardly an answer, but an attitude—the mood of the unlit and the ungirt. It lies outside the scope of our narrative to discuss these novelists in their works, or to judge between the lotus and the laurel. The brief winter-sunshine of Russian fiction, reflected at first from foreign climes, is an afterglow of European literature. Gogol's *Dead Souls*, Goncharov's *Oblomov*, Turgenev's *Fathers and*

---

[1] Stephen Phillips, 1868–1915. His oblivion is as undeserved as the excess of praise which he encountered in the eighteen-nineties.

Sons, Dostoievsky's *Crime and Punishment*, Tolstoy's *Anna Karenina* and *War and Peace* are supremely great novels, the stature of which is not diminished by the shortness and lateness of that wintry sun. We admire them the more for their lack of links in place and time. They came suddenly out of contacts which were broken off, and a revolution vaster in experimentation than that of France at the end of the 18th century, from which the light was spread, has made the breach more formidable and complete.

§ 5. LYRISM AND LIBERTY.

The alliterative heading above is deliberately chosen. For we want to emphasise the connection, not necessarily illicit but undesirable, between parties better kept separate. It was a connection which confused for many years the barriers of lyrical poetry. Keats had described the formal school as

> ' a schism
> Nurtured by foppery and barbarism,'

and declared that the poets of the schism had ' blasphemed the bright Lyrist to his face.' Apollo's plight was, perhaps, not so bad as his eager young champion imagined. But there was this unfortunate belief that lyrism was a ferment of liberty. We note it as early as 1770, when an anonymous pamphleteer declared that a ' romantic notion of liberty ' was getting hold of ' the lower sort of people in England. The less the manufacturing poor have of it,' he added, ' the better for themselves and the State.'[1] We note it in 1790, when Burke assailed Rousseau, and Wordsworth prayed for the success of French arms in the hope of promoting British freedom. And we note it again in 1830, to select a third signal example, when Macaulay in the *Edinburgh Review* denounced Southey for asking : ' How is it that everything which is connected with manufactures presents such features of unqualified deformity ? ' Here's wisdom ! quoth the statesman to the poet, in the very spirit of a Bumble or a Squeers :

[1] Quoted by Dr. W. J. Warner in *The Wesleyan Movement in the Industrial Revolution*. London, 1930, p. 19.

' Rose-bushes and poor-rates, rather than steam-engines and independence. . . . We despise those mock-philosophers who think that they serve the cause of science by depreciating literature and the fine arts. But if anything could excuse this narrowness of mind, it would be such a book as this. It is not strange that, when one enthusiast makes the picturesque the test of political good, another should feel inclined to proscribe altogether the pleasures of taste and imagination.'

It is unnecessary to remark to-day that the ' manufacturing poor ' have had more and not less of liberty since the date of that pious aspiration for the welfare of .' the lower sort of people ', and that Southey's plea for preserving beauty in a countryside devoted to manufactures is no longer regarded as an excuse for proscribing lyric verse. Rose-bushes and steam-engines are not mutually exclusive, and independence, though not of the *laissez-faire* variety, is compatible with a measure of protection which has travelled far beyond the range of the old poor-rate.

These are commonplaces, despite the apprehensions of 1770 and 1830. But it is important to re-state them, because they were not commonplaces in the long years of the Industrial Revolution. Bumble, however much heightened by caricature, was a real figure in the sphere of local government, and Mr. Squeers was not less real as a schoolmaster. There were features of ' unqualified deformity ' in public life both here and abroad, which Dickens, Ruskin and others did well to oppose.

Within the four corners of this contrast, which persisted from the middle of the 18th century, when social reform first began to frame demands, lies the splendid confusion between lyrism and liberty, which, as in the Southey-Macaulay instance, brought poets and politicians into conflict and provoked the latter to object to the beautiful as the test of the good.

' *Le Lyrisme* '. What was this Lyrism precisely ? Like all labels, it is difficult to define, because it was affixed to the phenomena as a means of identifying them. It is better to untie the bundle than to start from the name.

The foregoing paragraph tells us something about it. It

was more than the poetry which it evoked. It was an aspect of a movement astir in Europe at a particular time. In literature, which is our concern, and in French literature, which expressed it most clearly, the time lay between 1820 and 1843 and reached its zenith in 1830. We shall be able to justify these dates. Here we observe that it was the time which followed the Napoleonic wars and the defeat of Bonaparte at Waterloo; the time of reviving individualism, of heads lifted from the oppression of a great fear and of a force which seemed irresistible. It was a time of risen nationalism, exultant over the drabness of discredited cosmopolitans and republicans. The restored Bourbon in Paris (Louis XVIII, 1814–24) was to renew the splendour without the terror of Louis Quatorze. East and South had come into ken, as an outcome of Napoleon's campaigns and as an inspiration to Byron and Pushkin. Literature enlarged its bounds and admitted a new vocabulary into the preserves of Malherbe and *l'Académie*. Base words were mixed with noble as they have been mixed since Tennyson's day in the soldier-lore of Mr. Kipling and the sailor-lore of Mr. Masefield.[1] Metres, too, were liquefied and broken down. Verse-endings were no longer solid barriers, as in the former practice of the French rule, and the last defence of Classicism was shattered when an epithet was separated from its substantive by the pause between one verse and the next.

It sounds ridiculous, of course. *Le Lyrisme* as a European movement seems to be dissolved in laughter when we reduce it to so trivial an event. But little things may typify big; a small symbol may reveal a great series, as the pressure of a button in London may set in motion huge works in a distant land. It is not the symbol which matters, but its significance, and that of the men who manipulate it, and it is in this sense that we are to appraise the culmination of French *Lyrisme* in the separation of *dérobé* from *l'escalier* in the opening scene of *Hernani* by VICTOR HUGO (1802–85) at the Théâtre Français in Paris on February 25, 1830. It was a

---

[1] The drift of the reading public away from the stately muse of Sir William Watson, another too-much-neglected poet who was overpraised in the eighteen-nineties, is largely due to his inhospitality to the lower order of words.

challenge to tradition and authority, which, in current phrase, the young poet got across the footlights. Lyrism vindicated liberty.

First of all, omitting the prior signs, there were Voltaire and Rousseau and the French Revolution itself. There was the Oath of the Tennis Court on June 20, 1789, and the Fall of the Bastille on July 14. Wordsworth was in France in 1790, picking up the stones of the Bastille, and meditating how joy for one could become joy for millions. In 1798 came his *Lyrical Ballads*—observe lyrism following liberty—in collaboration with Coleridge, and the *Athenæum* of the Schlegel brothers in Berlin. Mme. de Staël was the *commis-voyageuse* of Romanticism, which took its various shapes in England, France, Germany and Russia. Travel, adventure, colour were all extracted from and added to common life, bringing the distant near and revealing distance in near things—an edge of wonder in the familiar face. This phrase of George Meredith recalls us to a name omitted hitherto and by no means one of the greatest names which might be cited in our present context. Yet CHARLES LAMB (1775–1834), essayist and poet, was among the romantic founders, and his *Tales from Shakespeare*, written with his sister, Mary (William and Dorothy Wordsworth were another brother and sister, with the sister content to suppress her individuality), opened the gate for children which Schlegel and the graver Shakespeareans were opening for adults in the same epoch. No small part of the lyric-romantic movement, renewing experience and transmuting it, is contained for attentive ears in Lamb's stanzas, *The Old Familiar Faces*, which by a happy coincidence, were composed in 1798, the year of departure from the poetic conventions of the 18th century :

' I have had playmates, I have had companions,
  In my days of childhood, in my joyful school-days,
  All, all are gone, the old familiar faces . . .

I loved a love once, fairest among women ;
  Closed are her doors on me, I must not see her—
  All, all are gone, the old familiar faces . . .

> Ghost-like, I paced round the haunts of my childhood.
> Earth seemed a desert I was bound to traverse,
> Seeking to find the old familiar faces ' . . .

The ghosts are readmitted to literature : the ghost in *Hamlet*, as we are aware, with the rest, out of the limbo to which Boileau had remanded him ; and we return under Lamb's safe and gentle guidance to the more conscious renovation of the temple by Boileau's repentant fellow-countrymen. So we may justify the dates mentioned above. The *Méditations poétiques* of ALPHONSE DE LAMARTINE (1790–1869) were published in 1820, transferring to French lyric verse the qualities found in the prose of Rousseau and Chateaubriand. ALFRED DE VIGNY (1797–1869) was a direct forerunner of Hugo by his narrative poem on Moses, *Moïse*, 1822, his historical novel, *Cinq Mars*, and his dramatic *Chatterton*, 1835. STENDHAL (1783–1842), the pen-name chosen by Henri Beyle, wrote his *Racine et Shakespeare* in 1822, which ranged him on the side of the new Romantics, and his famous novels, *Le Rouge et le Noir*, 1831, and *La Chartreuse de Parme*, 1839. The year 1823 stands out for the establishment of *la Muse française* as the organ of the young poets, who fore-gathered in the *Cénacle* founded by CHARLES NODIER (1780–1844) in the Arsenal, now known as the Mazarin Library, of which he was appointed librarian at the beginning of 1824. On February 11, 1827, came the production of *Henri III et sa Cour*, the romantic play by ALEXANDRE DUMAS (1803–70) the elder, followed in order of significance by Vigny's Othello-play, *Le More de Venise*, on October 24, 1829, and then by Hugo's *Hernani*, by which the year 1830 acquired fame in French literary annals as *Mil-huit-cent-trente*. Prior to this play was the preface to Hugo's *Cromwell*, 1827, which has been described without exaggeration as the Oath af the Tennis Court of the new lyrism; and concomitant with the play were the ebullitions of the young parties to that oath, among which the capers and *gilet rouge* of THEOPHILE GAUTIER (1811–72) have passed out of gossip into history. Finally, the *Burgraves* of Hugo, produced on March 7, 1843, is commonly taken as the close of the Romantic period in the French theatre.

We come back now to the challenge itself with a better power of appreciation. The ardent spirits of *Le Lyrisme* wanted to do something shocking and irreversible, something symbolically final which should lift the dead hand from living drama. The dramatic Unities[1] had been broken down already. Formulated in the 17th century and founded, it was believed, on commonsense, they exactly suited the stage and genius of Racine and were observed for just on two hundred years. ALESSANDRO MANZONI (1785–1873), the long-lived Italian novelist, whose *Promessi Sposi* ('The Betrothed,' 1825–27) won the praises of Scott and Goethe and the untiring admiration of his own countrymen, had deliberately employed the illusion of more than one place and time in tragic plays which were more remarkable for their choric odes (*le lyrisme* again) than for their dramatic value. Stendhal defended this relaxation in his *Racine et Shakespeare* (above), following closely in his argument an essay by Dr. Johnson in *The Rambler*, 1749, where the right of appeal was admitted from the critics' to nature's law. To break these, then, in 1830, was not to violate propriety. It was still irregular, but it was no longer a violent act, which would cause Gautier to dance in a red waistcoat and date an epoch from *Mil-huit-cent-trente*. The shock-tactics for the routing of Malherbe craved a more revolutionary innovation. 'Enfin Malherbe vint', Boileau had said of him,

'Et reduisit la Muse aux règles du devoir.
Par ce sage écrivain la Langue reparée
N'offert plus rien de rude à l'oreille epurée.
Les stances avec grace apprirent à tomber,
Et le vers sur le vers n'osa plus enjamber.'

This was the Romanticists' opportunity, the occasion for their Napoleon touch. 'In the Romanticist army', wrote Gautier, with his dark chestnut hair flowing down his back, 'everyone was young, as in Napoleon's army of Italy. What a time it was in which to be alive! Scott, Byron and Shakespeare were being discovered for the first time in France.' So *le vers* should dare *enjamber sur le vers* for the first time in France since Boileau had banned Shakespeare and had taught Thomas

[1] See page 187 above.

Rymer his bad poetics.[1] So *l'escalier* at the end of one verse
was qualified by *dérobé* at the beginning of the next, and the
Muse broke a *règle du devoir* and set at nought the classic law
of *enjambement*. It was a real thrill, like the fall of the guillotine
on a royal neck, and lyrism and liberty were both served by it.
' The Romantic movement,' we read, ' was felt in Spain, Italy
and Russia, but in no degree comparable to that of its activity
in France, England and Germany. The wealth of its artistic
production is prodigious, and it is impossible to estimate which
of the arts reached the point of highest emotional expression
in this new burst of creative inspiration '; and the writer
duly notes ' the heroic passion of Romanticism ' in Wagner,
and its sensitiveness and melancholy in Chopin.[2] Rousseau,
too, had written on music for Diderot.

Victor Hugo. There is more to Hugo than his *première* of
Hernani, however significant it is as a landmark in European
literature. He outlived 1830 through fifty-five changeful years,
and a French critic, Edmond Biré (in four volumes, 1883–94),
distinguishing between his appearances *avant* 1830, *après* 1830,
and *après* 1852, is not kind to him in his later phases. But we
remember that France, too, changed, and that an active writer
who tried to be consistent was fighting against time itself—
always a losing fight. We prefer to recall that Hugo was hailed
by Chateaubriand, Rousseau's disciple, as ' enfant sublime '
and by Swinburne as the apogee of genius and goodness, two
testimonies which can hardly be gainsaid. All through his
long career, like Tennyson, who loved him, he was a poet.
Hs passes the difficult test, in which even Wordsworth failed,
and in which Keats and Shelley were not tried, of not declining
in old age from his youthful promise. In this respect the
greatest poet of France is comparable to Goethe, the greatest
poet of Germany. His *Quatre Vents de l'Esprit*, 1882, had the
force and colour of his *Odes et Ballades*, 1826, and his *Art
d'être Grandpère*, 1877, is grandfatherly only in its topic. Some
of his plays have been mentioned : Cromwell, Hernani
(Castilian honour), Lucrezia Borgia, and Mary Tudor were
among their subjects, and their medium was lyrical melodrama.

[1] See page 216, above.
[2] *Gautier and the Romantics*, by J. G. Palache, London, 1927 ; p. 32.

More permanently famous are his romances : *Notre Dame de Paris, Les Misérables, Les Travaileurs de la Mer, L'Homme qui rit, Quatre-vingt-treize*, etc., ranging from 1831 to 1879. His noblest verse is contained in *Les Châtiments*, 1853, and *La Légende des Siècles*, i, 1859, ii, 1887; and his *William Shakespeare*, 1864, is selected for obvious reasons from his critical writings.

Two things, perhaps, stand out : his love of the sea and his command of language. He mustered his words with Rabelaisian gusto and mastered them with Tennysonian skill. He cultivated them both for sound and for sense, missing no nuance of association and hesitating at no experiment in their extensive use. M. Lanson, the historian of French literature, refers particularly to his brilliant metaphors, to his local and technical vocabulary, to his curious power over emphatic adjectives with a vague connotation, such as *étrange, horrible, effrayant, sombre*, etc., and to his manipulation of substantives in apposition : *le bœuf peuple, le pâtre promontoire*, etc., by which comparison is resumed in an imaginative effect on identity. And, as to Hugo's metrical devices :

' On devra étudier ', he writes, ' la première *Légende des Siècles* presque vers par vers, pour comprendre la délicatesse, la puissance et la variété des effets que le poète fait rendre à toutes les formes de vers, et particulièrement à l'alexandrin ; c'est là qu'on devra chercher, en leur perfection, les types variés du vers romantique '.

We may quote a more general piece of eulogy. Catulle Mendès (1841–1909), a younger French Romanticist, whose opinion may be set against Biré's, wrote :

' qu'il y a dans Victor Hugo toute l'Humanité ; il contient aussi tout l'univers, visible et invisible. Il est les mers, les montagnes, les ciels, le ciel ; et dans tout ce qui existe il offre asile a tout ce qui vit '.

Praise could hardly be higher, and if we may select more particularly the first identification, ' il est les mers,' we would recall his period of residence in the Channel Islands, while he was a political exile from Paris, and the appeal of his sea-verse to our own sea-poet, Swinburne.

Leopardi. In Italy GIACOMO LEOPARDI (1798–1837) belongs

to the same great epoch. He was always an invalid and died young, but his mental vigour and love of life conquered his physical infirmities, and he spent his strength with royal lavishness as scholar, lover, patriot and friend. He belongs, too, to the Greek succession and claims his place among the Hellenists in § 3 above ; indeed, in his native Italy, Leopardi is linked directly to Petrarch across the five centuries which have no power to divide them. Like Petrarch, he was a Humanist, and his ode to Angelo Mai (1783–1854), the learned Cardinal who had unearthed the MS. of Cicero's *De Republica*, recalls the very spirit of the earlier Ciceronian. Appropriately, he edited the poems of Petrarch for a Milanese publisher, Stella, whose name, like that of Cottle in Bristol, should be mentioned for the sake of his generosity to poets. Leopardi fulfilled the Renaissance striving by adding Hebrew studies to Greek, and his patriotic verse responded to the same test as Wordsworth's, that of instant revival in the Great War of the 20th century. The odes to Mai, to Italy, to Dante and to *la Ginestra* (broom) rank highest in Italian poetry, alike for matter and for form, and a recent English editor writes of him :

' It is his signal distinction to be the only Italian poet and one of the only poets of modern Europe to have completely acquired the Greek style at its simplest and clearest, while at the same time retaining his own world of ideas.'[1]

We stop here. The road is long, and it would take us too far to pursue it step by step to the borders of our own day. There is no *finis* to art, no end to the poets' endeavour to interpret phenomena to man. But the French Revolution marks a stage in that process, a definite though not a final stage in the process begun when modern Europe recovered and revived the pagan view. Such degree of liberty, social and intellectual, as men then foresaw for enjoyment, however dimly and incompletely, was achieved in that last *émeute*, with its sequel of literature in the beginning of the 19th century. The record of the next hundred years may be briefly noted in a concluding section.

[1] *The Poems of Leopardi*, by G. L. Bickersteth. Cambridge, 1923.

II. EPILOGUE

THE pagan view has been recovered. He who ran could read. John Keats, a surgeon's apprentice and a stableman's son, enjoyed the freedom of Greece and Rome. More fortunate in this respect than Petrarch, a leisured scholar in the Euganean Hills, the ancient classics were an open book to him. There is more than an accidental likeness in the tastes of the two poets, and more than an accidental contrast in the means of satisfying their need. The history of European literature is epitomized in that record : Petrarch, at the beginning of the 14th century, without a Greek-Italian lexicon or grammar, importuning Boccaccio in Florence to get someone, however uncouth, to decipher his precious manuscript of the *Iliad*; and Keats, at the beginning of the 19th, sailing securely to the realms of gold under George Chapman's Elizabethan flag, the conscious heir of Antiquity and its interpreters. Still taking Homer as our symbol of the civilization which spread from Greece, and remembering the concomitant labours of Homeric scholars and critics, from the *editio princeps* of Chalcondyles in 1488 to the *Prolegomena* of F. A. Wolf in 1795 (the year of the birth of Keats), we reach a clearer conception of what is meant by the recovery of the pagan view. Petrarch and Keats, the two eager Grecians, are pre-Renaissance and post-Renaissance types.

To Keats's equipment of Chapman's Homer was added the legacy from the Navigators and Reformers. He reminds us himself of the first part of it :

> ' Then felt I like some watcher of the skies
>   When a new planet swims into his ken ;
> Or like stout Cortez when with eagle eyes
>   He stared at the Pacific—and all his men
> Look'd at each other with a wild surmise—
>   Silent, upon a peak in Darien.'

293

v

The double view with its widened outlook had been enlarged
further by the Hebraists. Cortez and Erasmus were contemporaries. The Reformation marched with the Renaissance.
Pico della Mirandola, Johann Reuchlin and Martin Luther,
with an increasing sense of pragmatic values, had applied the
methods of Greek scholarship to the literary and textual study
of Holy Writ, and the *Authorised Version* in England was
published when Milton was three years old. So, the freemen
of Hellas and the ocean highways enjoyed, too, the freedom of
the Bible, and Chateaubriand's *Génie du Christianisme*, 1802,
was at once its *Prolegomena* and its *Lyrical Ballads*.

It was in some respects a fearful freedom. Red war accompanied its beginnings and devastated Luther's native
country from 1618–48, laying it bare of culture for well-nigh
a hundred years; and when 'the mysteries of kings', in the
famous phrase of Erasmus, were unveiled in 1789 as completely as 'the mysteries of Christ', red war was renewed
in Europe and in European colonies overseas. The sense of
fear infected literature. The unveiler was loaded with war-
guilt. Wordsworth, who had rebelled against his countrymen
when

' Britain opposed the liberties of France ' (*Prel.*, xi, 175),

lived to lament that

' Frenchmen had changed a war of self-defence
     For one of conquest ' (*ibid.*, 207).

Nelson, who defeated the conqueror, cherished a 'natural
hate ' for the French, and Tennyson declaimed in well-known
words against 'the red fool-fury of the Seine'. Since the
Golden Calf was cast in the desert, men had found it hard to
be kind to their deliverers.

There were still more mysteries to be unveiled. In a
generation weary of revolution this sense of rending a veil
and of destroying more idols of the tribe acted as a foe to the
progress which Macaulay trusted so firmly. Even he had
underrated its pace. Writing in 1830, in the course of the
essay quoted above, he said of his country :

'We firmly believe that, in spite of all the misgovernment of her rulers, she has been almost constantly becoming richer and richer. Now and then there has been a stoppage, now and then a short retrogression; but as to the general tendency there can be no doubt.'

Note riches as the measure of national progress. Southey was to found his political creed on 'bills of mortality and statistical tables.' Using these evidences, Macaulay went on:

'If we were to prophesy that in the year 1930 a population of fifty millions, better fed, clad and lodged than the English of our time, will cover these islands, that Sussex and Huntingdonshire will be wealthier than the wealthiest parts of the West Riding of Yorkshire now are, that cultivation, rich as that of a flower-garden, will be carried up to the tops of Ben Nevis and Helvellyn, that machines constructed on principles yet undiscovered, will be in every house, that there will be no highways but railroads, no travelling but by steam, that our debt, vast as it seems to us, will appear to our great-grandchildren a trifling incumbrance, which might easily be paid off in a year or two, many people would think us insane.'

To us who have survived 1930 the insanity is by way of under-statement. Railroads and steam-power have been superseded; the machines have diminished employment to an extent which countervails the better food, clothes and houses; and a vaster debt than oppressed our great-grandparents makes a tragedy of our anticipated financial ease. There were two tendencies at work in the eighteen-thirties, not the one only of which Macaulay was so well assured. His 'richer and richer' vision did not appeal to all friends of the poor. CHARLES DICKENS (1812–70), for example, continuing the purposeful novel which Samuel Richardson had helped to popularize, exhibited the evils of the social system in plots expressly directed to expose the operation of the poor-law (*Oliver Twist*), private schools (*Nicholas Nickleby*), industrial conditions (*Hard Times*), the Court of Chancery (*Bleak House*), selfish wealth, etc., etc. The purpose never detracted from the warmth and humour of the treatment. It is by his delineation of character in sharply contrasted black and white that Dickens, a realist in topic and an idealist in temperament, won and kept his hosts of admirers. France has rivalled England in appreciating him, and his fondness for the road and the stage-coach, the inns of England, her water-ways and barges, the mean streets and queer, urban people who retarded by the mere force of their existence the rationalization of economic life throughout the first half of the 19th century, preserved the tradition of Chaucer in a harder and more positive age. JOHN RUSKIN, too, (1819–1900), had no use for orthodox tenets on the topic of national wealth, and the immense vogue which he gave to the landscape-painting of J. W. M. Turner (1775–1851) helped to bring men back to a taste for the imponderable values of sea-scape, sunshine and mountain scenery as a set-off to prosperity and material power.

Certain classes of the population—we trench now in what has been ridiculed as Victorianism and deplored as the Victorian tragedy—dug themselves into the safe places of the middle-classes, developed a Nonconformist conscience, and took successive halfpence off the income-tax. These were the classes girded at by MATTHEW ARNOLD (1822–88). Yet Arnold for all his belief in Hellenism (he even invited us to ' hellenize with free-trade '), was a less than perfect Grecian. He aspired to, but could not attain, Goethe's calm. He divided his allegiance to a muse less strenuous than melancholy with essays in criticism of society and literature. He was notable in the epoch of the Crystal Palace, the positive product of a German brain, for his appreciation of aspects of the French genius, which reminded him of the Greek. But his appreciation was halting and academic. It missed the bold, objective note and the virile humour of his contemporary, GEORGE MEREDITH (1828–1909), a blithe novelist but an obscure poet, whose vindicatory *Odes in Contribution to the Song of French History* were inscribed appropriately to JOHN (Viscount) MORLEY (1838–1923), author of liberal monographs on Rousseau, Diderot and Voltaire as well as, later, of the official biography of Gladstone.

Another champion of the French spirit, though his approach to it differed both from George Meredith's and Matthew

Arnold's, was the poet, ALGERNON CHARLES SWINBURNE, (1837–1909), sea-lover and disciple of Victor Hugo, who, though too passionate a beauty-adept for the taste of business-men of the mid-Victorian epoch, invented melodies which will not perish and tempered his exceeding love of liberty with a patriotism at once fine and true :

' All our past proclaims our future : Shakespeare's voice
    and Nelson's hand,
Milton's faith and Wordsworth's trust in this our chosen
    and chainless land
Bear us witness : Come the world against her, England
    yet shall stand.'

Swinburne brings us at once to a group of writers who retired from the more typical Victorian foreground into a cult of art or beauty for its own sake. They are found on both sides of the Channel. The Frenchmen, in train to Hugo, formed a retinue known as the Parnassians, after their three volumes of verse, *Le Parnasse contemporain*, 1866, 1869–70 and 1876. Several names are of account in this connection. CATULLE MENDÈS, the convener of the group, was the son-in-law of Gautier, whose *Rapport sur le Progrès de la Poésie depuis 1830* served as handbook to the movement in the start of which he had been prominent.[1] AUGUSTE VACQUERIE (1819–95), another Hugo-worshipper, and SULLY PRUDHOMME (1839–98) merit notice. The group-leader was LECONTE DE LISLE (1820–94), who brought home from his birthplace in the Tropics a fertile fancy for images and diction which suited the exoticism of the new *Parnasse*.

The English group was a little earlier in time and the impression of retreat which it produces is more definite. There is a close connection between the Oxford Movement in the Church and the Pre-Raphaelite Brotherhood in painting and poetry. The former started in 1833, when on July 14, JOHN KEBLE (1792–1866) preached the Assize sermon in St. Mary's, Oxford, on ' National Apostasy ', and it may be

[1] The quotations from Mendès on pages 196 and 199 above are taken from his own *Rapport sur le Mouvement poétique française de 1867 à 1900*, a valuable compilation with a biographical dictionary.

said to have closed in 1845, when JOHN HENRY (afterwards Cardinal) NEWMAN (1801–90) was received into the Church of Rome. Meanwhile, the frescoes in Italian churches and cognate monuments of medieval sacred art appealed to the same consciousness as the usages of the Roman Church, and likewise afforded a refuge from the commonplace—*was uns alle bändigt, das Gemeine*. They corrected the taste for the animals and pastures of Landseer, Sidney Cooper and other painters, patronized by merchant-princes for the decoration of suburban and provincial dining-rooms; and when we recall that the esoteric sign, P.R.B., was first affixed to the pictures of the Brotherhood in 1848, and that their organ, *The Germ*, was first published in 1850, we mark a new antidote to the principles incorporated in the Great Exhibition of 1851. EDWARD FITZGERALD (1809–83), the intimate friend and exact contemporary of ALFRED (Lord) TENNYSON (1809–92), opened an avenue remote from Hyde Park. He made an instant appeal to the tastes trained by the Pre-Raphaelites by his languorous quatrains, 1859, of the *Rubáiyát* of the Persian astronomer-poet, Omar Khayyám. There was the Orient, there was music, there was beauty, and there was a philosophy of life, composed partly of the hedonism discouraged by the merchant-princes, partly of the mysticism encouraged at Oxford. Tennyson himself in certain aspects was a forerunner of the Pre-Raphaelites : his *Lady of Shalott*, 1832, influenced the mannerisms of the group by its pictorialness, its choice of subject, its refrain and its liquid diction of ' willows ', ' lilies ', and so forth. Keats, too, was a father of the movement, though he did not live to see his offspring, and in painting and poetry alike there were echoes and even strong voices of medievalism long after the doctrine of the Pre-Raphaelites had been resumed in a wider stream. Most immediate to the English group was DANTE GABRIEL ROSSETTI (1828–82), the Ronsard of the new Pleiad, which included his grave, shining sister CHRISTINA (1830–94) and the lesser light of their brother WILLIAM MICHAEL (1829–1919), who married a daughter of Ford Madox Brown, a kindred artist.

The service of Rossetti to literature was to keep the flag of beauty flying in an age of material aims. We remember

the excellent Dr. SAMUEL SMILES (1812–1904), with his essays
in industrial biography and his monographs on duty and
self-help—all calculated to accumulate the riches which
served as the measure of human happiness. We remember
John Halifax, the hero of a famous novel by DINAH CRAIK
(*née* Mulock; 1826–87), and how his virtuous and exemplary
career was bounded, however unconsciously, by self-seeking;
and we contrast with those figures, so rigid in their conventionality, 'La Belle Dame sans Merci' of Keats or Rossetti's
'Blessed Damozel'.

> 'I made a garland for her head,
>   And bracelets, too, and fragrant zone;
> She look'd at me as she did love,
>   And made sweet moan.

> 'She found me roots of relish sweet
>   And honey wild, and manna dew;
> And sure in language strange she said,
>   I love thee true.'

So, la belle Dame; and the Damozel:

> 'Her eyes were deeper than the depth
>   Of water stilled at even;
> She had three lilies in her hand,
>   And the stars in her hair were seven.
> Her robe, ungirt from clasp to hem,
>   No wrought flower did adorn,
> But a white rose of Mary's gift,
>   For service meekly worn;
> Her hair that lay along her back
>   Was yellow like ripe corn.'

There were no such fruits or cereals among the products
exhibited in the Crystal Palace. They were not the chosen
food of John Halifax or Dr. Smiles.

It is recorded that Tennyson succeeded Wordsworth as
Poet Laureate in November, 1850, and that he prefixed to
the seventh edition of his *Poems* in March, 1851, the noble

stanzas addressed ' To the Queen '. One of those stanzas, never reprinted, had been worded as follows :

> ' She brought a vast design to pass
> When Europe and the scatter'd ends
> Of our fierce world did meet as friends
> And brethren in her halls of glass.'

Why did he excise it and suppress it ? Was the union of Europe too brittle, and the brotherhood too fierce for friendship ? Or did the poet's sense of a beauty not of this world refuse the bleak glare of halls of glass ? We cannot say. But we observe that the lifework of WILLIAM MORRIS (1834–96), reconciling beauty with utility, added a tonic value to Pre-Raphaelite æsthetics. Like a new Dryden, he did not forget Chaucer. He remembered Spenser's purpose in the *Faery Queen*, from which all that beauty was derived :

> ' Fierce wars and faithful loves shall *moralize* my song ' ;

and we may say that Rossetti's service to literature included or was resumed in the revelation of taste which Morris practised and others preached. We may even say that such pure service included the saving of Tennyson for beauty through all his forward-striving vision into the science of his day. ' Tennyson saw dimly what Morris saw clearly,' we read[1] ; and the ray, however dim, came from Rossetti. Its source was found behind the bar of Heaven out of which the blessed damozel had leaned.

The ' sweetness and light ' desiderated by Matthew Arnold, and distributed between Rossetti and William Morris, were combined in Tennyson to the high purpose which made him peculiarly the poet of the Victorian age. He served both beauty and utility, attaining at his best to beauty in use and to use in beauty. His *Maud*, his *Locksley Hall*, his *Princess*—

> ' Why should not these great Sirs
> Give up their parks some dozen times a year
> To let the people breathe ?'—

---

[1] H. Walker, *The Literature of the Victorian Era*, Cambridge, 1910 ; p. 533.

are replete with this special excellence, and his *In Memoriam*, for all its luxury of woe, made a popular philosophy of the creed :

> ' Ring out the want, the care, the sin,
>   The faithless coldness of the times ;
>   Ring out, ring out my mournful rhymes,
> But ring the fuller minstrel in.'

Where the light failed, the sweetness surpassed. It was an exact student as well as a lifelong admirer of Tennyson who bore witness that

> ' More and more a wiser sense divines
>   What in quick heats of youth
> He deemed the form of beauty in your lines
>   To be the soul of truth '[1] ;

and, though some of Arthur's knights proved false and others fickle to their vows, so that the beautiful overbore the useful, and Tennyson, in the *Idylls of the King*, was oppressed by the weight of an

> ' imperfect tale,
> New-old, and shadowing Sense at war with Soul '—

the material with the spiritual—yet we are always aware of *Merlin and the Gleam* :

> ' There on the border
>   Of boundless Ocean,
>   And all but in Heaven
>   Hovers the Gleam.'

The ocean of Keats, the heaven of Rossetti.

So, the retreats served their fair purpose. The Oxford Movement and the Pre-Raphaelite Brotherhood, seeking like means to different ends, had routed the commonplace and the conventional, with results of so wide a range that more pity was extended to sinners and better patterns were stamped on

[1] Sir Herbert Warren (1853–1930).

English wall-papers. Mr. Galsworthy's readers will add that strange fancies entered the unquiet mind of Soames Forsyte.

Beauty, immured in a retreat, might founder by its own excess : We recall the exhibitionism of OSCAR WILDE (1856–1900), and the satire poured on the æsthetes by Sir WILLIAM GILBERT (1836–1911) and Sir ARTHUR SULLIVAN (1842–1900). Salvation came by contact and intercourse. The fresh wind blown from the heights fell in varying degrees on Tennyson himself, as has been indicated, and on his great contemporary, ROBERT BROWNING (1812–89), a man of love and vigour and sufficient learning :

> ' What had I on earth to do
> With the slothful, with the mawkish, the unmanly ?
> Like the aimless, helpless, hopeless, did I drivel
> —Being—who ?
> One who never turned his back but marched breast-forward,
> Never doubted clouds would break,
> Never dreamed, though right were worsted, wrong would triumph,
> Held we fall to rise, are baffled to fight better,
> Sleep to wake.'

There are those who still remember the publication of this ' Epilogue ' in Browning's *Asolando*, December, 1889, and the appearance in the same month of the same year of Tennyson's ' Crossing the Bar ' in *Demeter and Other Poems*. Never before had two master-poets taken leave of their generation so nobly. The wind blew, as we have said, on William Morris, guild-socialist and art-designer as well as ' the idle singer of an empty day ' ; on George Meredith, lover of gallant women, who was haunted in ' the woods of Westermain ' by the insistent voices of Earth ; on GEORGE ELIOT (Mary Ann Evans, 1819–80) and THOMAS HARDY (1840–1928), master-realists in fiction, and on other thinkers in terms of humankind whose work rebukes and will finally refute the denigration of the Victorian era. Lastly, for our present purpose, it blew on ROBERT BRIDGES (1844–1930), Tennyson's second successor as Poet Laureate, whose *Testament of Beauty*, on the eve of his death, assured the heirs of Antiquity recovered :

' Verily by Beauty it is that we come at Wisdom,
  yet not by Reason at Beauty : and now with many words
  pleasing myself betimes I am fearing lest in the end
  I play the tedious orator who maundereth on
  for lack of heart to make an end of his nothings.
  Wherefor as when a runner who has run his round
  handeth his staff away, and is glad of rest,
  here break I off, knowing the goal was not for me
  the while I ran on telling of what cannot be told.'

Perhaps it never will be told. Plato could not tell it, nor
Lucretius, nor Augustine, nor Dante, nor Shakespeare, nor
Goethe. Our destiny is the stadium, not the goal. But between
Faust and *The Testament of Beauty*, between the death of Goethe
in 1832 and the death of Bridges in 1930, CHARLES DARWIN
(1809–82) ran his course, and in November, 1859, seventy
years after the Fall of the Bastille, he published his *Origin of
Species*.

' Though considerably added to and corrected in the later
editions,' Darwin wrote, ' it has remained substantially the
same book. It is no doubt the chief work of my life. It was
from the first highly successful. The first small edition of
1,250 copies was sold on the day of publication, and a second
edition of 3,000 copies soon afterwards. . . . It has been
translated into almost every European tongue, even into such
languages as Spanish, Bohemian, Polish, and Russian. It has
also been translated into Japanese, and is there much studied.
Even an essay in Hebrew has appeared on it.'

These were the author's notes in 1876, written at Down,
now a national possession. The later story of *The Origin of
Species* has confirmed and enhanced its early record.

It is partly for Darwin's sake—note his birth in 1809, the
year of Tennyson and Gladstone, of Gogol and Edward
FitzGerald—that we have set this epilogue in an English
scene. We might have chosen France as our centre and dwelt
on the sequel to Hugo till the death of GUSTAVE FLAUBERT
(1821–80) and EMILE ZOLA (1840–1903), the novelists who
changed romanticism into realism. Or we might have chosen

303

Scandinavia, where the separation of Norway from Denmark on May 17, 1814, evoked a *Syttendemai-poesi*, the ecstasy of which was resumed, as Norse independence grew, in the graver and ampler tones of HENRIK IBSEN (1828–1906) and B. M. BJÖRNSON (1832–1910), poets and dramatists, of S. L. E. LIE (1833–1908) and ALEXANDER KIELLAND (1849–1906), poets and novelists. But these, too, were affected by Darwinism. These, too, except for Darwin, would have written their social novels and plays without access to the philosophy of evolution. We equated just now Darwin's book with the Fall of the Bastille, 1859 with 1789. It may seem an odd collocation, and odder still in a history of literature. But the equation of revolution with evolution is plainly not so far-fetched, and both alike were terminal expressions of long-antecedent thought. The Humanism of the 12th to the 14th century which extracted the pagan view out of its occultation in the Dark Ages of the West, was continued by the Humanists of the 18th and 19th, who inquired, even unto force, into the foundations of society and the origin of species. Their inquiries shook the temple-pillars. The Bastille was merely a symbol of the ruin wrought by Voltaire and Rousseau, and walls firmer than of stone fell at Darwin's assault. Sir Arthur Keith, in his Presidential Address at the British Association in 1927 said that the effect of *The Origin of Species* was to bring about ' a sweeping revolution in our way of looking at living things and to initiate a new period in human thought.' With all allowance for the enthusiasm of the disciple to whom we owe the possession of Down, the word ' revolution ' is not an over-statement.

' The Darwinian Period, in which we now are,' ran Keith's peroration to that statement, and, since we are in it, judgment must be suspended. One thing is clear, however. Those who were afraid of revolution and resisted the rending of the veil from the mysteries of Christ and kings renewed their fight in the 19th century and left a stricken field. Perhaps we may date the last encounter at June 30, 1860, when the British Association was sitting in Oxford. Dr. Draper of New York had read a paper in Section D on *The Origin of Species*, published in the previous November. Dr. Samuel Wilberforce,

Bishop of Oxford, whose *Quarterly* article on the subject was to appear a few days later, ridiculed Darwin and Huxley,[1] and, turning towards the latter with a dulcet smile, asked him ' as to his belief in being descended from an ape. Is it on his grandfather's or his grandmother's side that the ape ancestry comes in ? ' Huxley accepted the challenge :

' I am here only in the interests of science,' he said, ' and I have not heard anything that can prejudice the case of my august client. . . . I should feel it no shame to have risen from such an origin (as the monkey) ; but I should feel it a shame to have sprung from one who prostituted the gifts of culture and eloquence to the service of prejudice and falsehood.'

Accounts agree as to the impression produced, and the occasion has become historic. This unrehearsed scene at the session of Section D in 1860 was confirmed, as we have seen, at the Meeting in 1927, and the intervening sixty or seventy years broke down in all departments of thought not prejudice only and falsehood but the fear which motivates their manifestation. So the aim of the early Humanists was fulfilled : man was afraid no longer to know :

> ' Who loves not Knowledge ? Who shall rail
> Against her beauty ? May she mix
> With men and prosper ! Who shall fix
> Her pillars ? Let her work prevail,'

Tennyson wrote, and none presume to seal her springs.

We remark for historical accuracy that this open mind to science was attained in that mid-19th century when prosperity in trade marched with orthodoxy in faith, and ' " Safe as the Bank " was the proverbial yoke-fellow of " True as the Gospel " '.[2] The reconcilement of ' knowledge ' and ' faith ', two modes of approach to experience, the mutual respect of Tennyson and Darwin, and the representation of the Royal Society at the poet's funeral in the Abbey, because, as Huxley wrote to Tyndall on October 15, 1892, Tennyson was ' the

---

[1] Thomas Henry Huxley, (1825–95).
[2] *The Victorian Sunset*, by Dr. E. Wingfield-Stratford, London, 1932, p. 14.

first poet since Lucretius who had understood the drift of science '[1] : this liquidation of differences, with its ample promise of common aims, was the boon to the future of the very epoch, 1850–70, which in other aspects was typically ' Victorian '. It is a paradox, but there it is. The disease and the antidote were co-existent, and the definitive historian of literature, from the eighteen-thirties, when Tennyson emerged, till 1930, when Bridges died, will treat the liberal speculation as more significant that the conservative inhibition.

Our own object is less laboriously discharged. We have traversed not a century but a millennium, not a country but a continent. On so long a journey the reporter travels light, carrying but little exact scholarship and visiting only the chief sights. These conditions governed our choice of a rapid survey of European literature from the time when it began to reform itself on the recovered patterns of the Greek and Roman Classics to the time when the freedom of learning had broken the last barriers to the pagan view. There is a value in such a survey, if it be completely made, which will increase the higher value of more intensive study of shorter tracts. As to our competence, they will judge who have followed the present history to the border of a time when knowledge is swimming into human ken more quickly than ever before—even more quickly, perhaps, than the capacity of the mind to absorb it. As to the value, that is not for us. However incompetent the writer, there must be value for the reader in the discipline of comparative literature. A company of nations is growing up, in league by poverty and principle to avoid the ordeal of war. The historian recalls in this connection the words of Dean Inge, worthy successor in St. Paul's Cathedral to Dean Colet, the friend of Erasmus :

' The Humanism of the 15th century was more literary and artistic than scientific, but it was ready to welcome scientific research, and would in a short time have freed itself from the ecclesiastical shackles which hampered its development. The outbreak of fierce religious war in the 16th century destroyed the hopes of the Humanists.'

[1] See Dr. L. Huxley's *Life and Letters* of his father, Vol. III, p. 270.

He recalls, too, the words of George Saintsbury, who, more than any teacher in this faculty, has adorned it with monuments of humane learning :

' It is not at all impossible that, in the immediate or at least the near future, there may be something of a return to that comparative study of European literature, that absence of sharp national divisions, which existed to some extent in the Middle Ages, and was interrupted, partly by ecclesiastical, partly by literary causes, at and after the Renaissance.'

It is, therefore, as a very slight contribution to the cause of international union, of which literature is a handmaid, that this book is humbly, yet proudly, dedicated.

INDEX

w

w*